THE ILLUSIVE TRADE-OFF

Intellectual Property Rights, Innovation Systems, and
Egypt's Pharmaceutical Industry

Studies in Comparative Political Economy and Public Policy

Editors: MICHAEL HOWLETT, DAVID LAYCOCK, STEPHEN MCBRIDE, Simon Fraser University

Studies in Comparative Political Economy and Public Policy is designed to showcase innovative approaches to political economy and public policy from a comparative perspective. While originating in Canada, the series will provide attractive offerings to a wide international audience, featuring studies with local, subnational, cross-national, and international empirical bases and theoretical frameworks.

Editorial Advisory Board

For a list of books published in the series, see page 231

BASMA I. ABDELGAFAR

The Illusive Trade-off

Intellectual Property Rights, Innovation Systems, and Egypt's Pharmaceutical Industry

UNIVERSITY OF TORONTO PRESS
Toronto Buffalo London

© University of Toronto Press Incorporated 2006
Toronto Buffalo London
Printed in Canada

ISBN-13: 978-0-8020-9180-2
ISBN-10: 0-8020-9180-6

Printed on acid-free paper

Library and Archives Canada Cataloguing in Publication

Abdelgafar, Basma I.
The illusive trade-off : intellectual property rights, innovation systems
and Egypt's pharmaceutical industry / Basma I. Abdelgafar.

(Studies in comparative political economy and public policy)
Includes bibliographical references and index.
ISBN 0-8020-9180-6

1. Pharmaceutical industry – Egypt.   2. Drugs – Egypt – Patents.
3. Intellectual property (International law)   I. Title.   II. Series.

HD9673.E3A33 2006   338.4'761510962   C2006-903341-2

This book has been published with the help of a grant from the Canadian
Federation for the Humanities and Social Sciences, through the Aid to
Scholarly Publications Programme, using funds provided by the Social
Sciences and Humanities Research Council of Canada.

University of Toronto Press acknowledges the financial assistance to
its publishing program of the Canada Council for the Arts and the Ontario
Arts Council.

University of Toronto Press acknowledges the financial support for its
publishing activities of the Government of Canada through the Book
Publishing Industry Development Program (BPIDP).

Contents

Preface

This study analyses the implications of the World Trade Organization's Agreement on Trade-Related Aspects of Intellectual Property Rights (TRIPS) for the pharmaceutical industry and public health sector in Egypt using a national system of innovation (NSI) approach. My main arguments are (1) that there is no robust method for determining the appropriate balance between innovation and technological diffusion, which subjects intellectual property policy to political influence rather than economic calculation; (2) that attempts to establish positive links between strong patents and research and development, foreign direct investment, trade, and technology transfer through the use of conventional economic models have yielded few conclusive results; and (3) that adequately understanding the implications of stronger intellectual property rights (IPRs) for the pharmaceutical industries of developing countries requires an examination of relevant aspects of their respective national systems of innovation.

Historically, Egypt had maintained a relatively lax pharmaceutical patent regime that was effective in expanding local manufacturing capabilities and stimulating competition. However, the development of key elements of the NSI necessary to enable the industry to move towards greater innovation was largely neglected. Thus, while the industry managed to capture a significant share of the local market, its growth remained heavily dependent on the imitation of foreign technologies. To curb competition in the 1990s foreign firms began to press the Egyptian government for immediate changes to the IPRs regime. Although these demands were rejected, Egypt's accession to the WTO-TRIPS ensured that IPRs would soon be strengthened.

The choice to delay full implementation of the Agreement until 2005 reflects concerns over the appropriateness of its standards given the country's weak innovation and institutional capabilities. The industry's low levels of research and development (R&D) and heavy reliance on technology licensing have been reinforced by its limited ability to draw on the support of the science and technology system, which itself is characterized by weak R&D efforts and poor financial services. In a rush to beat the strengthening of national patent standards, local actors have been moving quickly to introduce health biotechnology products based on foreign technologies. Yet time is quickly running out. Serious challenges facing the biopharmaceutical innovation system are likely to cripple the industry's ability to benefit from stronger IPRs, while clearly augmenting the position of foreign title-holders. For the most part, the new IPRs regime is expected to act as little more than a rent transfer mechanism from local pharmaceutical producers and consumers to foreign actors.

Acknowledgments

Much of this book is based on my doctoral dissertation, which was successfully completed in January 2003. This work would not have been possible without the unyielding support of my thesis supervisor, Manfred Bienefeld. I also owe a debt of gratitude to my two other committee members: Phil Ryan for his encouragement in times of great need; and Bruce Doern for his tacit confidence. It was Calestous Juma, however, who convinced me that this work must be published.

I am grateful to my father and mother, Ibrahim and Afaf Abdelgafar, for their infinite patience and encouragement, for helping me to translate numerous documents, and for taking care of my children, Billal, Yasmeen, and Hanna. I am thankful to Mohammad Zebian, my husband, for never accepting the possibility of my quitting. Thanks also to Shrouk Abdelgafar and Ayman Abdelaal, my sister and brother-in-law, for their support throughout. This was truly a family affair.

There are so many people that have been an integral part of this lengthy process that I want to acknowledge including the team at the University of Toronto: Peter Singer, Abdallah Daar, Halla Thorsteinsdóttir, and Uyen Quack; my dearest and loyal friend who helped with various aspects of the research, Mohamed Barakat; my great support and cheerleader throughout my studies at Carleton, Iris Taylor; and the many wonderful individuals who assisted with my field research in Egypt.

This research was facilitated by the generous financial support of Carleton University, The Social Sciences and Humanities Research Council of Canada, and the Health Services Research Foundation of Canada. I have also drawn on subsequent research that was generously sponsored by the Canadian Program on Genomics and Global

Health and the University of Toronto's Joint Centre for Bioethics. The findings, interpretations, and conclusions in this book, however, are entirely my responsibility and should not be attributed to the individuals or organizations named above.

Abbreviations

CIPR	Commission on Intellectual Property Rights
CPT	Consumer Project on Technology
DCMA	Drugs, Chemicals, and Medical Appliances, General Organization for
DSU	Dispute Settlement Understanding
EMR	exclusive marketing right
EU	European Union
FDI	foreign direct investment
GATT	General Agreement on Tariffs and Trade
GEBRI	Genetic Engineering and Biotechnology Research Institute
GMP	Good manufacturing practice
GSP	Generalized System of Preferences
HIV/AIDS	Human Immunodeficiency Virus/Acquired Immune Deficiency Syndrome
IDA	International Dispensary Association
IFPMA	International Federation of Pharmaceutical Manufacturers Associations
IMF	International Monetary Fund
IPC	Intellectual Property Committee
IPR	Intellectual Property Right
MFN	most favoured nation
MNE	multinational enterprise
MOA	Ministry of Agriculture
MOH	Ministry of Health
MOSR	Ministry of Scientific Research
MSF	Médecins Sans Frontières

MUCSAT	Mubarak City for Scientific Research and Technology Applications
NGO	Non-governmental organization
NODCAR	National Organization for Drug Control and Research
NRC	National Research Centre
NSI	National System of Innovation
OECD	Organization for Economic Cooperation and Development
PhRMA	Pharmaceutical Research and Manufacturers of America
PMA	Pharmaceutical Manufacturers Association
QUAD	EU, Canada, and Japan
R&D	research and development
SOE	state-owned enterprise
S&T	science and technology
TAC	Treatment Action Campaign
TRIPS	Agreement on Trade-Related Aspects of Intellectual Property Rights
TWN	Third World Network
UNCTAD	United Nations Conference on Trade and Development
UNDP	United Nations Development Program
UNICEF	United Nations Children's Fund
USAID	United States Agency for International Development
USTR	United States Trade Representative
VACSERA	Biological Products and Vaccines Holding Company
WHO	World Health Organization
WIPO	World Intellectual Property Organization
WTO	World Trade Organization

THE ILLUSIVE TRADE-OFF

Intellectual Property Rights, Innovation Systems, and Egypt's Pharmaceutical Industry

1 Introduction

From the mid-1980s to the conclusion of the Uruguay Round of multi-lateral trade negotiations in 1994, the governments of the developed countries, led by the United States, were strongly promoting the global harmonization of intellectual property rights (IPRs) against strong opposition from the developing countries. At the heart of the disagreement was a demand for the mandatory extension of patent protection for pharmaceutical products, with potentially serious implications for domestic pharmaceutical industries and health sectors in developing countries. Previously, many countries, including Egypt, had been rather lax in their protection of IPRs for pharmaceuticals in the belief that this was conducive to the creation of a local industry because the early stages of such industrial development generally necessitate heavy reliance on imitation and the adaptation of existing technologies. Nevertheless, the demand for a stronger and more internationally harmonized IPRs regime by the industrial countries eventually resulted in the World Trade Organization's Agreement on Trade-Related Aspects of Intellectual Property Rights (TRIPS), the most ambitious and binding global IPRs agreement in history.

Stronger patent protection for pharmaceutical products will likely affect the drug industries and health sectors in developing countries in many ways because of its impact on prices, investment decisions, trade flows, local research and development (R&D), and the scope for effective technology transfer. Both in the short and the long term, these effects could turn out to be negative for all developing countries that remain heavy importers of technology and drugs. In the short term, even the resident representatives at the International Monetary Fund (IMF) accept that benefits of stronger IPRs are most likely to accrue principally to those who own the existing intellectual property rights and that their gains will come at the expense of those who must rely on their ability to acquire – or to use – those technologies at minimum cost (Harmsen and Subramanian 1994, 12). As for the long term, a United Nations Conference on Trade and Development (UNCTAD) report noted that 'in those nations in which technological development is at a rudimentary stage and to which technology transfer and diffusion is limited, with little in the way of offsetting local innovation, there could be a net cost' (1997, 19).

This observation highlights the importance of studying national systems of innovation (NSIs) in order to better understand the implications of TRIPS for developing countries. A national system of innovation constitutes the framework that determines a country's potential for building and attracting knowledge-intensive industries, for example, pharmaceuticals. The three primary components of an NSI are the structure and capabilities of the firms in an industry, the scientific and technological infrastructure of the economy, and government policies. From this perspective IPRs are only one aspect in a country's complex set of institutional arrangements that are necessarily embedded in a historical, social, economic, and political context. It follows that the implications of IPRs reform will depend on the specifics of national settings.

Using a national system of innovation approach, this study seeks to examine the implications of TRIPS for Egypt's pharmaceutical industry and public health sector. The case of Egypt is interesting because it provides fertile ground for such an assessment from a developing country perspective. It also provides an example of the impact that domestic and global political forces are having on the formulation of economic and technology policies in developing countries.

The study centres on four main points:

1 There is no robust method of determining the appropriate balance between innovation and technological diffusion, known as the core intellectual property trade-off, without specifying numerous parameters. This inevitably complicates the exercise and leads to a situation where intellectual property policies are especially subject to political influence rather than economic calculation. Thus, it cannot be said that the standards espoused by TRIPS are based on sound economic knowledge.

2 Attempts to establish positive and reliable links between strong IPRs

and research and development, foreign direct investment (FDI),[1] technology transfer, and trade have largely failed. Claims that strong IPRs would yield major benefits for developing countries are not conclusively supported by the conventional economic models on which they are based or by the available evidence. Such claims are often qualified by references to other significant national factors.

3 To adequately understand the implications of stronger patent protection for the pharmaceutical industries of developing countries we must consider relevant aspects of each country's national system of innovation. A weak NSI means that stronger pharmaceutical patents will likely have both short- and long-term adverse implications for a country.

4 Finally, the implications of stronger pharmaceutical patent protection for developing countries cannot be analysed from an economic perspective alone. The intimate relationship of this industry to public health also warrants consideration. It is feared that stronger patent protection may threaten drug accessibility, both supply and affordability, which can have serious, even tragic, social consequences.

The Case of Egypt

Historically, Egypt's lax pharmaceutical patent policy promoted the development of a domestic industry. Law No. 132 of 1949 limited the protection of pharmaceutical processes to a period of ten years from the date of filing and protected a product only if it used the particular production process described in the patent application. As a result local manufacturers were often able to evade such patents by introducing minor molecular manipulations that qualified as new production processes, thereby expanding local manufacturing capabilities and increasing competition with foreign firms. In addition domestic producers were able to benefit from strict price controls and from a foreign trade policy that limited the number of pharmaceutical substitutes that could be sold on the Egyptian market at any one time. Such policies were not in violation of the General Agreement on Tariffs and Trade (GATT) since the latter allowed for infant industry exceptions, protection for industrial development purposes, and quantitative restrictions for the maintenance of balance-of-payments equilibrium (Hudec 1987, 27). In general, Egypt's pharmaceutical policy sought to develop a domestic industry and to foster its technological capabilities so that it could provide affordable medicines for most of the country's poor people. A strong domestic pharmaceutical industry that was locally controlled was deemed most conducive to this end, since reliance on foreign investments or imported drugs would be too costly, and in some cases, too unreliable.

The relatively unrestricted international availability of technology up until the mid-1980s for the development of indigenous R&D and manufacturing capabilities in the pharmaceutical industry, coupled with a significant number of science graduates produced by President Nasser's education policy, facilitated the growth of Egypt's domestic industry which was initially dominated by the public sector. President Sadat's market-opening policies of the late 1970s paved the way for increased private investments, with the effect of rapidly expanding local pharmaceutical production, which continued to benefit from the imposition of import controls on drugs whose active ingredients were similar.

Aside from these economic and technological aspects, Egypt's earlier pharmaceutical patent policy reflected the political and social conditions of the time. A strong historical legacy extolled the virtues of socialist self-reliance and put a premium on objectives such as national self-sufficiency in drug production. These goals were supported not only by state officials and local investors, but also by society at large, since it appeared to benefit from the provision of cheap local substitutes for expensive foreign drugs. Surprisingly, opposition from foreign investors remained relatively limited until the mid-1980s; this was largely because such policies were common in many other countries, and because patent owners actually enjoyed a form of tacit protection since the Egyptian Ministry of Health had generally taken a very pragmatic line, often delaying for considerable periods of time the approval of locally manufactured drugs that were based on the manipulation of foreign-owned patents. More importantly, however, Egypt's lax patent law, like that of other developing countries, was supported by the balance of prevailing global political forces. By the mid-1980s, however, the global pharmaceutical industry, together with other IPR-sensitive industries, began accusing developing countries of 'unfair' practices, claiming that this resulted in a loss of billions of dollars of their 'rightful' profits. Intensive lobbying gradually led the industrial countries, foremost the United States, to demand that developing countries should reform their IPRs regimes. It was within this context that foreign investors in Egypt began to demand such changes, and vehement opposition from local manufacturers led to an intense struggle at the national level.

Egypt was getting caught in an international shift of political forces and interests, without which it would be impossible to understand why a battle over pharmaceutical IPRs developed in this particular country with its very small domestic industry and even smaller productive capacity. Of the entire global pharmaceutical market in the mid-1990s approximately 30 per cent of sales were by U.S. firms, 30 per cent by European Union (EU) firms, 21 per cent by Japanese firms, and the remaining 19 per cent by the firms of all developing countries combined, with Egyptian firms accounting for a mere 0.3 per cent (Al Ansari 1999, 13). The Egyptian market as a whole spends less on pharmaceuticals in one year than the United States does in four days (Pearl 1996, 1). The majority of pharmaceuticals that were being copied in Egypt were relatively older drugs whose patents had already expired even in places like the United States and Europe with their stronger IPRs (ibid.). Subramanian and Abdel-Latif noted that the share of patent infringing activity – or of production based on 'illegal' imitation – had always been low and estimated it at 4 per cent of total sales (1997, 10).

The recent shift in IPRs policy has resulted from global developments. The implications of these changes for Egypt's pharmaceutical industry and consumers can be assessed only by analysing the situation from a national perspective, and such an analysis must begin by recognizing that Egypt's earlier pharmaceutical policy produced some impressive results. Local manufacturers had supplied 29 per cent of the total quantity of drugs produced in Egypt in 1962, but that share had gradually increased to over 65 per cent by 2000 as local manufacturers gained experience. As a result, locally owned firms could provide consumers with more affordable medicines as they increased competition with the multinational enterprises (MNEs) operating in Egypt. Because local companies do not operate under the sorts of restrictions usually imposed on foreign-owned subsidiaries by their parent companies, they were the driving force behind the growth of exports from this sector. The past decade has witnessed the emergence of the health biotechnology sector which some have attributed to the industry's concerted efforts to beat the introduction of stronger IPRs in 2005.

Despite these successes in terms of growth and market share, Egypt's pharmaceutical industry failed to develop a capacity to innovate that could have assured its continued growth and evolution. In large part this was due to the small size of the industry and the high and rising costs of R&D. The policy of self-sufficiency compounded these problems by giving priority to increased production, while neglecting drug quality, and by implementing pricing policies that were designed to make drugs affordable but that took inadequate account of commercial realities. This constrained the industry's ability to modernize and to invest in R&D. Moreover, the same subsidies that protected the local industry and that allowed drug prices to be kept low also served to eliminate much needed competition that may have diminished duplicate drug provision within the industry.

After more than forty years of development Egypt's pharmaceutical industry has remained primarily one of formulation – or of assembly. This is largely because it has not developed the R&D capabilities required to manufacture the main active ingredients for more independent local drug production, but also because foreign investors have not honoured their commitments to eventually begin producing some of these basic ingredients in Egypt. As a result the industry continues to import more than 85 per cent of its raw materials, leaving domestic producers in a very vulnerable position vis-à-vis foreign supply sources. Today, the devaluation of the Egyptian pound and strict price controls are threatening the very existence of the industry (Mostafa 2004).

Egypt's science and technology (S&T) policies have not promoted appropriate linkages and relationships between national R&D institutes and the pharmaceutical industry. The results are an underutilization of the country's scientific capacity and increasing reliance on foreign technology suppliers. In short, Egypt has neglected a fundamental requirement of technological progress – the creation of a strong NSI – which means that the industry's future capacity for growth is limited and that it remains extremely vulnerable to any adverse changes in the terms on which technology could be acquired and copied. This context gives TRIPS such special significance and led me to make it the central focus of this book.

On a more general level, the 1980s changed the economic and political conditions within which Egypt's pharmaceutical policy was made. As was the case in so many other developing countries, by the mid-1980s the two oil crises, a sharp rise in international interest rates, and the collapse of many commodity prices left Egypt's economy with an unmanageable foreign debt and forced it into negotiations with creditors who made continued access to credit conditional on an extensive package of market-liberalizing policies. Among other things, this soon imposed severe constraints on the government's ability to continue to support the modernization and development of the country's pharmaceutical sector. Faced with demands for privatization and for the removal of tariffs and subsidies, the Egyptian government was forced to allow private market decisions to increasingly shape local industrial and innovation policies. This made it more and more difficult for the government to promote long-term investment for national development and to protect the poor by ensuring continued access to affordable drugs.

In time, these developments led to the emergence of major contradictions within the state apparatus. On the one hand, the need to manage the foreign debt and the perceived need to attract more foreign direct investment compelled the state to accept the market-driven policies advocated by international creditors, led by the World Bank and the International Monetary Fund. On the other hand, the continued desire in some quarters to build a strong NSI suggested a need for more (not less) government involvement in the economy. The perceived need to ensure Egyptians' access to affordable drugs led many government officials, particularly those from the Ministry of Health, to oppose the elimination of subsidies, the liberalization of prices, and the removal of import restrictions on popular medicines. These dilemmas persist.

Meanwhile, the main condition that had enabled the growth of Egypt's pharmaceutical industry was being destroyed as weak IPRs regimes in developing countries came under attack from the developed countries under pressure from their pharmaceutical lobbies. They charged that lax IPRs, in combination with improved information and communication technologies, were facilitating undue imitation and adaptation of technologies that had mostly been created in the industrial countries and that this significantly heightened global competitive pressures in ways that would undermine much needed technological progress, especially in R&D-intensive sectors like pharmaceuticals. In response the developed countries began to emphasize the need for stronger and more effective intellectual property protection. In the pharmaceuticals sector patents are the most effective and the most widely used instrument for such protection.

This demand for stronger protection of IPRs was spearheaded by the

United States, which increasingly acted unilaterally in targeting and punishing countries that refused to accede to its demand that those trading with the United States should harmonize their patent protection of pharmaceuticals with that prevailing in the United States. Indeed, the United States stood out in its willingness and its ability to take unilateral action in response to industry pressures, even when these violated existing international trade law.[2] From the latter half of the 1980s into the 1990s the United States made increasing use of its power to threaten, or to take, measures against developing countries that refused to grant more extensive patent protection to pharmaceuticals in line with U.S. demands (Correa 1995; Nogues 1990; Primo Braga 1990). This was the context in which the developing countries gradually moderated their opposition to the proposed changes in the global rules on patent protection. They did so to avoid punitive, unilateral threats and sanctions from the United States in exchange for some semblance of international 'due process.' It is misleading to suggest that developing countries' acceptance of these new rules implied that they believed these rules to be in their interests.

TRIPS was eventually signed on 15 April 1994 as part of the Final Act of the Uruguay Round; it is administered by the World Trade Organization (WTO). In essence, the agreement requires national treatment and most-favoured nation (MFN) treatment to be extended to the nationals of other member states.[3] It also demands the harmonization of the intellectual property policies of all member states, bringing them largely into line with U.S. practice. In pharmaceuticals, TRIPS demands the granting of product and process patent protection for a term of not less than twenty years from the date of filing. These rights must be granted irrespective of the place of invention or of whether the patent owner chooses to service the market in question through local production or imports. TRIPS restricts the use of compulsory licensing,[4] which has long been used by many member states to promote domestic manufacture of pharmaceuticals. All countries were to implement the provisions of TRIPS within one year, but developing countries were given five years to achieve full compliance, in light of their more vulnerable economic and social circumstances. In addition, they were granted another five years to extend full patent protection to all industrial sectors that had previously not been subject to patent protection under domestic law. Full compliance was required within ten years, or by 2005.

To ensure compliance, the WTO established a dispute settlement mechanism to deal with any international conflicts over IPRs. All disputes that cannot be *satisfactorily* resolved at the national level can be referred to an integrated Dispute Settlement Understanding (DSU) that is administered by the WTO. If a violation is established under this system, the 'wronged' country is given the right to retaliate against the offending country in *any* area covered by the WTO agreement, not just in the sector where the violation occurred. This leaves developing countries in a position where non-compliance can become extremely difficult and costly, while their ability to threaten large industrial country offenders remains very limited.

Opinion over the economic implications of TRIPS has been highly polarized. Developed countries have consistently maintained that a globally harmonized IPRs regime offers an impressive array of global benefits, including increased R&D, FDI, trade flows, and technology transfers to developing countries. But the proponents of a globally harmonized IPRs regime have also been careful to remind developing countries that they would be well advised to accept this new regime since these promised benefits are reinforced by the threat that any country that fails to comply will be increasingly isolated from access to global markets. Few countries can afford to allow themselves to be so isolated. At the same time developing countries argued for a more flexible global IPRs regime, one that would give countries substantial freedom to determine the appropriate design of national IPRs policy to reflect their own national goals, circumstances, and priorities. Their greatest concern was the fear that their pharmaceutical industries and their public health systems could not respond constructively to the drastic patent reforms being proposed. However, the ability of the developed countries to neutralize these developing country demands was bolstered by their enormous advantage in information and power and by their ability to exploit the interplay of complex domestic interests in the developing countries themselves.

At the end of the day it is true that Egypt, like most other developing countries, acceded *willingly* to the WTO agreement and is therefore committed to its implementation. Indeed, many Egyptian policymakers see the discipline imposed by the WTO as an integral and inevitable aspect of the state's current economic policy regime which focuses on full integration into the global economy. However, Egypt's bureaucrats do not unanimously share this view, and it is definitely not shared by the local pharmaceutical industry. There is widespread agreement that TRIPS will be associated with serious costs in the short run because of the challenges it poses for local industry and for public health. The government has decided to take full advantage of the transition period provided within TRIPS, but without a national strategy of how to deal with these challenges and of how to use the transition period to maximize the benefit-cost ratio for Egypt, this transition will probably only serve to postpone the inevitable.

Organization of the Book

Chapter 2 explains the background of this study and is concerned with the establishment of universal IPRs standards or the policy process through which TRIPS was created. It discusses the role of MNEs, industrial country governments, in particular that of the United States, and the World Bank and IMF in effectively transforming the global IPRs regime along lines largely defined by the United States. The chapter examines the arguments presented by the developing countries in opposition to these proposed changes and their eventual acquiescence to industrial country demands. With the Egyptian experience as our focus, we see how international and domestic political forces constrained the governments' policy choices during and after the Uruguay Round. The chapter illustrates how the pervasiveness of power and information asymmetries throughout the reform process had a definitive impact on the final outcome of the Uruguay trade negotiations.

Chapter 3 explores whether there is an economic basis for the standards espoused in TRIPS. This chapter is primarily concerned with conventional intellectual property theory, as this is the fundamental theory underlying the globalization of IPRs. To this end, I examine the core intellectual property trade-off and the attempts that have been made by various scholars to determine optimal patent strength. The chapter also reviews studies that have sought to establish links between strong IPRs and R&D, FDI, trade, and technology transfer. This discussion is instrumental for assessing the claims of the proponents of a stronger and globally harmonized IPRs regime. The chapter demonstrates that the substance of TRIPS is not based on sound economic theory, particularly when considered from the perspective of developing countries, since these countries often face different opportunities and constraints when seeking to develop or acquire new technologies.

Chapter 4 outlines the way in which a national system of innovation approach can be used to assess the implications of stronger intellectual property protection for the pharmaceutical sectors of developing countries. It emphasizes the importance of understanding the specific characteristics of the innovation process within a development context and shows that these have far-reaching consequences for the plausibility of the core intellectual property trade-off. The chapter argues that it is the strength of key pharmaceutical/health aspects of a country's national system of innovation that determine the extent of innovative activities and, hence, the ability of the country's pharmaceutical firms to take advantage of the new IPRs standards. National systems of innovation include three key elements: the structure and capabilities of domestic firms (in this case pharmaceutical firms), the scientific and technological infrastructure of the particular country, and the existence of suitable and coherent government policies. The chapter demonstrates that the innovative behaviour of a country's pharmaceutical firms is affected by a whole host of factors and that the definition of a country's optimal IPRs regime ought to take such factors into account.

Chapter 5 is the first of two chapters examining the case of Egypt. It focuses on key aspects of the historical evolution of Egypt's pharmaceutical industry. The aim of the discussion is to demonstrate (1) that a relatively weak pharmaceutical patent policy was instrumental in fostering the emergence of a vigorous domestic industry; (2) that the industry that emerged achieved this approximate self-sufficiency in ways that were desirable from a public health point of view; and (3) that the industry had limited innovative capacities, which is not surprising given the economic strategy of the government beginning in the mid-1970s. These historical realities conditioned the domestic response to a strengthened patent regime today.

Chapter 6 is concerned with how the contemporary pharmaceutical industry was affected by Egypt's traditional IP policy given some of the key pharmaceutical/health aspects of the national system of innovation. It examines the achievements of the industry and the challenges facing it, which come not only from foreign sources but also from weaknesses in the scientific and technological support structure and from the development of the pharmaceutical industry itself. The purposes of the discussion are to assess the plausibility of the claims being made by the proponents of stronger IPRs and to offer explanations as to why certain outcomes are deemed more or less likely, as well as to identify those aspects of Egypt's NSI that require improvement or transformation in light of these circumstances.

Finally, chapter 7 presents an analysis of recent international events that have transpired as a result of the continuing disagreement between developing and developed countries over the impact of TRIPS on local pharmaceutical industries and public health systems. The chapter also examines recent changes in Egypt's patent law within this context. It is argued that, although the developing countries have come a long way since the Uruguay Round negotiations when they were pressured and threatened into accepting TRIPS, they remained largely unable to counter the proposals of the industrial countries during negotiations concerning TRIPS and public health that led to the creation of the Doha Declaration during the Fourth WTO Ministerial Conference in November 2001. This has given rise to a problematic acceptance of the core requirements of TRIPS by developing countries and obscured the necessity of more critical negotiations regarding the impact of the core TRIPS requirements on innovation and technological diffusion in the developing world.

2 Establishing the New Global IPRs Regime

This study was born of an interest in examining the implications of an international agreement about which there continues to be considerable disagreement. This chapter is concerned with exactly how this *agreement* came into existence, and to this end it examines the policy process through which it was created. This discussion is important for several reasons. First, it will help to clarify why developing countries acceded to TRIPS, despite their significant reservations concerning the probable economic and social outcomes for them. Second, it will provide insight into the weight of the various competing objectives that entered into the decision to adopt the new IPRs regime. Thus, it will enable us to understand more fully the new global IPRs policy and the likelihood of its effective implementation in a development context.

To illuminate these issues this chapter is divided into four main parts. The first part examines the main forces that gave impetus to global IPRs reform, with a special focus on the role of the pharmaceutical industry. The second explores the involvement of the U.S. government in supporting the demands of its industries for a globally strengthened and harmonized IPRs regime, and the initially strong opposition of developing countries to such changes. The next part takes a close look at the role of Egypt in the international negotiations that led to TRIPS. Finally, a brief account is given of the events that occurred in Egypt in the aftermath of the Uruguay Round in response to foreign pressure to forego the grace period for which provision is made in the agreement.

Global Realities

Coping with Competition

The intensified efforts to establish a globally harmonized IPRs regime can be attributed to changing technologies, changes in the strategies of multinational enterprises responding to increasing global competition, and changes in government policies. Since the 1980s accelerated technological advance, resulting primarily from linking new information and communication technologies with the biological sciences, has given high technology an increasingly important role in shaping global competitiveness and trade flows in the global pharmaceutical market. Companies wishing to participate in the new 'life sciences' industry, with its rapidly moving technological frontier, have had to increase their R&D expenditures but, of course, with no guarantee that these investments will bear fruit. With R&D expenditures allegedly ranging anywhere between 12 per cent (Merck) and 18 per cent (Pfizer) of pharmaceutical sales (Barr 1999, 38), companies have strategically searched for ways to enhance the earnings to be generated by these investments. They and 'their' industry analysts argue that the key to ensuring R&D investments and progress in the pharmaceuticals field lies in the provision of strong intellectual property protection.

While the accelerating pace of technological change makes more rapid and more innovative changes in pharmaceutical products and processes feasible, it also means that domestic and international competitors can imitate new technologies more quickly and easily and with higher levels of quality control than used to be possible. The growth in the strength of generic companies worldwide reflects this intensified competitive pressure and is a major factor in the global industry's discontent with the prevailing intellectual property rights regimes in many countries. Generic drug firms offer the patient/consumer alternatives, similar or identical to their brand name counterparts, but at much more affordable prices. Relatively lax patent provisions and/or lax enforcement of these provisions, as well as the imposition of strict compulsory licensing regimes in many developing countries, facilitated this growth. Indeed, for many developing country governments generic drug producers represented the primary health care and competitiveness tool. Moreover, the expanding cost containment policies of governments around the world struggling with public sector deficits also facilitated the rapid evolution and expansion of generic industries in both developed and developing countries.

During the 1980s many governments in the industrialized world promoted competition by generic drug firms to lower public health expenditures. In 1984, for instance, patent reform in the United States encouraged competition between generic and brand name companies by no longer requiring the imitator to duplicate many of the pioneer's clinical tests in order to gain market approval. Instead, the generics only had to demonstrate bio-equivalency, which can be done much more readily and at relatively low cost. This was soon followed by the elimination of antisubstitution laws, which had prohibited pharmacists from recommending generic drugs in place of equivalent but more expensive brand names, thereby making consumers more aware of more affordable drug alternatives (Grabowski and Vernon 1986, 195; Nogues 1990, 94). In Canada, prior to 1993, the existence of compulsory licences allowed generic companies to compete with their brand name counterparts even before their patents had actually expired. As a result, 'big pharma' was becoming increasingly impatient with the growing role of generic drug producers in the public health care systems of some of their largest markets.

These concerns were exacerbated by the recognition that the patents of many popular brand name drugs were to expire at the end of the 1980s so that the market for patent-expired drugs reached U.S.$10 billion[1] (Nogues 1990, 95) and it was expected that by the year 2001 this would rise to U.S.$30 billion worldwide (Industry Canada 1997, 12). Not surprisingly, those drug giants who were about to see U.S. patents expire on several of their most lucrative drugs were seriously concerned about the resulting slow-downs in earning growth.

In response to these pressures multinational enterprises began to source their scientific and technological operations strategically all over the world, while setting up alliances with their major oligopolistic rivals (Chesnais 1992, 291). This led to a flurry of merger and acquisition activity in the 1990s, concentrating the industry's structure dramatically and bolstering its global political power. At the end of this process the global industry was dominated by a small number of gargantuan MNEs headquartered in the United States, the United Kingdom, Japan, Germany, France, Switzerland, and Sweden. By this time the top ten corporations accounted for 47 per cent of the $197 billion global pharmaceutical market (Rifkin 1998, 68), and the industry remained consistently among the most profitable, as it has been since the Second World War.

Against this background the global pharmaceutical industry, in concert with other IPR-sensitive industries,[2] initiated an intense campaign against the inadequacy of the existing global IPRs regime. The weight of the industry was such that the industrial country governments, and in particular that of the United States, were very likely to listen. According to Stalson, concerted pressures for stronger IPRs commenced in the late 1970s when 'the sponsors of this effort began to gather information, to supply the U.S. government with evidence of the alarming effects that international policy was having on legitimate production and trade, and to alert their counterparts in Europe and Japan of the losses facing their domestic industries if concerted efforts were not taken to halt infringement activities' (1987, 3). By 1986 U.S. industry alone claimed that it had lost $25 billion in sales due to infringements of their IPRs, with the bulk of this activity allegedly taking place in developing countries (Richards 1988, 93).

Despite the leverage that the big business lobby could exert in the industrial countries, it seemed clear from an early date that pressures to reform national IPRs regimes in developing countries would probably have to be externally imposed. In most of these countries there was insufficient internal pressure for reform due to their lower levels of technological development and conflicting economic policy goals (Haagsma 1988, 66). Corporate giants experienced considerable difficulty in coordinating their lobbying efforts in various developing countries, which was compounded by the fact that they generally made only limited contributions to economic and technological development in most of the developing world. These factors had traditionally led the developing countries to be very cautious when trying to attract foreign investments, especially in the pharmaceuticals sector, where public health objectives had to be seriously considered alongside the usual commercial priorities.

From the outset industry leaders insisted at both national and international levels that stronger IPRs were needed to build the confidence of investors in R&D, largely by reducing the threat of early competition from imitators. They claimed that stronger IPRs were necessary as incentives for continued investments in innovation and to 'encourage foreign investment from industries that otherwise would hesitate to expose their most important ideas and inventions to theft' (Leahy 1988,

78). This position was put forth especially strongly by the pharmaceutical industry, which argued that existing efforts to curb 'piracy' through individual litigation were highly inadequate and that the 'deterrent value of a strong patent enforcement program' would be of great benefit to the industry (Clemente 1988, 134). Indeed, they claimed, 'there is very little an individual company can do on its own to improve the level of intellectual property protection in countries in which it operates. But in concert with each other through trade and professional organizations or, more important, in concert with the appropriate representatives of the U.S. government, a company can help to achieve significant improvement' (Keefauver 1988, 149). The introduction and inclusion of IPRs in the GATT Uruguay Round agenda must be seen as a direct result of these strong and concerted efforts of U.S. brand name multinationals, which succeeded in getting the U.S. government to act on their behalf.

The executives from both Pfizer and IBM who sat on the President's Committee for Trade Negotiations had expressed particularly strong interest in bringing IPRs under the purview of GATT. To this end, they had rallied other IPR-sensitive industries, including the creative arts, electronics, software, and chemicals, behind an Intellectual Property Committee (IPC)[3] that was established initially to lobby the U.S. government, but eventually it extended its activities to Europe and Japan. The proponents of stronger IPRs contended that weak and non-uniform IPRs regimes worldwide were a major source of trade distortion and, as such, should be dealt with by GATT. Not only did industry leaders seek the imposition of higher IPR standards on developing countries, but they also sought to secure their commitment to enforce these standards at the national level. This, they believed, would best be accomplished through the establishment of a dispute settlement mechanism that would legitimize cross-retaliation in cases of non-conformity. The demands of the so-called IPR-sensitive industries were eventually drafted in a consensual document, based on industrial country standards, for a global approach to intellectual property protection (Sell 1998, 137).

U.S. Involvement and Developing Countries' Opposition

By 1983 the United States was facing an erosion of its competitive advantage in high value added goods while experiencing massive trade deficits. Under these circumstances some critics of the liberal trading system claimed that GATT was becoming less and less consistent with U.S. business interests. Since U.S. exports had become increasingly characterized by high technology industries, these soon came to see themselves as victims of a very lax global IPRs regime whose 'failures' were becoming more apparent as countries around the world liberalized their markets. The persistent MNE lobby was therefore able to convince the U.S. Congress 'that inadequate intellectual property protection in foreign markets [was] a real and tangible barrier to the growth of trade in copyrighted materials and patented inventions' (Leahy 1988, 78).

In response to this, but also to stem possible rejection of its basic pro-GATT policy, the Reagan administration sought to broaden congressional support by increasing the scope of GATT in ways that would promote additional U.S. economic interests abroad. Thus, in January 1985 the President's Commission on Industrial Competitiveness suggested that the 'strengthening of intellectual property rights at home and abroad should be a priority item on the nation's policy agenda' (Benko 1987, 1). This led President Reagan to emphasize the importance of linking IPRs to trade. Furthermore, according to Hudec, 'in exchange for being able to use GATT trade retaliation to open and protect their foreign markets, the export industries benefiting from these new obligations could be expected to join the coalition in support of GATT' (1991, 109). This was a judicious calculation.

The resulting criticism of the prevailing IPRs regime focused on the Paris Convention and the Universal Copyright Convention, which would have to be strengthened to meet new and more rigorous standards. The lobby argued that the minimum standards of the Paris Convention (patents and trademarks), the Berne Convention (copyrights), the Rome Convention (neighbouring rights), and the Washington Treaty (integrated circuits) would all have to be raised. Acceptance of all of these changes was to be made mandatory for joining the new trade regime. In May 1986 the economic summit of the Group of 7 industrialized countries, meeting in Tokyo, endorsed these proposals, although this meeting did not necessarily support all of the substan-tive changes being proposed by the United States. The appropriate-ness of having GATT deal with matters of intellectual property, which had traditionally been the domain of the World Intellectual Property Organization (WIPO), however, soon began to raise serious concerns worldwide.

For the developing countries the plan to link trade talks with IPRs was unacceptable. Previous opposition to the inclusion of trade in counterfeit goods in GATT, during the Tokyo Round (1974–9), had led to its eventual abandonment by the developed countries. Despite the challenge posed by their limited power and resources, the developing countries again vehemently opposed the inclusion of IPRs in the Uruguay Round. Led by India and Brazil, they voiced concerns about the inclusion of IPRs in the trade agenda on a number of grounds, ranging from divergent ideological beliefs to conflicting economic interests (Primo Braga 1991, 174). In general, they argued that their industries were not yet ready to comply with the international IPR standards that were being promoted by the United States and its industrialized allies. In fact, they suggested that the efforts of developing countries to catch up economically were heavily dependent on their ability to imitate existing technologies, as had historically been done by the industrialized countries. Nationally specific IPRs regimes were therefore needed to facilitate domestic innovation through reverse engineering and imitation based on liberal and affordable access to global technologies.

In the area of patenting many developing countries had established national regimes that excluded certain products or industries altogether from such protection. To protect the public interest they had excluded areas like pharmaceuticals, foodstuffs, and plant varieties from patentability. In developing countries where IPRs regimes did exist, enforcement was usually lax enough to permit the implementation of divergent policy initiatives that were considered of high national priority. The developing countries insisted that trade negotiations were not an appropriate mechanism for altering the prevailing global IPRs regime. They proposed that the current regime should be reviewed within the framework of WIPO, suggesting that it play a more prominent role in the Uruguay Round and that it should, in all cases, remain the primary forum for discussing international IPRs and their administration. The strength of their opposition on this point temporarily brought the initiation of the Uruguay Round of trade negotiations to a halt in 1985. In response, and to demonstrate the gravity of the situation, the U.S. administration made its participation in the Uruguay Round conditional upon inclusion of the reform of the global IPRs regime in its deliberations. Even so, the developing countries maintained their strong opposition to negotiating IPRs within GATT; but by 1986 America's full resolve to include IPRs in the discussion was made unambiguously clear when the United States threatened to use its right to call a special session with or without consensus if the developing countries did not acquiesce (Hudec 1991, 181). In the meantime, the U.S. government's behaviour had given further indication of the hard line that it proposed to adopt on this question. Just prior to the GATT negotiations, the United States held bilateral discussions with more than thirty countries, in which the United States had tied stronger intellectual property protection to a country's eligibility for the Generalized System of Preferences (GSP) benefits (Gadbaw and Richards 1988, 7). By the time the trade negotiations began, there was little doubt that IPRs would play a large role in them.

Washington's aggressive stance on IPRs was part of its wider strategy on trade reform, which became apparent when the U.S. Congress enacted legislation to give the president authority to use trade law to demand stronger intellectual property protection in foreign markets (Gadbaw and Richards 1988, 5). However, by far the most significant piece of legislation was the 1988 U.S. Omnibus Trade Act, designed to enhance the usefulness of bilateral trade negotiations to open recalcitrant markets. The act's amendment of Section 301 of the Trade Act of 1974 was the most important development in this regard since it legitimized U.S. retaliation against 'unfair practices of foreign governments which can be unjustifiable, unreasonable, discriminating or which burden or restrict U.S. commerce' (Nogues 1990, 84). Subsequently, the Office of the Trade Representative (USTR), the Department of Commerce, and the Department of State were given the lead in implementing this policy. These actions were effectively unilateral since the use of sanctions under Section 301, or the denial of GSP benefits under Section 502, were being used to bring about policy change in the targeted country without multilateral consultation or approval (Haagsma 1988, 67). Moreover, 'given that the GATT did not allow governments to use trade retaliation to attack inadequate intellectual property regimes, all the retaliation called for by the Special 301 appeared to be GATT illegal' (Hudec 1991, 227). Nevertheless, the United States persisted in its aggressive behaviour, in part to impress big business and its trading partners with the potential benefits of greater GATT-induced discipline.

A comprehensive review by Sykes of the effectiveness of trade sanctions imposed under Section 301 found that they had been relatively successful in enforcing U.S. interests abroad (1992, 263). This was not only so in cases where countries were overtly violating international agreements, but also where they were merely taking advantage of loopholes or ambiguities in the law, that is, interpreting the law in accordance with their own national priorities, as opposed to those of the United States. The success of such sanctions was particularly evident where the country was also a GSP beneficiary. Indeed, trade sanctions became so popular as a measure to open foreign markets that U.S. industry feared that GATT negotiations would actually undermine the level of intellectual property protection that could be sought via bilateral means (Bale 1988, 124). Among the first successful cases in which the United States used these powers to challenge another government's weak pharmaceutical patent protection was that of South Korea in 1985. In this case it did not take long before the South Korean government enacted product patent protection for pharmaceuticals and improved its enforcement procedures. According to Gerald Mossinghoff, president of the U.S.-based Pharmaceutical Manufacturers Association (PMA), 'the Korean case was a major step forward and set an important example of what could be accomplished using trade instruments to achieve intellectual property objectives' (in Sell 1998, 188). However, by 1989 South Korean firms were under fire again, this time because of charges brought against them by the pharmaceutical giant Bristol Myers Squibb, which led to the opening of a new Section 301 complaint laid by the U.S. Trade Representative (Sell 1998, 190).

In 1987 the threat of sanctions under Section 301 was actually carried out for the fist time when the PMA initiated a case against Brazil for 'inadequate' patent protection for pharmaceuticals. When the Brazilians refused to reform their system accordingly, the United States placed a 100 per cent retaliatory tariff on a wide range of Brazilian exports to the United States, including pharmaceuticals, paper products, and consumer electronics, which totaled U.S.$39 million (Sell 1998, 190). When patent reform was eventually introduced in the Brazilian legislature in 1991, it stipulated that stronger protection would only be afforded to drugs manufactured in Brazil. But this did not satisfy the PMA, which insisted that Brazil remain on the USTR's Watch List (Sell 1998, 191). In general the threat of sanctions seems to have been enough in most cases to induce change. As a result, it is widely believed that the eventual willingness of many developing countries to increase the level of patent protection that they afford to pharmaceutical products is largely to be understood as a 'response to trade retaliation, or the threat thereof, rather than a premeditated policy shift' (Primo Braga 1990, 47).

Thus, despite their reservations and in spite of domestic pressure urging opposition, the developing countries eventually concluded that, given the strength of corporate interests and their lobbying power in the United States, they were likely to continue to confront endless Section 301 threats in the future, so that negotiating intellectual property rights in GATT was probably the 'lesser evil' (Hoekman 1994, 113). The 1988 ministerial mid-term review of the Uruguay Round, in which the developing countries first agreed to expand the scope of the discussions, must therefore be interpreted from this perspective. The agreement among ministers on what TRIPS negotiations could and should include was not based on some newly found consensus as to its benefits, but rather it reflected the circumstantial coercion of the developing countries to accept these demands. Under these circumstances, the members *agreed* in this review to discuss the applicability of GATT principles and of relevant IPRs conventions; the adequacy of standards concerning the availability, scope, and use of trade-related IPRs; the most appropriate means of enforcement; dispute settlement between member states; and an interim agreement to encourage maximum participation of the developing world (Namfua and Yusuf 1991, 4).

Yet participation of the developing countries was marred by the frequent inability of their delegations to deal with the complexity of IPR issues or with the number of issues tabled during this round more generally. For most of the developing countries the Uruguay Round was a completely new experience. Although they had been a part of the GATT 'system' for some time, their marginal role in the negotiating procedures during the previous rounds meant that they were largely unprepared for the expanded role that they would be asked to assume during this latest phase of the Uruguay Round. For most of the postwar period these countries had been accorded rights of membership in GATT, but with few reciprocal obligations demanded of them. They therefore had little historical experience on which they could rely during the negotiations that were triggered by these developments.[4]

Egypt during the Uruguay Round

Egypt has been an active participant in GATT negotiations since the early 1960s. Yet it was not until the Uruguay Round that such participation became premised on achieving certain trade and economic policy, as opposed to political policy, objectives. The Uruguay Round was a totally new experience for Egypt's policymakers and foreign affairs specialists, most of whom had very little knowledge of how such negotiations actually proceeded. Nevertheless, many of them believed that Egypt's active participation in this process and its eventual accession to the World Trade Organization would result in net benefits for the country. These benefits would largely stem from subjecting the traditional areas of textiles and agriculture to GATT discipline, which Egyptian policymakers felt would serve as a counterbalance to the simultaneous inclusion of IPRs and services.

Egypt's delegation at the negotiations comprised officials from both the Ministry of Foreign Affairs and the Ministry of Economy. These people were not technically qualified to handle many of the issues tabled during the round, and they expressed surprise at their volume, complexity, and scope and complained of very little time to prepare serious counterproposals. Their ability to call other national experts for assistance was constrained by several factors including certain systemic rigidities,[5] difficulties in identifying the experts required, and funding in bringing such experts to Geneva. Finally, internal divisions within the delegation between the two ministries on how to tackle some of the issues at hand made a daunting task even more difficult.

The apparent lack of coordination between Egypt's ministries caused much confusion during the Uruguay Round. There were differences not only between the two ministries that comprised the delegation, but also between other ministries that had a stake in the issues under discussion. In truth, despite Egypt's initial rejection of TRIPS, some internal interests were in support of it. These included, among others, Egyptian publishers, filmmakers, software developers, and agricultural interests, all of whom argued that Egypt had a comparative advantage in these areas and that lax IPRs, especially in the Arab world, had cost them billions. They insisted that Egypt should support the proposed reform of the international IPRs regime. However, their position was strongly countered by the Ministry of Health on the grounds that any such reform would have a significant impact on drug accessibility in Egypt and that, in turn, would adversely affect the majority of Egypt's poor and strain the country's limited health care resources. The internal struggle that emerged, therefore, reflected a wide range of interests, and it was further compounded by the complexity of the agreement and by the short time by which it would have to be implemented. The national committee that was established by Egypt's cabinet to consider the various issues emerging in the course of the Uruguay Round negotiations was largely ineffective. According to one foreign affairs specialist, the people delegated to this committee by various interest groups were often incapable of providing the negotiators with timely and effective information. For instance, those representing the banking sector showed little enthusiasm for the issues at stake by remaining largely 'inward looking.' Other industries put forward representatives who had little knowledge of the negotiating process and hence the type of information they would have to provide if their views were to be given any weight.

In the end many believe that Egypt's negotiations were a 'one-man show,' with some weak supporting actors. Although various domestic interests had submitted opinion papers to the ambassador in charge of the negotiations, it appears that because of the weaknesses of these submissions and a lack of accountability to his domestic constituents, the ambassador paid little attention to them. The concessions that were made during these negotiations were essentially made by the ambassador, who then justified them to the government on the basis of studies done by the negotiating team, which relied heavily on discussions with other developing country delegations and the resources of the U.N. Conference on Trade and Development. Indeed, the Egyptian delegation often found itself turning to foreign information sources such as the United States Agency for International Development (USAID), even when it knew full well that the latter did not necessarily share Egypt's interests.

In line with the general developing countries' stance, Egypt initially opposed the inclusion of IPRs in the Uruguay Round and then, once the issue was on the agenda, it was an active participant in seeking amendments to the industrialized countries' proposals regarding IPRs. However, when President Reagan made a personal appeal to the heads of state of recalcitrant developing countries, urging them to back down and to comply, the Egyptian government decided that it did not want to be among the opposition's frontrunners and therefore softened its stand. Of course, it was further encouraged in this by sustained pressure from the multilateral financial institutions and from the U.S. government which implicitly and explicitly suggested that continued strong opposition could call into question future U.S. aid flows to Egypt which amounted to U.S.$815 million per annum, military support, and freedom from Section 301 threats. The carrot that was added to the stick took the form of a promise to push companies to invest in Egypt, but policymakers largely thought of this as inconsequential. As one government official put it, 'you can only give red lights to businesses thereby stopping investments; green lights mean very little.'

With its arm twisted, the Egyptian government chose to play a limited role in the negotiations as a whole and allowed India and Brazil to take the lead and the heat in matters of disagreement, especially those with the United States. In the final analysis, policymakers believed that membership in the WTO, and acceptance of its attendant agreements, was necessary for the country's transformation into a fully fledged outward-oriented market economy, driven by the private sector. It was a necessary step in Egypt's attempt to integrate with the global economy and to become an equal or 'level' player. At the same time, and maybe even more importantly, it was also seen as a necessary step if Egypt was to avert the threat of U.S. economic sanctions for non-compliance.

In the Aftermath of the Uruguay Round

Egypt signed the WTO agreement on 15 April 1994 although it was not until 16 April 1995 that the People's Assembly ratified TRIPS.[6] As in other developing countries, Egypt's domestic pharmaceutical industry has been greatly troubled by the changes that TRIPS introduced. Although Egypt's pharmaceutical industry is not nearly as significant as that of India or Brazil, since it remains primarily one of formulation and exports very little, it is an important actor because national manufacturers satisfy over two-thirds of Egypt's drug consumption needs. Manufacturers explain their relative success in this regard by pointing to Egypt's lax patent law (Law No. 132 of 1949), which only allowed for pharmaceutical process patents for ten years from the date of filing. This form of protection enabled manufactures to work 'around' patents by making minor molecular manipulations that potentially qualified as new processes. This policy of limited patent protection allowed the pharmaceutical industry to develop to the point where 93 per cent of the domestic market of LE 5 billion[7] was domestically produced, with locally owned and public sector firms supplying about two-thirds of this 93 per cent, foreign-owned firms supplying about one-third, and with only 7 per cent being met by imports. This suggests that the domestic industry was a formidable source of competition, often providing drugs at a fraction of the cost of foreign equivalents primarily because of its ability to import raw materials from cheap international sources – one of the many things that will be restricted once Egypt changes its patent laws to conform to TRIPS. This has naturally been a cause for concern among Egypt's health authorities, who are responsible for ensuring drug accessibility for the majority of Egypt's people and whose ability to meet this obligation will be greatly challenged as a result.

Partly in order to assuage such fear, TRIPS allowed developing countries a 'grace period' of five years, before they had to be in full compliance. But, despite this allowance, increasing pressure was brought to bear on the Egyptian government soon after ratification of the agreement in 1995 for immediate implementation of its provisions. This gave rise to an intense struggle mainly between foreign and local pharmaceutical firms in an effort to sway government opinion. At numerous meetings, conferences, and seminars the potential implications of TRIPS on Egypt's pharmaceutical industry and on its health sector were hotly debated, with each side calling on 'their' international group of experts. Foreign pharmaceutical firms demanded immediate implementation of TRIPS, on the ground that the provision of strong patent protection would enhance technological development by encouraging highly risky investments in R&D. According to the website of the Pharmaceutical Research and Manufacturers of America (PhRMA),[8] Egypt will benefit from increased patent protection since it is 'indispensable for economic development and growth.' It goes on to state that the 'historical record of industrialized countries demonstrates that intellectual property protection has been one of the most powerful instruments for economic development, export growth and the diffusion of new technologies.' Several factors undermine the plausibility of these broad assertions.

First, it was by now well known that these corporate advocates tended to exaggerate the technical risks associated with R&D. As Lall (1974, 156) argued:

> If the claim of exceptional risk were valid, we would expect an analysis of the data to show that risk and uncertainty, as opposed to other factors, exercised a significant influence on the profitability of drug firms; furthermore, we would expect the industry to show considerable fluctuations in its earnings relative to less risky industries and we would expect to find drug firms which were exceptionally unproductive of innovations to show relatively low returns. None of these factors are supported by the evidence: econometric analysis of the determinants of profits *does not* show that risk is a very significant variable; the industry has consistently earned profits higher than the average; and firms producing few innovations have nevertheless shown very high profits.

Pharmaceutical firms tend to undertake research projects whose probability of success is normally between 50 and 70 per cent (Bonin 1991, 276). In cases where a firm is not achieving desired results, or where the results are not likely to be as profitable as first anticipated, certain projects may be abandoned.

Second, one has to wonder why the foreign firms approached the situation with such a heavy hand if the economic benefits from early implementation were so indisputable. From the very start, they relied extensively on the resources and support of PhRMA, U.S. diplomatic representatives, the U.S.-Egypt President's Council, and the Pharmaceutical and Health Committee of the American Chamber of Commerce in Cairo, which had all been mobilized to exert pressure on the Egyptian government. Through official diplomatic channels, U.S. officials repeatedly reinforced these efforts with strategic threats that included placing Egypt on the Special 301 List, and then later on the Priority Watch List, which threatens a country with economic retaliation, including the removal of GSP benefits, if it does not agree to deal with the complaint against it.

Third, the pharmaceutical industry was unable to create a concerted lobby to offer significant commitments in the form of R&D or other investments in exchange for early implementation of TRIPS. Unlike in Brazil, where it is estimated that early implementation attracted *promises* of U.S.$1.2 billion in pharmaceutical investments (Pearl 1996, 12), the industry in Egypt was unwilling to make similar commitments. This greatly weakened the position of the foreign firms in relation to that of the local firms, where the opposition was fierce and unified. As the prospects of increased investments in R&D seemed less and less likely, only a couple of MNEs, Pfizer and Glaxo Wellcome, continued to put overt pressure on the government, while the other MNEs chose a less confrontational stand. These factors combined to adversely affect the credibility of the foreign industry's arguments. In contrast, the local firms mounted a relatively unified and well-planned campaign. Their two most outstanding tactics were (1) to identify themselves as agents of the state and hence as being interested in social equity and justice and (2) to use a lot of nationalist rhetoric to defame the leaders of the foreign firms. Both the Federation of Egyptian Industries and the Union of Pharmaceutical Industries organized conferences and seminars, which brought international experts from India, Argentina, and Canada to warn against the dangers inherent in stronger patent protection for pharmaceuticals.

Throughout these debates the industry argued forcefully against the strengthening of patent protection under TRIPS. Their strongest point of attack was the impact that they claimed TRIPS would have on drug prices, with some of their estimates reaching mythical proportions. They also argued that stronger patent protection would probably lead to market monopolization by foreign firms, that imports would likely rise, that the positive results from stronger patent protection were only likely to materialize in countries with higher levels of economic development, and that the strategic nature of pharmaceutical products means that competition in this sector has to be expedited, not stifled. To convey these messages effectively, local industry leaders held closed-door sessions with the prime minister and with ministers from departments with a direct stake in TRIPS as it related to pharmaceuticals. They sought to convince the government of the country's need of the full grace period, and these efforts were ultimately successful.

Consequently, in August 1996, the Ministry of Scientific Research sent an official communiqué to the prime minister informing him of the conclusions that it had reached after several meetings with technical experts, industry leaders, and representatives from various other ministries. The letter outlined the anticipated positive and negative impacts both of postponement (to the maximum period allowed) and of immediate implementation. As for the positive impacts of postponement, the letter suggested that postponement would (1) allow sufficient time for Egypt to absorb the costs of applying the agreement, (2) protect the present low level of drug prices for a time, and (3) enable Egyptian firms to adjust constructively to the new IP regime. The negative implications of postponement included (1) loss of foreign investment to other countries, (2) retarding the drive towards market openness, and (3) increasing the cost of a transformation that had to be undertaken. The positive implications of immediate implementation included (1) possible attraction of foreign direct investment; (2) possible enhancement of strategic alliances and contracts with foreign technology suppliers; (3) creation of a healthy tension between local and foreign firms, thereby facilitating the transformation; and (4) for Egypt to become a regional leader on IPR issues. The expected negative effects of immediate implementation included (1) the acceleration of adjustment pressures on all relevant national activities and (2) having to deal prematurely with new international legal challenges.

The letter also included an attachment from the Chamber of Chemical Industries urging that the grace period be fully utilized. The attachment stated that this would (1) give drug companies a chance to develop further (raw material manufacturing capabilities, alliances, and supplier networks); (2) enable firms to register products that would lose their protection during the grace period according to the old patent law (the number of these products was estimated at 300 and their price would be reduced to one-tenth in the event that this was permitted); (3) allow time for the standard of living to rise so that people would be more able to afford the price increases that usually accompany stronger patent protection for drugs; and (4) enhance the possibility of coordinating the activities of drug manufacturers and research centres at the Scientific Research Academy and the schools of pharmacy and medicine. Finally, they demanded that the provisions of the agreement not be applied to drugs registered before its signature, dashing the foreign industry's hopes for 'pipeline' protection.[9]

In response to these arguments and concerns, the letter to the prime minister recommended that the government take advantage of the full five-year grace period allowed for all industries and the full ten years allowed for the pharmaceutical industry. This opinion was fully endorsed by the Ministry of Industry, the Ministry of Military Production, the Ministry of the Economy and Foreign Commerce, the Union of Egyptian Industries, and the Drug Manufacturers. Indeed, Egyptian policymakers and leaders of the local pharmaceutical firms were not convinced of the potential advantages of stronger patent protection for pharmaceuticals, while they were aware of the difficulties that such a policy shift would have on the development of the local industry and on public health.

But the opposition did not fade away. Egypt's decision to take full advantage of the grace period merely led to an intensification of pressures by foreign interests. This led President Mubarak to try to put an effective end to these persistent demands and this bullying, especially by the United States, by making a public announcement that the full grace period would be taken. Thereby he sent a clear signal that it was politically unacceptable for foreigners, including Americans, to overtly push the issue within Egypt since any attempt to do so would mean total disregard for the president's decree. Henceforth, U.S. pressure would have to be exercised through less visible channels, or from abroad.

Conclusion

Since the 1980s the global pharmaceutical industry has been aggressively pursuing changes in the international IPRs regime. The intensification of efforts to this end can be attributed to changes in technology and to intensifying global competition from generic drug producers in the developed and developing countries. Generic drug producers generally provide more affordable alternatives for consumers around the world. Nevertheless, the strength of the global pharmaceutical industry when combined with that of other so-called IPR-sensitive industries has allowed it to gain the upper hand in the international policy process. Indeed, it has allowed the industry to play an unprecedented role in the history of GATT. James Enyart of Monsanto noted that 'we [MNEs] went to Geneva where we presented [our] document to the staff of the GATT Secretariat. What I have described to you is absolutely unprecedented in GATT. Industry has identified a major problem in international trade. It crafted a solution, reduced it to a concrete proposal and sold it to our own and other governments ... The industries and traders of world commerce have played simultaneously the role of patient, the diagnostician and the prescribing physician' (Sell 1998, 54–6). Ultimately, however, it was the willingness of the U.S. government to threaten, or impose, sanctions on countries that refuse to accept their demands for stronger patent protection, and the broad support of the international financial institutions for such policy changes, that had a definitive impact on the creation of a stronger global IPRs regime. Paradoxically, it was later revealed that certain U.S. officials believed that the standards inherent in TRIPS had gone too far. Joseph Stiglitz observed that 'in the final stages of the Uruguay negotiations, both the White House Office of Science and Technology Policy and the Council of Economic Advisers worried that we had not got the balance right – that the agreement put producers' interests over users'. We worried that, with this imbalance, the rate of progress and innovation might actually be impeded. After all, knowledge is the most important input into research, and overly strong intellectual-property rights can, in effect, increase the price of this input' (2002). Stiglitz's concern highlights the necessity of balancing the interests of producers of new knowledge with those of users, not only in developing countries but also in developed countries. 'Overly' strong IPRs result in overpricing knowledge, and in doing so 'we retard its diffusion and beneficial effects on living standards' (ibid.).

These concerns were not publicized by the United States, let alone heeded during the negotiations, as the developing countries were largely coerced into accepting relatively strong IP standards. Under these circumstances, many countries, including Egypt, hoped that the inclusion of the more traditional areas like agriculture and textiles would somewhat balance industrial countries' demands for new rules regarding IPRs and services. Yet major concerns remained over the potential adverse implications of stronger patent protection for local pharmaceutical industries and for public health. This is why the Egyptian government chose to take full advantage of the grace period allowed by TRIPS.

The remainder of this study is dedicated to examining the implications of TRIPS for the pharmaceutical sector and for public health in a developing country like Egypt. The next chapter assesses the economic arguments dealing with IPRs, and especially with patents, with a view to determining the extent to which this literature can further our understanding of the appropriateness and the potential impacts of TRIPS for developing countries.

3 Intellectual Property Theory and TRIPS

This chapter offers an analysis of the theoretical foundation of intellectual property rights, with a focus on patents. A basic intellectual property trade-off exists between innovation and technological diffusion. Striking a balance between the two depends on the specification of numerous parameters in any particular setting. Because of the complexity of this task, analysts often reach conflicting conclusions regarding the optimal strength of patents – that is, the desirable extent of their duration and scope. Even the impact of patents, assuming different levels of protection, is very difficult to determine. Economic studies that have sought to establish the link between stronger patent regimes and (1) research and development, (2) foreign direct investment, (3) technology licensing, and (4) trade have failed to establish consistent or reliable conclusions and to provide a convincing economic justification for the new IPRs regime, particularly for the developing world. These studies have, however, served to draw attention to the importance of the wide range of factors that collectively influence the nature of these four relationships. This ambiguity means that in the real world patent policies cannot simply be derived from economic analysis but are significantly subjected to the influence of competing special interests, as demonstrated in the previous chapter.

This chapter sets the stage for the identification and development of an appropriate analytical framework for assessing the medium- and long-term economic implications of TRIPS for developing countries and their pharmaceutical industries. To this end, it addresses the following four issues: the definition of the concept of intellectual property rights, with a special focus on patents and the relevant aspects of TRIPS; the core intellectual property trade-off that is assumed to exist between innovation and diffusion and the problem of striking a balance between them; the extension of this trade-off to the global level, with a focus on implications for developing countries; and finally, the links between stronger and harmonized patent regimes and R&D, FDI, technology licensing, and trade. In all cases, special attention is paid to the relevance of these issues for the developing world.

The Economics of Intellectual Property Rights

What Are Intellectual Property Rights?

Intellectual property rights are regarded as temporary monopolies granted and regulated by the state to permit the commercial exploitation of intellectual creations. IPRs are classified in two main categories: (1) those applying to industrial property, which includes patents, trademarks, and industrial designs among others; and (2) copyrights, which apply to property that is related to art, music, and literature. Because pharmaceutical technologies are the primary focus of this study, we will be concentrating specifically on patent protection, the single most important intellectual property instrument in that sector.

A patent is a legal instrument that prevents others 'from the unauthorized use, sale, or manufacture of the product or process claimed by the patentee, [patents] are intended to protect embodiments of inventive activity rather than abstract thoughts' (Lesser 1990, 6). As with other forms of intellectual property, a patent provides its owner with an exclusive monopoly over an invention for a finite duration within a given territory – or 'legal space.' Traditionally the basic design of patent law was determined at the national level, but with the creation of TRIPS the minimum standards of protection have been largely relocated to the international level. For an invention to be patentable most patent regimes require that the invention exhibit three characteristics: (1) novelty, the invention must be new; (2) utility, the invention must do what it is intended to do; and (3) non-obviousness, the invention must represent a non-trivial extension of the state of the art. The determination of these criteria is not detailed in TRIPS and so remains completely within the purview of national authorities. These same authorities must also ensure that the inventor includes sufficient disclosure of the invention in the patent application so that, theoretically at least, any person skilled in the art could reproduce the invention. This requirement serves to enhance knowledge dissemination by making public the technical features of a process or product that might otherwise be kept a secret by the inventor. This is intended to counter the inherently negative impact of patents on diffusion.

The extent of the privileges granted to a patentee depends on the strength of the patent, which is defined by its scope and duration. The scope of a patent is defined by the extent to which it provides a 'protected sphere around the characteristics of the invention' (Dasgupta 1988, 7). Thus, a patent determines not only when an identical invention can be marketed, but also how similar an invention can be to the original, without infringing the latter's patent. A patent is strongest · when it protects a product, since then it impedes others from finding different ways of producing, using, or importing the patented product, and when it applies for a long period of time. A product patent confers monopoly rights over a product irrespective of the production technique, while a process patent merely confers monopoly rights over a particular production technique. The latter was a popular form of protection in developing countries, because it permitted firms with limited resources to work around a patent by creating identical but cheaper products, using new processes.

Prior to TRIPS, recourse against patent infringements could *only* be sought through national legal systems that provided for 'appropriate' sanctions and their enforcement. As noted earlier, however, with TRIPS national IPRs regimes have become subject to the discipline of the World Trade Organization. Now, any disputes that cannot be *satisfactorily* resolved at the national level can be referred to the WTO's integrated Dispute Settlement Understanding, and violations of TRIPS can lead to trade sanctions in *any* area covered by the WTO.

TRIPS and Patents for Pharmaceuticals

Before the WTO, intellectual property rights were not defined or managed at the international level to any significant degree. Even so, there was an international intellectual property regime comprised of several treaties and conventions administered since 1970 by the World Intellectual Property Organization. This system tended to be extremely flexible, with few substantive standards, voluntary state membership, and no effective dispute settlement or enforcement mechanisms, leaving countries free to adopt divergent national approaches to IPRs, in general, and to patents for pharmaceuticals, in particular. Thus, some countries provided pharmaceutical product and process patents, others provided process patents only, and still others provided no protection at all. In addition, it was common to find wide discrepancies in the terms of patent protection between countries.

TRIPS changed this situation dramatically. This agreement requires that all countries adopt patent protection regimes in conformity with the standards set in the leading industrial economies, irrespective of their appropriateness for developing countries. Accordingly, all member states of the WTO now have to grant strong patent protection for pharmaceutical products and processes. Specifically this agreement demands the following:

1 Member states may not exclude any field of technology from patent-ability as a whole, and they may not discriminate as to the place of invention when the rights are granted as long as the invention meets the criteria of patentability, that is, novelty, utility, and non-obviousness (Article 27);
2 national patent laws must provide for a minimum patent term of twenty years of protection from the date of filing (Article 33);
3 the patentee's bundle of exclusive rights must include the right to supply the market with imports of the patented product (Article 28) which is subject to the principle of exhaustion (Article 6);[1] and
4 compulsory licences are permitted but only under highly restrictive conditions stipulated in the agreement (Article 31).

As noted in the introduction, developing countries were given until 2005 to fully implement the TRIPS provisions relating to pharmaceuticals, and the least-developed countries were given until 2006, which has subsequently been extended to 2016, with the possibility of further extensions. Countries that make use of these transition periods are obliged to set up a 'mail' or 'letter' box system for accepting the filing of new applications for patents for pharmaceutical products during that period, and they are further bound to grant exclusive marketing rights to the applicants for a maximum period of five years or until the patent is either granted, or rejected, during the transition period (Article 70.9). These provisions will be referred to throughout this book.

The Core Intellectual Property Trade-off

This basic definition of patents tends to imply that knowledge is a standard economic good to which property rights can be clearly assigned and enforced. Yet it is widely known that knowledge is actually a *public good*, which means that it is non-rivalrous and non-excludable. It is non-rivalrous because it has joint consumption properties, meaning that the use of an idea by one person does not diminish its use-value to others; it tends to be non-excludable because it is costly and difficult to prevent others from using an idea without paying for it.

Kenneth Arrow was one of the first economists to discuss the ways in which patent protection might, or might not, be used to rectify the misallocation of resources associated with public goods like knowledge; he argued that knowledge is characterized by three essential features: indivisibility, uncertainty, and inappropriability (1962, 609). Indivisibility here means that the acquisition of a 'unit' of knowledge is a one-time event, after which that knowledge can be used repeatedly without incurring further costs (Dasgupta 1988, 2). Uncertainty is associated with knowledge production because it is especially difficult to estimate the required levels of investment in research and development (particularly in the early stages) or to foresee the potential outcomes or returns. Yet perhaps the greatest problem associated with the production of knowledge, and the one that has attracted the greatest interest, especially from mainstream economists, is its relative inappropriability. This means that, in the absence of legal protection, it is difficult or impossible to appropriate the returns generated by such investments in knowledge production. The problem of inappropriability is exacerbated by the fact that the social and economic value of an invention often far exceeds the immediate, or direct, returns to the inventor due to the presence of positive externalities, or spillover effects. That is why the benefits of 'increases in generally accessible new information' (Rosegger 1986, 129) are usually not adequately reflected in market prices, which impairs the ability of inventors to appropriate the full social value of their invention. This pervasive disincentive to investments in innovation is the main reason that market forces alone would usually lead to underinvestment in R&D.

Mainstream theorists have extensively explored market failure in the production of knowledge. In the extreme case, if one assumes zero dissemination costs in a free market, once a piece of knowledge has been discovered, it would become freely available to all, and the inventor would receive no compensation for the time and resources expended in making the invention in question. In theoretical terms, once a unit of knowledge exists in such a world, the market price for this unit of knowledge would tend to approach zero, preventing the innovator from appropriating any of the associated benefits. For investment in 'research and development to be worth considering, a firm must be able to sell its results, directly or indirectly, for a price. But who would be willing to pay for a commodity that once produced, becomes available to all in unlimited quantity?' (Mansfield 1988, 12). Therefore, the challenge in attempting to provide incentives for the efficient development and production of new knowledge rests in balancing this need to provide incentives for the inventor with that of ensuring the efficient use of existing knowledge for the benefit of society. This is the basic tension or trade-off that exists in any intellectual property system. According to UNCTAD, 'on the one hand, *static efficiency* requires providing wide access to users at (probably low) marginal cost. On the other hand, *dynamic efficiency* calls for providing incentives to improve property or invest in new information for which the value exceeds development costs' (1997, 13). If we accept this trade-off, then the main challenge in designing appropriate patent systems lies in finding an appropriate balance between these two objectives.

Attempts to Find a Balance

Unfortunately, there is no robust method of determining such a balance, as is clearly demonstrated in the literature on optimal patent duration and scope. One of the earliest systematic studies dealing with the optimal duration of patents was that by Nordhaus (1969), who treated it as a maximization problem given certain assumptions. He concluded that patents should be of finite duration and that the length of the period depended on elasticities of demand, the social discount rate, and the significance of the invention. Specifying these parameters is very complex and the results inevitably ambiguous. Nordhaus's most important conclusion was that a uniform patent duration across products and industries is never optimal. This conclusion has found widespread support from analysts like Stoneman, who concluded that various detailed 'observations suggest that different industries, different technologies, different market demands necessitate different optimal patent lives' (1987, 106).

Attempts to determine the optimal scope of patents have faced similar challenges. According to Dasgupta, the scope of a patent 'should be defined as narrowly as is compatible with incentives on the part of the private sector to produce property' (1988, 8). Gilbert and Shapiro concurred with this finding, observing that the 'optimal patent policy calls for infinitely lived patents whenever patent breadth [scope] is increasingly costly in terms of dead weight loss' (1990, 111). In other words, longer patent lives are optimal so long as their scope is kept relatively narrow.

By pointing to the possibility of costly imitation, Gallini, however, suggested quite the opposite. She submitted that lengthy, narrow patents will invite competitors to invent around a patent, thereby displacing the patentee's output and thereby undermining the rewards and incentives for research (1992, 52). This leads to the conclusion that an optimal patent should eliminate entry completely for a time, which is best achieved by making the patent short and broad (ibid.). Klemperer also concluded that the optimal scope of patents will vary across different classes of products, but for him this is because lengthy and narrow patents are less effective when consumers are easily able to substitute a 'less-preferred' product for the protected one. In this case, the patent holder must lower prices to limit the number of consumers who would turn to other substitutes (1990, 115). Determining the optimal scope of a patent must therefore come down to an empirical question depending on the feasibility of 'inventing around a product' in any particular case. Once again this implies that determination of the optimal scope of a patent will be extremely complex and inevitably ambiguous, and it will differ for different products.

Finally, it is important to remember that the conclusions regarding the optimal scope and duration of patents will change if one drops the usual assumption that the existence of a patent does not affect subsequent innovations (Gallini 1992, 62; Gilbert and Shapiro 1990, 112; Klemperer 1990, 127). This assumption is unrealistic, since in reality, innovation is almost always an incremental, cumulative, self-perpetuating, and interactive process (Rosenberg 1976; Freeman 1987; Dosi 1988; Grossman and Helpman 1991; Lundvall 1992; Freeman and Soete 1997). In other words, innovation should be thought of as a process in which 'resources and knowledge may be combined to produce new knowledge, some of which then spills over into the research community and thereby facilitates the creation of still more knowledge' (Grossman and Helpman 1991, 17). Indeed, Dosi suggested that these continuous, positive feedbacks are probably a major reason why we have not seen the emergence of a 'stationary state' in the modern economy (1988, 1138).

Concern with the dynamic, path-dependent nature of innovation has been the main focus of a body of work concerned with innovation as a process. The main significance of this work is that it challenges the basic idea that there is a fundamental conflict between the need to accelerate the diffusion of existing knowledge and the desire to promote innovative activity through incentives. In fact, what this work suggests is that diffusion also accelerates innovation. Thus, Scotchmer and Green concluded that the pace of innovation is dependent on the degree of protection granted to the original innovator, with less protection leading to more rapid innovation (1990, 132). In other words, since rapid disclosure of incremental technological improvements is socially desirable, they suggested that narrow patents are preferable because they permit subsequent additional innovations to be developed and patented without infringing on prior patents (1990, 144). Bessen and Maskin went further in suggesting that when innovation is sequential and complementary, it follows that only limited intellectual property protection is desirable; indeed, they argue that 'imitation *promotes* innovation and that strong patents [long patents of broad scope] *inhibit* it' (2000, 2).

This discussion has shown that there is no robust method for determining the optimal duration or scope of patents. Conceptually, optimal patents will necessarily depend on the specification of numerous parameters in specific contexts. This undoubtedly raises serious concerns regarding the intellectual property framework, as established by TRIPS, which demands that all countries wishing to participate in the global economy must now adhere to one relatively uniform set of IPRs, not only across products, but also across countries. Theoretically speaking, however, there is no basis for the demand for uniform minimum standards of patent protection at the national and international levels.

Extending the Trade-Off to the Global Level

The international strengthening and harmonization of patent regimes is aimed at reducing the extent of imitative activities in developing countries, especially with regard to pharmaceuticals, and this could have a significantly negative impact on the welfare of these countries, and on global welfare generally (Grossman and Helpman 1991). This follows from the single fact that the main purpose of a patent is to exclude others from the use of the protected knowledge, for a period of time, thereby making imitation – and competition – more difficult and costly. Since developing countries are major importers of technology, and since their firms and residents account for less than 10 per cent of all patents (UNDP 2001, 3), changes in the international IPRs regime are going to affect these countries disproportionately. In these countries, stronger patent rights will tend to suppress industrial and innovative activities that are based on adaptation and imitation, forcing them to the sidelines not because they are inefficient, but because they are no longer allowed to compete.

For imitation to be commercially successful two conditions must be fulfilled: (1) the imitating producer must be able to command positive profits in competition with the pioneer, and (2) patent laws must be lax enough to make this possible by not imposing prohibitive costs (Grossman and Helpman 1991, 281). Until recently, these conditions appear to have held in many developing countries with low manufacturing costs and lax patent laws. Grossman and Helpman contended that this situation can enhance 'global' welfare because developing countries have a comparative advantage in manufacturing and a comparative disadvantage in R&D. Therefore, 'the transfer of technology to these countries may cause resources to be released from the manufacturing sectors in high income countries which then find their way into industrial research labs' (ibid., 282). This creates a win-win situation in which the short-term benefits from greater competition and lower prices are complemented by the long-run benefits of more rapid innovation. Although the Grossman and Helpman theory has not been subjected to empirical testing, it does open the possibility that exclusion through the use of patents will have harmful international welfare effects not only on developing countries but developed ones as well.

This discussion implies that patents should generally be designed to suit national priorities and capabilities, and for this they need to be limited geographically. Deardorff suggested that this should be the case even if stronger patent protection does accelerate the overall global pace of technological change. The reason is 'that extending this [high level of] protection to other countries is very likely to be harmful to them, in spite of the fact that they may benefit from increased inventive activity. In those circumstances, if the world as a whole does gain from extending patent protection, it is only in the inventing countries that these gains are experienced, and in fact, they gain even more than the world as a whole because they gain at the rest of the world's expense' (1992, 36). Deardorff's model reflects the fact that patent protection leads to monopoly profits and a more concentrated market structure, so that consumer choice is distorted by higher monopolistic prices, while consumer surplus is diminished in the importing markets. Although this may lead to more innovation globally, this activity is likely to be concentrated in the industrialized countries. As such, its net impact on the developing world is likely to be negative since the costs of extending the monopoly privileges to those who own the technology are likely to exceed the benefits for the developing world (ibid., 49).

Subramanian's models, based on pre- and post-patent reform market structure scenarios in several developing countries, confirm these insights. According to these models, the short-term impact of increased global patent protection on the pharmaceutical industries of developing countries is likely to be negative. Subramanian concluded that the biggest losers would be the larger developing countries which have significant domestic pharmaceutical industries that depend heavily on imitation of existing products. These countries would face grave difficulties with respect to the patentable drug market where they would incur heavy annual losses as a direct result of the introduction of significantly stronger patent protection (Subramanian 1995, 254–5). Even relatively smaller countries like Egypt would suffer major setbacks as a result of a significant transfer of profits to the patent owners. Subramanian and Abdel-Latif suggested that if Egypt were to implement TRIPS it should expect drug prices to rise and welfare to fall; their estimates of the short-term losses that would result from reduced consumer and producer surpluses in Egypt range between U.S.$28 million and U.S.$114 million per annum, or about 3 to 12 per cent of the industry's entire annual output (1997, 15). Although these particular estimates depend on certain assumptions about market structure and size, price elasticities, and the timing of the changes in the patent laws, they do suggest that the losses to Egypt would be significant and that these losses would mirror the gains that would accrue to the foreign producers.

It is important to recognize that these studies only consider the impact of stronger patent regimes on industrial production in developing countries. Other studies have suggested that a stronger and more harmonized global IPRs regime would have a positive impact on the behaviour of multinational enterprises. Such benefits would potentially be shared with developing countries in the form of enhanced flows of foreign direct investment, increased technology licensing, improved trade flows, and higher investments in research and development in knowledge-intensive goods. The following section considers each of these possibilities.

Patents, FDI, Technology Licensing, Trade, and R&D

Proponents of a strong global IPRs system, including the International Federation of Pharmaceutical Manufacturers Associations (IFPMA) and the Pharmaceutical Research and Manufacturers of America (PhRMA), have made numerous claims with regard to the alleged benefits of such a policy shift for the developing countries. According to them TRIPS should enhance FDI, technology transfer to, and trade flows from developing countries by bolstering the incentives for foreign enterprises. In addition, they claim that strong IPRs regimes will promote national and international R&D, with the former contributing to a better use of domestic resources.

Patents and FDI

An extensive review of the literature that has sought to test the hypothesis that there is a positive link between strong patent regimes and foreign direct investment has revealed that any such relationship is ambiguous at best, and contradictory at worst. While there are some theoretical reasons to expect a positive relationship between patents and FDI, particularly for the pharmaceutical sector, that link turns out to be difficult to establish empirically, largely because so many other factors affect FDI, including productivity, education, skills, physical infrastructure, trade barriers, and the transparency of government policies (Primo Braga et al. 1998, 16; Maskus 1998, 11). On balance, 'consensus seems to exist that the main factor explaining FDI flows is the / "economic environment" prevailing in a particular country' (Correa 1995, 175). It should not be surprising then that countries like South Korea, Taiwan, Singapore, Thailand, Brazil, and Mexico, which have often been accused of providing inadequate IPRs, were the highest recipients of FDI during the 1980s, at least until their overall economic situation deteriorated, particularly in the two Latin American countries just mentioned (ibid.).

Other studies have suggested that the presence of strong patent regimes may actually diminish the level of FDI since FDI is sometimes used as a mechanism to maintain control over proprietary information in countries with weak patent systems (Primo Braga and Fink 1997,

113). Under these conditions, as patent strength increases 'firms would tend to choose more technology licensing and joint ventures and less FDI' (Maskus 1998, 12), and in some instances they might reduce their involvement in a particular economy primarily to arm's-length trade. The incentive to invest directly in a country is weakened by TRIPS because it limits a host country's ability to grant compulsory licences or to insist on the local working of patents.

Patents and Technology Licensing

Many analysts have suggested that the strength of patent protection is a key determinant of technology licensing, which is preferred by multi-nationals when 'location advantages favor production in the foreign country and title holders prefer to externalize their proprietary assets' (Primo Braga and Fink 2000, 16). These advantages include attractive profit opportunities, reasonable costs associated with the technology transfer, and conducive regulatory policies, of which strong patents are just one aspect (UNCTAD 1999, 18). Several surveys have indicated that U.S. companies place a high premium on the availability of strong patent regimes when transferring advanced technologies (Primo Braga et al. 1998, 9; Taylor and Silberston 1973, 258–9). Nevertheless, the legal strength of the licensing agreement and the estimated capacity of the buyer to absorb the technology are of even greater importance (Nogues 1993, 42). Because of the importance of factors other than strong IP regimes, the existing survey-based and econometric evidence on the link between patents and technology licensing reveals no more than a weak link, at best (Primo Braga and Fink 2000, 17–18). It is also worth noting that this evidence tends to be based on revenues from royalties and licensing fees, which tell little about the substance and nature of such contracts, particularly with regard to the extent to which knowledge and technology are *actually* transferred during the process.

A major concern regarding the link between stronger patent protection and technology licensing is the cost implication that this may have for developing countries, especially in the field of pharmaceuticals, where the vast majority of product and process patents, particularly those of synthetic drugs and fermentation techniques, are owned by MNEs. Some analysts have suggested that stronger patents can lead to lower licensing costs since it 'becomes easier to discipline licensees against revelation or appropriation of proprietary technology' (Maskus 1998, 16). Others insist that when strong patents are the basis of technology transfer agreements, excessive direct and indirect costs are often imposed due to the frequent existence of too many restrictive clauses (Kirim 1985, 221; von Wartensleben 1983, 173–4) and the reduced bargaining power of the technology purchaser. A study commissioned by WIPO found that 'the major cost implication' of TRIPS for developing countries will result from expected increases in the cost of technology acquisition (Sherwood 1996, 12). These costs are comprised of two components: (1) the increased costs of technology that had been used previously but without the permission of the right holder or under a weaker patent policy and (2) the costs of obtaining technology that could not be imitated previously and could not be acquired willingly from the right holder (ibid.). These costs may be amplified when the effects of technology licensing arrangements undertaken by MNEs and their subsidiaries in developing countries are taken into account. In doing so rents are transferred from the developing country to the country of the parent firm in the form of royalty payments. As a result of these two outcomes, the costs of technology licensing between developed and developing countries are expected to constitute an increasing share of global trade and could double or even triple foreign exchange outflows from developing countries (RAFI 1989 in de Almeida 1995, 222).

Patents and Trade

The impact of stronger patent protection is likely to be most apparent in the altered volume of international trade in technology-sensitive goods. Strong patent regimes augment the market power of multinational firms and enlarge their market size by curtailing imitation. Although in theory stronger patent protection should have an effect on both arm's-length trade and intrafirm trade, it is difficult to predict how a market is going to be supplied by the patent holder when imitation is suddenly displaced.

According to Primo Braga and Fink (2000, 5) the level of intellectual property protection in a particular country may influence trade in one of two ways: (1) by influencing firm decisions regarding how to supply the market and (2) by prohibiting imports from sources where production is still based on imitation. Because of the ambiguity of these impacts, these authors point to the importance of empirical evidence to resolve this question. Studies that have attempted to model the relationship between stronger patent protection and trade flows, however, have resulted in few clear or robust conclusions. Ferrantino found that while a country's adherence to international IPRs conventions had no effect on U.S. interfirm trade, there was a weak negative relation for U.S. intrafirm exports, that is, intrafirm exports tend to be higher in countries with weak protection (1993, 328). In a replication of Ferrantino's study, Primo Braga and Fink found a significant positive coefficient only for arm's-length trade, while the coefficients for intrafirm trade and establishment trade were insignificant (2000, 6).[2]

A study by Maskus and Penubarti found that 'the empirical results strongly suggest that exporting firms discriminate in their sales decisions across export markets, taking account of local patent laws' (1995, 244). It also found that bilateral imports are larger for countries with stronger patent laws, especially among the larger developing countries. Yet a second study, using a different country set and data source, found that the impact of IPRs on trade flows is weaker in larger developing countries and stronger in smaller ones (Primo Braga and Fink 2000, 6). Inevitably these results are specific to the particular econometric approaches used, and these were explicitly static in nature. It is clear, as Maskus and Penubarti have also concluded, that there are few unambiguous predictions about the effects of patents on trade flows (1995, 230).

Patents and R&D

Perhaps the most important claim made by the supporters of TRIPS is that strong patents are a necessary incentive for firms to carry out adequate levels of R&D. By allowing for a limited period of exclusivity, patents enable firms to charge prices well above manufacturing costs and hence to earn *adequate* returns on their innovative investments to encourage continuing high levels of R&D investment. Again, neither the theory nor the evidence lend strong support to this argument. Relatively few studies have addressed the implications of such a policy change for R&D in developing countries.

Most analysts agree that there is some link between patents and R&D, but there is little agreement over whether this relationship is beneficial. Some believe that strong patents lead to an excessive duplication of R&D as firms compete for the patent *prize* (Barzel 1968; Loury 1979; Stiglitz 1986; Dasgupta 1986); however, others see patents as *barriers to entry*, which mitigate competitive pressures on innovative firms, leading to a reduction in duplicative R&D (Loury 1979, 408).

There is disagreement over whether patents are the most important incentive for investment in R&D. It has been argued that commercial returns from being the first to invent are often sufficient to sustain R&D activities, even in the absence of patent protection (Rosenberg and Mowery 1989, 15). This implies that the probability of success, market size, and the purchasing power of consumers are also significant factors. Indeed, de Almeida observed that 'in a wide variety of industries, investments in R&D are made by firms for maintaining their technological leadership and market position and they would do so regardless of the availability of patent protection' (1995, 221). This conclusion seems to be supported by the evidence. Thus, we find that pharmaceutical R&D in the United States continued to rise over the years without complementary changes in that country's patent policy. Nogues noted that in spite of more stringent industry regulations and the introduction of administrative procedures, which decreased effective patent duration between 1938 and 1962, R&D continued to rise over this period (1990, 89). During the 1980s in the United States, the ratio of pharmaceutical R&D investment to sales increased steadily from approximately 10 per cent to 16 per cent (ibid.) despite the industry's persistent complaints of inadequate global IP protection.

Similar patterns have been observed in other countries. In Japan, a large survey of 2,390 corporate researchers revealed that patents were considered less important when appraising R&D decisions than competition and academic or technical interest (Evenson 1990, 39). More historically oriented studies reinforce these conclusions. Schiff (1971) found no evidence that the absence of patent laws in the mid-nineteenth and early twentieth centuries led to a paucity of R&D in the Netherlands or Switzerland (in Scherer 1977, 36). If anything he found that a lack of patent protection aided the industrialization process by enabling unrestricted importation of technology from other countries to support the development of stronger domestic industries. Indeed, even in sectors where technology was not borrowed, industry flourished and in many cases, excelled (ibid., 37). Similarly, Switzerland had a very well-developed chemical industry by the late nineteenth century, and its strength in pharmaceuticals continued despite very limited patent protection (ibid., 39).

Echoing these observations, a comprehensive study sponsored by the U.S. National Bureau of Economic Research found that 'despite the significance of the policy changes and the wide availability of detailed data relating to patenting, robust conclusions regarding the empirical consequences for technological innovation of changes in patent policy are few' (Jaffe 2000, 1). These 'disappointing results' were attributed to the extreme complexity of the economic environment within which the innovation process is necessarily embedded and suggested that this makes it extremely difficult to isolate the specific influence of changes in patent protection on either innovation or profitability (Jaffe 2000, 1–2). The study highlights the difficulty of reconciling 'patent theory' with history and with the empirical evidence.

When it comes to the developing world, these problems are even more pronounced, in part because what little evidence does exist on the link between patent regimes and R&D tends to be drawn from the industrialized world. Yet those who have promoted TRIPS have consistently claimed that a stronger, more harmonized global patent regime would increase R&D spending by both domestic and foreign firms in the developing world. It should be clear by now that such claims cannot be supported by means of the available empirical evidence. Indeed, they are particularly implausible when applied to the pharmaceutical industries that have grown up in some developing countries that have the necessary domestic capabilities. Almost without exception, such industries are heavily dependent on the production of existing drugs or compounds (imitation), which undergo little or no molecular manipulation. It is precisely these types of activities that will be curtailed by TRIPS, with adverse effects on domestic R&D capabilities, insofar as such imitative activities help to create the human and institutional capacities needed if R&D is to be strengthened and deepened in these countries in the longer run.

This strengthening and deepening of R&D is an important issue in its own right since it ultimately determines the extent of the benefits that a national economy can hope to reap from its R&D activities. Many analysts believe that the R&D undertaken by multinational corporations in the developing world can be problematic in this regard because their global corporate interests will generally lead them to try to protect their IPRs and to ensure that it is they who reap the bulk of any technology rents. This means that, although MNEs will usually adapt the scale and type of their R&D activities to a host country's market conditions and socioeconomic circumstances (Chesnais 1992, 278), they will generally focus any local R&D activities on the adoption or, at best, the adaptation, of their existing proprietary technologies (Correa 1995, 178) or possibly on the local provision of certain R&D support services (Chesnais 1992, 278), including seminars, physician training, and clinical trials. In both cases the gains to the local economy would tend to be relatively limited.

Of course, there remains the possibility that the developing countries could benefit substantially from the increased pharmaceutical R&D that might occur in the industrial countries as a result of the strengthening of patent rights under TRIPS. This is indeed a logical possibility but it is a far from certain outcome. First, as has been shown, there is no guarantee that implementation of TRIPS would actually lead to increased R&D in the industrial countries. Yet even if that were to occur, there is no guarantee that the health sectors or the people of the developing world would share significantly in the resulting benefits, either because such research usually does not address their health needs and/or because the resulting drugs are too costly for most consumers (or health services) in the developing world.

Conclusion

This chapter has considered various facets of patent theory. It has examined the basic intellectual property trade-off, the problems inherent in determining optimal patent duration and scope, the implications of extending the patent regime to the global level, and the impact of patents on FDI, technology licensing, trade, and R&D. The aim of the discussion has been twofold: first, to establish that the rules espoused in TRIPS cannot be justified by invoking the most widely accepted theory of patents or the available empirical evidence; and second, to demonstrate that patents cannot be analysed or evaluated in isolation from their economic and social circumstances. Both the theory and the evidence reviewed suggest that any serious evaluation of the likely impact of TRIPS must be based on a broad understanding of the ways in which a particular technology and sector are influenced by key aspects of the national environments within which they are embedded.

Insofar as the question of patents is framed in terms of the basic intellectual property trade-off, the task for the policymaker is to find an optimal balance between the incentive to innovate and the need to promote technological diffusion for the benefit of society. This chapter has shown that this balance will depend on the particular characteristics of the industry, the product, the production process, and the demand for that product or process. This is true of both the optimal period and the optimal scope of a patent. Yet even this does not fully capture the complexity of the problem, since these relationships are also likely to be path dependent, so that the outcome also rests on whether one looks at innovation as a relatively discrete, one-time event, or as part of a continuous process.

Not surprisingly, this complexity increases further when one tries to define optimal patents at an international, or global, level. Here the key question turns out to be whether 'imitation' is deemed beneficial or detrimental to innovation. Those who emphasize its benefits will argue for relatively lax patent regimes, which allow technology to be widely imitated at low cost in the developing world. They contend that this will potentially serve the interests of the developing world both in the short and the long run. In the short run it will mean additional employment, higher levels of investment, and lower drug costs, in the case of the pharmaceutical industry. In the long run, it may be an important part of the learning process through which people, and national economies, must develop the human skills and the institutional capacities needed to increase future productivity, shape future patterns of comparative advantage, and increase the scope for future national R&D. Those who emphasize its costs will argue for stronger, more harmonized patent regimes because they claim that these will increase global R&D to everyone's benefit, while promoting FDI, technology licensing, and trade to offset the acknowledged short-term costs to the developing world of shifting to such a regime. On balance, the short-term costs to the developing world of a shift to stronger patent rights are clear and substantial, while the long-term benefits are ambiguous and uncertain. It should therefore come as no surprise that the developing world has been far less eager to support such a policy shift than the industrial world and its corporate lobbies.

The deep divisions that have come to the fore in the debate about optimal patent regimes can be seen to be rooted in the fact that the benefits, costs, and risks associated with particular policy regimes differ dramatically for the various protagonists. These competing interests play an important role in even the most 'scientific' policy discussions because the extreme complexity of the issue ensures that all conclusions will be relatively uncertain, and therefore legitimately contestable, especially when one is dealing with longer-run outcomes. In this context the disproportionate power of some of the protagonists has allowed them to impose a relatively uniform, harmonized patent regime in the form of TRIPS on a deeply divided and highly unequal world, even though it is well known that optimal patents depend on the specific characteristics of the product or process to be protected, as well as on the circumstances of the surrounding economy and the nature of the innovation process that it is seeking to influence. In other words, the emergence of TRIPS must primarily be understood by looking at the competing interests that have dominated this policy process.

TRIPS is not necessarily undesirable for pharmaceuticals, or for the developing world in general, or for Egypt, in particular. To determine that, it will be necessary to assess the implications of this agreement, with its relatively uniform, minimum requirements for strong patent protection to the particular circumstances of Egypt. In doing so, it is critical to acknowledge that the impact will differ depending on the state of the technology, industry, and sector; the scientific and technological infrastructure of the country; and the administrative and political capacity of the government to design and implement suitable policies to complement any patent regime that it might choose. Only by incorporating this wide range of factors in our analysis of the implications of TRIPS for the pharmaceutical industry and the health sector of Egypt, as one representative developing country, can we hope to understand and explain how diametrically opposed conclusions can both appear to be plausible outcomes of ostensibly scientific inquiries.

4 A National System of Innovation Approach to Understanding the Implications of Stronger Pharmaceutical Patent Protection for Developing Countries

Chapter 3 discussed the core intellectual property trade-off that is commonly assumed to exist between innovation and technological diffusion and established that innovation is far too complex a process to be attributed to any one particular incentive, including patents, as most mainstream intellectual property models imply. This chapter outlines the basis of a national system of innovation (NSI) approach to assessing the implications of stronger patent protection for the pharmaceutical sectors of developing countries. The NSI approach views patents, and IPRs more broadly, as only one element in the complex system of institutions and incentives that shape a country's technological and economic performance. It highlights the importance of three key factors that must all be assessed in determining whether a developing country will be capable of capturing some of the potential benefits (or of minimizing some of the potential costs) associated with stronger IPRs regimes. They are the structure and capabilities of its pharmaceutical firms; the scientific and technological infrastructure, including its universities and public research institutions; and the existence of coherent and stable government policies relating to the pharmaceutical industry. All three of these elements need to be considered and analysed if one is to assess the chances of a beneficial and successful transition to a TRIPS-compliant regime.

At one level, this implies that the effects of IPRs reform will vary from industry to industry, and within an industry, from firm to firm. It also implies that individual cases do not exist in isolation but as part of a system, such that the net effect of stronger IPRs on a country's pharmaceutical industry is more likely to be positive when its national system of innovation is relatively well developed.

This chapter has three main parts. In the first the concept of a national system of innovation is defined, focusing on the particular characteristics of *innovation* in a developing-country context where the core intellectual property trade-off cannot be easily applied because in such a context innovation is largely based on the adoption, adaptation, and improvement of existing knowledge, which is itself highly dependent on effective diffusion. Such a systemic approach emphasizes the need to go beyond particular incentives, like IPRs, to understand the driving forces behind successful innovation. In the second part the three key components of any NSI – firms, scientific and technological infrastructure, and government policies – are examined with a focus on the conditions prevalent in many developing countries. In the final section I demonstrate how certain aspects of a country's national health system can overlap with national systems of innovation to influence the innovative behaviour of pharmaceutical firms.

The Concept of a National System of Innovation

It is difficult to define what is meant by a national system of innovation with great precision. Indeed, there are a number of approaches to the study of such a system, as reflected in the works of authors like Freeman (1987), Porter (1990), Nelson (1993), and Lundvall (1992). Each approach differs in emphasis and focus, and each raises many problems and leaves many issues unresolved. What they have in common is that they are all based on the methodological premise that 'the national system may represent a level of analysis that is not entirely reducible to its individual components' (McKelvey 1991, 121). In other words, the total is different than the mere sum of its parts. For the purpose of this study, a national system of innovation 'is constituted by elements which interact in the production, diffusion and use of new, and economically useful, knowledge and that national system encompasses elements and relationships, either located within or rooted inside the border of a nation state' (Lundvall 1992, 2).[1] The relationships are path dependent, so that each country's historical experience, language, and culture will influence the performance of its NSI (ibid., 13). While such an approach to the study of innovation opens the door to new levels of understanding, it also increases complexity and reduces the scope for certain kinds of analytical rigour and for the generation of widely applicable generalizations.

In this study I emphasize 'national' systems, as opposed to regional or international ones, largely because the specific design and implementation of public policy remains primarily a national function, although that is never exclusively so, and it can be argued that in some cases this balance has gradually been shifting. As Nelson has observed, 'much of the current interest in national systems of innovation reflects a belief that the innovative prowess of national firms is determined to a considerable extent by government policies' (1996, 287). In turn, the success of any policy, and the likelihood of its being effectively implemented or institutionalized, depend on local economic, social, and political circumstances (Pack and Westphal 1986, 103). This makes it challenging when governments seek, or are obliged, to implement international obligations that conflict with national priorities and local circumstances.

In this study, innovation systems, production systems, and the peculiarities of institutional set-ups are regarded as largely national phenomena embedded in specific historical, social, and cultural contexts (Lundvall 1992, 13; Porter 1990, 19). Thus, the implications of any pharmaceutical patent reform cannot be examined apart from the national system within which this reform is to be implemented. Although there is no implied presumption that these national systems are purposely constructed and hence function in a coherent manner, a minimum level of coherence and stability is undoubtedly required if such a national system is to attract and retain investments in innovative activities, whether from domestic or foreign sources. According to the Organization for Economic Cooperation and Development (OECD), the 'creation and diffusion of technology and its transformation into commercial products depends as much on the vitality of the whole set of relationships as on the individual performance of any given element of the system' (1992, 22). From this perspective the implementation of TRIPS in developing countries raises obvious concerns, since it takes little or no account of the specific circumstances or the basic logic of their innovation systems. Indeed, in many senses this new regime has been effectively imposed on an often-reluctant developing world, without consideration of the specific nature of the innovation process, as it generally exists in such a context.

Innovation in a Development Context

It is essential to understand the specific characteristics of innovation in a development context for two primary reasons. First, it is important to assess the relevance of the core intellectual property trade-off under those circumstances, and second, to ensure that the concept of an NSI is based on an appropriate understanding of the innovation process for the developing world.

The core intellectual property trade-off between innovation and technological diffusion is more complex than often suggested, and this is particularly true in a development context where the innovation process differs radically from the one posited by mainstream theory. As has been shown, in the economic literature on IPRs the central focus is on this conflict between innovation and diffusion. The standard argument suggests that intellectual property protection acts as a critically important incentive for innovation by restricting the diffusion of technology for a limited time, thereby allowing innovative firms to appropriate returns on their investments. The concept of innovation that is embedded in this argument, however, is highly restricted and does not take adequate account of the role that diffusion plays in the innovation process itself, particularly in the early stages of an industry's development. Once a link between innovation and diffusion is accepted as a possibility, it can be seen that under certain circumstances stronger IPRs can actually inhibit important aspects of innovation, by inhibiting diffusion.

Standard intellectual property theory tends to take a linear view of technological change and assumes that it occurs progressively and discretely in independent steps in a unidirectional manner. The process as envisaged begins with basic research, which eventually leads to innovation when it is applied to product and process development, then to production and marketing, and finally diffusion. Unfortunately, this view is not only oversimplified, it is essentially incorrect, and may well lead to the creation of incompatible incentive systems. The significant emphasis that this linear view has placed on research and its relation to other stages in the innovation process has had a profound impact on patent policy. Because the model implies that as research increases, so does innovation (Nelson 1996, 31) much mainstream analysis on innovation has simply focused on how to increase research, but without giving adequate consideration to other aspects crucial to the innovation process.

In this view, research has been conceptualized as being clearly divided between basic and applied. Basic research is defined as an activity whose output is unlikely to be a finished product (Mowery and Rosenberg 1989, 11) but which will generally be 'used only as an informational input into other inventive activities' (Dasgupta 1988, 5). Basic research, therefore, is likely to involve a search for fundamental, or pure, information for the advancement of science (Rosegger 1986, 6). Conversely, applied research is defined as an 'activity whose informational output is an input in the production of commodities' (Dasgupta 1988, 5) and it involves the search for 'practical' applications or technology (Rosegger 1986, 6). Basic research is treated as a public good since the payoff is uncertain and distant and partly because the results move rapidly into the public domain and the benefits are difficult to appropriate (Mowery and Rosenberg 1989, 10). Nevertheless, basic research is considered essential for technical progress because 'it enlarges the pool of knowledge from which innovative activities draw, and it is an essential input into the training of manpower for applied research and development activities' (OECD 1971, 14). For these reasons, basic research is mainly carried out in publicly funded laboratories and universities where incentives are linked to career structures that reward the dissemination of knowledge as rapidly as possible. In some cases, however, private firms may undertake basic research to try to be the first to innovate (Malecki 1997, 54), but generally these actors tend to focus on research whose 'technical surety' is much higher (Ostry and Nelson 1995, 110) and which promise specific results and profit opportunities in the relatively short run. As one moves from basic to applied research, both risk and uncertainty tend to decrease (Mowery and Rosenberg 1989, 11).

It is important to recognize that in reality the distinction between basic and applied research is not so clear-cut. In many cases basic research is done for 'practical' purposes, while applied research may have a significant basic component. Nevertheless, the distinction is important especially for understanding a significant inconsistency or 'paradox' between patent theory and patent policy. The logic of patents most directly fits situations where new knowledge is created in discrete, discontinuous steps that do not feed off each other. It fits less well where innovation is part of a seamless, continuous process in which every advance is the outcome of a diffuse and interdependent process where it is often hard to determine who actually 'made' a particular discovery. The innovation process, in reality, is never made up of discrete independent steps. It is always continuous and interdependent to a significant degree, but it is widely agreed that this is less true of basic research than of innovation. Yet, traditionally, patents have been much more widely used to reward innovation (or the results of applied research) as opposed to the results of basic research. Indeed, mainstream theorists have paid little attention to the way in which applied research is actually generated and diffused (Rosenberg 1976, 62), which is what would have to be done to derive truly effective incentives for such activities. In essence then patents provide incentives based largely on an understanding of basic research for actors undertaking applied research without an adequate understanding of that process.

This does not mean that patent protection is necessarily suitable for encouraging basic research even if the definition of knowledge inherent in patent theory is most closely associated with that activity. Since Washington passed the Baye-Dole Act in 1980, which permitted universities to patent technologies that they had developed, patents have been used more and more aggressively to protect research performed by these institutions. This trend, however, is highly contestable, as it does not seem to be responding to the need to stimulate basic research and the sharing of knowledge, while university research increasingly adopts a commercial focus. Allowing the patentability of public research obscures incentives and career structures that had long been designed so as to maximize the speed with which information is transferred and shared, as careers depended on being the first to publish important new findings. According to McDonagh this raises concerns about intellectual property and technology transfer: 'For instance, what is the relationship between patenting the products of research and the old, established way of getting information out of the lab and into circulation: publishing academic papers? There is a basic conflict between the goals of academia and industry when it comes to sharing knowledge' (2001). Unfortunately, the recent decline in government and corporate support for university research (Ostry and Nelson 1995, 10) may be giving rise to a vicious cycle as universities race to patent their research results in an attempt to augment needed funding levels. This will have a negative impact not only on 'the rate at which new understandings open up broad new technological prospects' (ibid., 112), but it will also serve to restrict the pool of knowledge from which researchers can freely draw, with serious long-term implications for the generation of new knowledge.

In effect, the linear model of technological change has created 'artificial conceptual disjunctions between innovative activity and other activities with which it is not only linked, but which in fact constitute major parts of the historical process of innovation itself' (Rosenberg

1976, 77). By oversimplifying the relationship between research and technical advance (Nelson 1996, 31), this model has induced analysts to focus on some aspects of the innovation process, while neglecting others that are equally important. As a result, IPRs policies have largely been based on a poor understanding of the innovation process, particularly in the case of developing countries.

Approaching the study of IPRs from an NSI perspective represents an alternative way of thinking that has much to recommend it. In doing so it is critically important to proceed on the basis of an accurate understanding of the innovation process. In this study the innovation process is conceptualized as a pervasive and dynamic economic phenomenon, following Lundvall's conceptualization: 'In practically all parts of the economy, and at all times, we expect to find on-going processes of learning, searching and exploring, which result in new products, new techniques, new forms of organisation and new markets' (1992, 8). Although in developing countries these activities are often happening at very different levels of sophistication than in industrial countries, they are happening nevertheless.

This understanding fits well into the approach taken by Ernst, Mytelka, and Ganiatsos, who suggested that when studying development it is useful to conceive of innovation as a 'process by which firms master and implement the design and production of goods and services that are new to them, irrespective of whether or not they are new to their competitors – domestic or foreign' (1998, 12–13). This emphasizes the importance of learning and of 'learning to learn'[2] which is defined as the development of 'problem solving capabilities that enable the firm to improve its productivity, to imitate and to adapt product, process and organizational technologies already developed elsewhere to local conditions' (Mytelka 1998, 4). Indeed, many of those who have studied imitation in developing countries have found that the process is akin to innovation in industrial countries (Baba and Imai 1992; Grossman and Helpman 1991; Dosi 1988; Rosenberg 1976). As Dosi observed, 'the partly tacit nature of knowledge and its characteristics of partial private appropriability makes imitation, as well as innovation, a creative process, which involves search, which is not wholly distinct from the search for 'new' developments, and which is economically expensive – sometimes even more expensive than the original innovation ... this applies to both patented and non-patented innovations' (1998, 1140). In the same vein, Mowery and Rosenberg argued that a significant research capability is required to 'understand, interpret, and appraise knowledge that is placed on the shelf – whether basic or applied' (1989, 15). It is, therefore, widely agreed that as with innovation, there is substantial uncertainty and risk associated with adopting and adapting foreign technologies to different national circumstances (Nelson in Pack and Westphal 1986, 105; Rosegger 1986, 177). Indeed, from the perspective of the firms undertaking these activities, the decision to adapt an existing technology 'may not look qualitatively different from a decision to innovate' (Rosegger 1986, 182).

Thus, in developing countries imitation often has many of the characteristics that are normally associated with the innovation process in industrial countries. Both involve ingenuity, scientific and technological skills, abilities to use specialized knowledge for problem solving, managerial abilities, and organizational effectiveness and flexibility – all of which influence production costs, market competitiveness, and hence the evolution of the industry (Pack and Westphal 1986, 105; Dosi 1988, 1120). Moreover, both innovation and imitation improve firms' technological absorptive capacity, defined as 'the ability of firms to learn and use the technology developed elsewhere through a process that involves substantial investments, particularly of an intangible nature' (OECD 1992, 17). The potentially close link between innovation and imitation is highlighted by the fact that innovation is, in large part, a self-reinforcing cumulative process. It is ultimately this characteristic that links innovation/imitation so closely with learning. Indeed, in many developing countries, the industrialization process has involved a significant accumulation of technological capability, despite the low levels of industrial and basic R&D, as producers have gained mastery over products and processes that were new to them and to the domestic economy (Grossman and Helpman 1991, 12; Pack and Westphal 1986, 105). The key to these developments in many developing countries has been the relatively uninhibited technological diffusion made possible, in part, by lax or even non-existent, IPR protection.

Many analysts would agree that the international diffusion of technology is closely linked to technological progress and economic growth, especially in the developing world (Rosenberg 1976; Perez 1988; Brown 1981; Grossman and Helpman 1991; Romer 1994; Freeman and Soete 1997). Insofar as this is true, the stronger patent laws embedded in TRIPS will impede diffusion and the learning and innovation to which it gives rise. Some would argue that it is of paramount importance to allow developing countries to benefit from the learning opportunities associated with effective technological diffusion. From this position the trade-off between technological diffusion and innovation inherent in TRIPS is indeed illusive.

Beyond IP Policy

The dominance of the linear model of technological change tends to focus attention on individual policy measures, like intellectual property protection, at the expense of a broader and deeper understanding of the many other factors that ultimately make up the innovation process. It follows from this that to understand the likely implications of TRIPS on the pharmaceutical industry and on public health it is necessary to understand the pharmaceutical/health aspects of the national innovation system into which it is being introduced. According to Correa, 'the patent system as an incentive to local innovation is unlikely to work, except in those countries where a significant technological infrastructure already exists, and where there are big enough firms to engage in substantial R&D efforts' (1998, 29). In other words, it is the NSI of a country, combined with its public health system, which should be the basis for the design and implementation of appropriate national intellectual property policy.

Although the suitability of IPRs regimes will have a significant influence on the shape and the success of a country's innovation system, sustained success also requires suitable and supportive framework policies that protect the economy from developing major, disruptive imbalances. Thus, it is widely understood that the need for radical budget cuts, or dramatic devaluations, or the instability generated by largely speculative mergers and acquisitions, all have the potential for destroying accumulated knowledge and technological capabilities (OECD 1992, 38). Indeed, as Rath reminded us, 'performance can stagnate and in fact negative learning can easily result from adverse policy and environmental factors' (1990, 1434). When patent policy is made without due regard for its appropriateness for the national setting, it is not difficult to see that it may meet with failure. Stronger pharmaceutical patents must be accompanied by a wide range of complementary policies and institutional reforms aimed at strengthening indigenous technological capabilities and safeguarding public health. Historically, the governments of the industrialized countries have complemented the often gradual introduction of stronger intellectual property rights with other domestic policies designed to ensure the continued development of their domestic pharmaceutical industries while also safe-guarding public health.

In short, the development of a national innovation system is generally the result of a long and continuous process of technological appropriation and development (Chesnais 1991, 158; OECD 1992, 17). This process is path dependent so that, in the words of the OECD report 'the countries, firms and institutions which have been able to exploit the opportunities over *many decades* and create a base for technological accumulation are the best placed to adapt to the transitions and transformations of structural change' (1992, 17; emphasis added). From such a perspective, the short transition periods granted by TRIPS are unlikely to give developing countries enough time to align their national innovation systems to their new international obligations, let alone to protect the ability of those systems to support and to strengthen indigenous technological capabilities within the context of the new global IPRs regime.

The remainder of this chapter explores three key elements of national systems of innovation that are fundamental to technical progress and that will therefore influence the outcome of the policy reforms entailed in TRIPS. These elements have been identified on the basis of a broad survey of the available literature on national systems of innovation which draws on the historical experience of several currently industrialized countries. Nevertheless, authors tend to differ with regard to the relative significance of each element. According to Nelson and Rosenberg, 'in a way these understandings do provide a common analytic framework, not wide enough to encompass all of the variables and relationships that are likely to be important, not sharp enough to tightly guide empirical work, but broad enough and pointed enough to provide a common structure in which one can have some confidence' (1993, 5).

This study focuses on Egypt's pharmaceutical sector within a national system of innovation framework. This means that it considers those elements of the national system of innovation that most directly affect innovation in the pharmaceutical industry. A sectoral focus is important because differences between the innovation processes in different industries are significant, so that each industry has its own unique characteristics that determine (1) its need for, or dependence on various elements like public research laboratories and universities and (2) its interactions with these and the more general systemic elements like government policies (Nelson and Rosenberg 1993, 13). Ultimately the task of assessing the implications of pharmaceutical patent reform in Egypt requires a critical examination of the structure and the capabilities of the firms that are involved in drug research and production. It may therefore be more apt to describe such an approach as a national innovation 'meso' system (Chesnais 1991, 160).

Key Elements of National Systems of Innovation

The Structure and Capabilities of Firms in an Industry

The role of the industrial firm is central to innovation no matter what definition of innovation is used. Although it is certainly not the sole contributor to technological change, the firm is nevertheless the main actor that transforms the knowledge gained from science and technology into products and services, 'hopefully' in response to market demand. Accordingly, it is quite appropriate that firms should be the primary targets of IPRs reform. However, firms differ in terms of their habits and practices with regard to innovation, and these will affect their response to any policy changes. According to Mytelka, firm strategies 'depend upon the set of habits and practices they have developed to deal with the challenges of change and competition. When these historical habits, practices and routines are generalized across many firms and achieve some measure of longevity, they become important elements in determining policy dynamics and hence policy outcomes. Only by understanding the historical habits and practices of targeted actors can policies be devoted to strengthen or change them' (1999, 19). What this means in practice is that industrialists who have long been dependent on the adoption and adaptation of foreign technologies may respond negatively to a strengthening of intellectual property rights since that is likely to impede technological diffusion.

In assessing firm responses to the introduction of stronger IPRs in the pharmaceutical sector we need to look at both research and development and production. As we do so, we need to bear in mind that the available evidence suggests that different types of firms will respond differently in many cases. Thus, it is widely believed that the responses of multinational subsidiaries operating in developing countries will often differ markedly from locally owned firms or from public sector firms. The discussion that follows is sensitive to such systemic differences while recognizing that within each group there inevitably will be differences between individual firm responses. These are issues that will become increasingly evident in our discussion of the case of Egypt in the following chapters.

Industrial Structure

Despite a vast and rich tradition, the link between industrial structure and innovation has not been conclusively established. According to standard industrial organization theory, largely based on Schumpeter's (1942) hypothesis, greater market concentration is associated with high levels of innovation. Empirical research, however, has revealed that greater market concentration may lead to quite the opposite: a decline in innovation due to less competitive pressures (Pavitt and Patel 1988, 46; Aghion et al. 2002, 1). Both proposed relationships lend support to the observation by Freeman and Soete that 'statistical generalizations about size of firm, scale of R&D, inventive output and innovation need to be heavily qualified ... simplistic generalizations about lower or higher concentration leading to better innovative performance cannot be sustained' (1997, 229).

A recent study by Aghion et al. (2002) found that when competition is intense firms tend to limit investments in innovation for fear that they will not profit sufficiently from the outcomes. Alternatively, when firms have too much power, they also tend to underinvest in innovation. Therefore, in situations of either monopoly or high competition firms are less likely to innovate than in situations that are between these two extremes. This suggests that strong IP rules that guarantee supernormal profits are likely to decrease innovation rather than encourage it.

In a developing country like Egypt, where innovation levels are dismal, this possibility is quite problematic. In accordance with Aghion's study, strong IPRs would sharply and abruptly decrease competitive pressures on foreign firms operating in Egypt and guarantee profit levels high enough so that local investments in R&D would no longer be considered necessary even in the event of major improvements to the NSI. For locally owned and public sector firms, innovation would also decrease, but in this instance it would occur as a result of too much competition resulting from the premature imposition of strong IPRs. In effect, TRIPS takes the level of competition far beyond that required to induce local firms to invest in innovation and may even deny them the possibility of building such capabilities.

Because of the complexity of the innovation environment in any

country, and particularly in developing countries where there are relatively few studies of the relationship between industrial structure and
innovation, one cannot make broad generalizations. However, low levels of pharmaceutical R&D and innovation are pervasive throughout
much of the developing world irrespective of market structures. This
may be an indication that the structure of firms in an industry only
becomes an important factor in innovation when an overall environment conducive to such activities already exists, or is established,
within a country.

In-house R&D and Production

In-house research is an important feature of many modern pharmaceutical firms, whether brand name or generic, and the literature suggests
four fundamental rationales for this. First, in-house R&D augments the
capacity of firms 'to recognize, evaluate, negotiate and finally adapt
the technology partially available from others' (Dosi 1988, 1132). In
effect, it allows firms to understand the strengths and weaknesses of a
technology, thereby permitting them to make improvements (Nelson
and Rosenberg 1993, 10; OECD 1992, 17). Second, in-house R&D allows
firms to draw more effectively on public research to adapt it to more
'practical' uses (Nelson and Rosenberg 1993, 10). In fact, although public institutes account for most basic scientific discoveries, the development of new technologies based on that research is largely the domain
of the private firm. Third, it is often suggested that in-house R&D
makes it is easier for a firm to integrate its R&D activities with developments in production and marketing (Nelson 1996, 62; Nelson and
Rosenberg 1993, 10). As research becomes more applied it has to be
linked to production design and marketing considerations, and these,
in turn, need to conform to a firm's specific capabilities and experience. Indeed, effective R&D tends eventually to be not only industry
specific, but also firm specific. This is the main reason why there are
limits to the effectiveness of separate stand-alone R&D facilities like
public or university laboratories. A final important reason for in-house
R&D is to allow a firm to keep new knowledge secret for as long as
possible, thereby giving the firm a head start on its competition (Nelson 1996, 63). Therefore, firms may prefer to rely on tacit knowledge
'embedded' in its staff and organization and avoid certain contractual
relations even when these are otherwise desirable (Mowery and
Rosenberg 1989, 6). Indeed, firms may even refuse to patent certain

processes for fear that this would allow competitors to decode the new knowledge that they have 'created.'

The extent of R&D undertaken by a national industry generally depends on the country's level of economic development and the degree of its international specialization (Freeman 1987, 16), so that there are significant differences in levels of R&D in developed and developing countries. The path dependency of the innovation process makes it very difficult to close this gap. Thus, according to Pavitt and Patel, 'lags in catching up with frontier technology often result from the lack of such [research] competence, rather than from legal, informational or other types of barriers to entry' (1988, 36). This underscores the importance of R&D in the early stages of development and the necessity of implementing policies and incentives that guarantee continued investments in R&D, as is the case in the OECD countries (Freeman 1987, 2). This is not to imply that expenditure on R&D is synonymous with innovation, but it does tend to be the most commonly used indicator of innovative activity by both policymakers and academics (Pavitt and Patel 1988, 38). But R&D is only one input into the innovation process. While it is true that levels of R&D help to determine the ability of firms to exploit existing knowledge, or to generate new knowledge, they miss an important additional source of technological capacity, namely, production engineering. However, it is difficult to integrate this sphere into the analysis since the distinction between R&D and these related activities, including the problem solving that is part of the production process and keeping abreast of competitors' new developments, is not easy to delineate (Nelson and Rosenberg 1993, 11).

Production itself is therefore an important determinant of a firm's response to the introduction of stronger IPRs. Since innovation is a cumulative process that involves learning by doing, by using, and by interacting with both other producers and users (Freeman 1987, 2), the system of innovation cannot be understood in isolation from the system of production. In this case, it is important to understand that TRIPS is likely to change the structure of pharmaceutical production in many developing countries as patent policies that have tended to favour local producers are amended in ways that strengthen the hand of foreign-owned enterprises. Production has a significant learning effect on the firm, and over time this can be expected to increase the firm's capacity to make use of scientific and technological research (Mowery and Rosenberg 1989, vii). Indeed, the resulting process of continuous innovation has been said to be 'the prerequisite of radical innovations' (Andersen and Lundvall 1988, 14). A good example is reverse engineering, which can be considered part of the production process and which, involves 'learning to produce by taking apart products and processes to find out how they work'; although such activities are not generally classified as R&D, they are very similar and can lead to similar outcomes (OECD 1992, 33).

As firms gain experience by engaging in production, they are able to combine their own knowledge with foreign technology, and this enhances their technological capabilities and strengthens their market position (OECD 1992, 263). Indeed, successful firms are the ones that achieve such combinations (Pack and Westphal 1986, 106). When there are learning effects, experience in production will lead to lower costs and that will generally lead to increased markets and an expansion of employment and production (Henderson et al. 1999, 282). This, in turn, creates better opportunities for innovation and the development of greater technological know-how (Rath 1990, 1434). The ability to gain experience in the production of new technologies by firms in developing countries, however, may be curtailed by the relatively high minimum standards established by TRIPS. In part, the development of technological capabilities in much of the developing world, as well as that which occurred historically in the industrial countries, has always been based on their relative freedom to adopt and adapt the technologies developed in more advanced countries, and this process was facilitated by the absence of strong IPRs (UNDP 2001, 102–3). From this perspective, TRIPS can be said to threaten the possibility for continuous learning and innovation in the developing world. In doing so, it will diminish the emergence of competitors that could, one day, have the capabilities to exploit frontier technologies, but that may be denied the opportunity under this new regime.

The Scientific and Technological Infrastructure

The scientific and technological infrastructure of a national economy is composed of a myriad of actors, including industry, relevant government departments, banks, public research institutes, and university laboratories. The need to understand the actions and interactions of these various actors arises from the fact that technological advance proceeds through the efforts of this complex community of actors, and that community always has a distinct national character (Nelson and

Rosenberg 1993, 15). The effectiveness of these actors, and of the 'system' of which they are a part, determines the level of support available to knowledge-intensive industries like pharmaceuticals, which will help determine the likelihood of such activities thriving in a particular location. In many developing countries the weakness of this scientific and technological infrastructure impedes innovation and that, in turn, helps explain the resistance of their domestic firms to stronger intellectual property rights. In other words, the weakness of the infrastructure makes it difficult for national firms to take advantage of the potential benefits of rights because the transition from imitation to innovation becomes more difficult, and this increases the dependence of domestic firms on foreign technology and imitation.

When examining the pharmaceutical sector, emphasis in the literature is often on the important role of universities and public research laboratories, which influence the innovation process in three main ways. First, universities are relied on for the training and retraining of scientists, engineers, and technically qualified personnel. It is important that university programs reflect the changing demands of the economy so that the skill composition of the labour force remains consistent with the demand for labour (OECD 1992, 268). Accordingly, in much of the developed world (and now in some developing countries) various arrangements and understandings have established closer links between industrial laboratories and the universities.

Second, as noted previously, universities and public laboratories are relied on for undertaking basic research. Research and development is generally considered the heart of the science and technology complex that 'originates a large portion of the new and improved materials, products, processes and systems, which are the ultimate source of economic advance' (Freeman and Soete 1997, 5). In the early stages of technological development, public R&D institutions play a particularly critical role by assimilating and diffusing foreign technologies at a time when dependence on such technologies is strongest (OECD 1992, 265). The importance of their role is especially great in the health sciences because health is largely a public good. There is much evidence to suggest that the discovery of new drugs is generally given strong impetus by public sector research, although often with interaction with the private sector. Indeed, it has been observed that 'all the countries that are strong and innovative in fine chemicals and pharmaceuticals have strong university research in chemistry and in the biomedical sciences' (Nelson 1996, 288). To be effective, however, these institutions must be dynamic and flexible so that, as private capabilities increase, they continue to be capable of generating appropriate knowledge inputs. It is important to keep in mind that the ability to establish and maintain this dynamism depends on the historic evolution of domestic science and technology institutions (OECD 1992, 267) and on available resources. Once more this underscores the need for much longer transition periods and much greater resources for developing countries than TRIPS currently provides.

Finally, public research institutes and university laboratories affect innovation through their interaction with industry and society at large. The presence of a professional R&D system is considered insufficient in the absence of viable linkages with other knowledge-intensive industries, industrial production, marketing, and the science and technology network in general (Freeman and Soete 1997, 275). In advanced countries 'university programs are not undifferentiated parts of a national innovation system broadly defined, but rather are keyed into particular technologies and particular industries' (Nelson 1996, 278). For instance, in the United States and Germany universities are the home of institutes designed to help particular industries (Nelson and Rosenberg 1993, 12). When these public institutions are supporting domestic firms, there tend to be direct interactions between faculty members or research teams and the relevant industries, often through various consulting arrangements (Nelson 1996, 288–9). The important point is that in such situations, 'the transfer of knowledge between science and technology is mainly person embodied: in other words, it takes place through people talking to one another, or through people moving from one institution to another' (OECD 1971, 14). This leads many to suggest that for scientists and industrialists to benefit significantly from one another, it is necessary to create structures and incentives conducive to personal interaction and collaboration (Mowery and Rosenberg 1989, 13).

Ultimately, science and technology can only flourish where there is a critical mass of professionals, backed by good facilities, effective information flows, and sustained funding. These are the main factors that are necessary for the continual advancement of knowledge and science (Rosenberg 1976, 167; Segal 1987, 87). In light of this, most governments fund basic research and higher education to a significant degree, but the organization, the means of funding, and the orientation of the research differ widely across countries (Nelson and Rosenberg 1993, 12). Nevertheless, they all have to face the same challenge, namely, that of integrating science and society, so that science can be responsive to social needs, because science in isolation is likely to become 'sterile and unproductive' (Mowery and Rosenberg 1989, 113).

The Coherence and Suitability of Government Policies

The third key factor of any national system of innovation that must be examined in order to assess the likely impact of stronger intellectual property protection on a developing country is the coherence and suitability of its government policies. This is so because the dynamics of government policies have an important influence on the 'resources, incentives and barriers' relating to all aspects of the innovation process (OECD 1971, 14). The idea is that intellectual property policy, and innovation or technology policy more generally, must be seen as part of a broader set of policies that may complement or contradict them, thereby affecting the opportunities and constraints within which innovative firms must operate (Mytelka 1999, 9). This broader policy framework is itself embedded within a set of sociopolitical conditions, which further determine the acceptability and effectiveness of different forms of government intervention (Pack and Westphal 1986, 103).

The NSI approach highlights the importance of examining policies that have an impact on cross-cutting issues like innovation, investment, competition, technological diffusion, trade, and in the case of pharmaceutical innovation, public health. Our task is to understand the main policies and public institutions that have traditionally served as effective complements to IPRs in developed countries and that may therefore deserve to be incorporated (in an appropriate form) into the national systems of innovation of developing countries. The discussion that follows focuses both on a number of general policy areas, including IPRs policy, competition policy, and technology policy, and some policy areas aimed specifically at the pharmaceutical industry.

INTELLECTUAL PROPERTY POLICY AND ITS IMPLEMENTATION
The level of intellectual property protection has traditionally reflected a country's level of technological and economic development, together with its national socioeconomic priorities. Thus, according to the U.N. Development Program's 2001 *Human Development Report*, 'many of today's advanced economies refused to grant patents throughout the 19th and early 20th centuries, or found legal and illegal ways of circumventing them – as illustrated by the many strategies used by European countries during the industrial revolution. They formalized and

enforced intellectual property rights gradually as they shifted from being net users of intellectual property to being net producers' (UNDP 2001, 102).

It is not surprising that the economies that performed well historically, especially in pharmaceuticals, have inevitably done so in an environment of lax IPRs, complemented by supportive government interventions that often included FDI restrictions and significant, selective trade barriers (Rodrik 1999, 1; Romer 1994, 65). The logic of these policy regimes is disarmingly simple. Relatively limited IPRs encourage the rapid adoption of existing technologies and this has been conducive to the development of local pharmaceutical industries. Indeed, the formative years of the pharmaceutical industry in industrialized countries were characterized by extensive international imitation. Many countries, including Japan, Switzerland, and Germany, actually delayed the extension of full patent protection to pharmaceuticals until their drug industries had become well established both in world and domestic markets (Frischtak 1989, 28). Other industrial countries, like Canada, reformed their patent laws as late as in the 1990s, with several others not doing so until the conclusion of the Uruguay Round,[3] and then only because of political pressures from stronger trade partners and certain domestic interests. Thus, the creation of stronger national IPRs regimes generally came rather late in the process of economic development, and they cannot therefore be credited with triggering the process of economic or industrial development.

In view of this historical reality, it is possible to say that developing countries, in general, are at present not ready for the changes implied in TRIPS or for the costs of their implementation. Until now their domestic systems of innovation and their socioeconomic priorities have rightly tended to favour lax IPR regimes. In cases where patent protection for pharmaceuticals was provided, the scope and duration tended to be limited. Limiting the scope of patent protection makes it easier for local firms or inventors to invent around a patent, which serves to encourage appropriate local R&D. Generally speaking, a relatively limited patent term enhances knowledge diffusion by reducing the time between the introduction of a new technology and its legitimate imitation. This encourages the rapid emergence of multiple suppliers of any new technology, which helps restore price competition. On balance, as Arrow observed, this has tended to ensure that knowledge is more widely and effectively exploited within any given society (1962, 614). The same could be said to be true of the global economy.

Theoretically, TRIPS provides countries with various policy options to partially address these and other concerns, particularly in relation to public health. Although TRIPS demands stronger patent protection levels than most developing countries have traditionally provided, especially for pharmaceuticals, it does allow some limited room for interpretation and hence for adaptation to domestic interests. There is no one correct way to interpret and implement TRIPS. Each country, whether developed or developing, must itself determine which interpretation of TRIPS best addresses its needs, especially in the pharmaceutical sector, which is linked to so many other issues ranging from industrial development to drug access and public health. Neglecting, or relinquishing, this right to adapt the agreement to domestic circumstances in response to international political pressure will mean that the adverse impact of stronger patent rights on a country's industrial development and public health will be greater than need be.

Competition Policy

Of all the related policy areas examined in the literature discussing IPRs in the context of developing countries, competition policy receives the greatest attention, which is not surprising, since patents are instruments in curtailing competition. According to Singh and Dhumale, competition policy may be defined as 'a body of laws, administrative rules and case law which are employed to deter restrictive practices so as to maintain fair competition' (in Correa 2000, 2). Experience suggests that several conflicts may emerge between competition policy and IPRs, including instances where intellectual property rights are used in a manner that violates the objectives and principles of such protection, which includes the extension of protection beyond its intended purpose, the restraint of trade, and the inhibition of technology transfer (UNCTAD 1997, 53). That developing countries are net technology importers, with weak or non-existent competition rules, raises legitimate concerns that stronger intellectual property rights may facilitate anticompetitive practices or abusive behaviour by patent right holders. Such behaviour includes cartel-like restraints, exclusionary conduct, monopoly leveraging by dominant firms, and practices or mergers that may dampen innovation and the impact of overly broad IPRs (UNCTAD 2001, 3).

The introduction of stronger patent protection will alter the competitive environment within which domestic firms must operate. It is plausible to argue that the premature imposition of stronger patent regimes is similar to the premature opening of markets to international competition, where 'potential opportunities' cannot be taken advantage of by a firm or industry because it is not yet in a position to do so. In a number of Latin American countries, the premature opening of markets has had significant adverse effects (Mytelka 1999, 22). Without adequate systems to facilitate the adjustment of domestic firms, many competitive enterprises in these countries went bankrupt, declined, transformed production to imports, or replaced some of their innovative activities with licensing (ibid.). Similarly, the premature imposition of stronger patent rights may lead to the misallocation of R&D resources and to the loss of dynamic gains that had traditionally resulted from the reverse engineering and sequential innovation through which local producers were able to access existing technologies. Competition laws should be designed to address these possibilities.

It is noteworthy that the strengthening of IPRs in developed countries has generally taken place within a 'framework of effective application of competition policy' (Correa 2000, 2). These countries have an extensive tradition of competition rules related to IPRs that evolved through legislation, case law, and enforcement procedures (UNCTAD 2001, 4). Developing countries, on the other hand, have little or no such experience partly because their ability to make coherent policy has often been compromised by a lack of resources and a lack of sovereignty due to their frequent inability to resist excessive foreign interference in their policy process.

Competition policies vary according to place and time, and it is widely acknowledged that economic, social, and cultural interests influence competition laws (Ullrich in Correa 2000, 3). In general, however, it is possible to say that anticompetitive behaviour is determined by several factors, including the extent of IPR protection, the economic and social significance of the product (or process) that is being protected, market structure, the nature of competitors, and the defined national goals (UNCTAD 1997, 3). All this makes the task of developing suitable competition policies very difficult, especially since developing countries cannot simply emulate developed country regulations both because their circumstances are so different and because developed country policies continue to be hotly contested and problematic. Yet despite the many difficulties, competition policy must be used to remedy anticompetitive practices that may arise with stronger IPRs

(Correa 2000, 4). Hence, as TRIPS is being implemented in the developing world, we see that most countries are creating new competition policies. These are not always uniform, and serious enforcement problems remain. One of the main enforcement problems stems from the fact that most of the intellectual property being protected in the developing world is owned by foreign enterprises. The enforcement of competition rules is most likely to affect such firms, and this means that developing countries will be unable to enforce those rules without international assistance and cooperation (UNCTAD 2001, 21), which, unfortunately, is not easy to obtain.

Governments must ensure that their new competition policies take account of TRIPS. In this regard, TRIPS Article 8.2 accepts that appropriate measures may be 'needed to prevent the abuse of intellectual property rights by right holders or the resort to practices which unreasonably restrain trade or adversely affect international transfer of technology.' Article 8.2 also stipulates that any remedies that are devised must be consistent with the general provisions of the agreement. Similarly, Article 40.1 acknowledges that IPRs 'may have adverse effects on trade and impede the transfer and dissemination of technology,' but it also establishes clear limits to the types of national action that can be taken in response to such adverse outcomes: such action must be 'consistent with the other provisions' of TRIPS and must allow for consultations between disputing members. In short, there is autonomy, but this autonomy is clearly and explicitly constrained.

Notwithstanding these limitations, it is crucial that developing countries devise effective competition policies that conform to their own national priorities and that address the potential problems that can arise with stronger patent rights under their particular circumstances. Indeed, developing countries must understand that 'defining and enforcing an adequate competition policy regarding the unilateral exercise or the contractual exploitation of intellectual property protection is not a secondary concern that might await the establishment of a TRIPS-compatible intellectual property system, but rather must go hand-in-hand with it' (UNCTAD 1997, 4).

Technology Policy

In this study we have noted that the basic rationale for IPRs – to inhibit the diffusion of new technology in order to guarantee the rapid development of new technology to be diffused in the future – is largely inapplicable to the conditions that characterize the early stages of development, when innovation and diffusion are largely complementary processes. We have also noted that one of the most outstanding outcomes of TRIPS will be the inhibition of diffusion for prolonged periods and an increase in the cost of technology acquisition for developing countries. This highlights the vital importance of active technology policies in the developing world to counter or minimize these adverse consequences.

Technology policy may be narrowly defined, in which case it is primarily concerned with the promotion of R&D, or it may be broadly defined, in which case it overlaps with elements of competition, trade, and financial policies. In reality, the diversity of government policies makes it difficult to make any broad generalizations. However, it is important to explore some of the more popular instruments of technology policy currently in place in many developed (and increasingly, in developing) countries to encourage innovation and technology transfer. Although the adoption, adaptation, and creation of new technologies are largely the responsibility of private actors, governments do have an impact on this process through their diffusion/technology policies. According to Stoneman and Vickers, diffusion policy should be thought of as extending beyond the simple provision or dissemination of information to include subsidies and any other incentives that speed up the adoption of new technologies and encourage investments in R&D (1988, ix). Indeed, as noted in the previous chapter, knowledge has many of the characteristics of a public good, and therefore too much competition will tend to lead to an underinvestment in such activities. For this reason, governments in both developing and developed countries have tended to promote such investment in a variety of ways. According to Ostry and Nelson, jointly funded R&D consortia by government and private firms are a standard feature of domestic technology policies in Japan, the United States, and Europe (1995, 87). This is also the case in the newly industrialized East Asian economies. For example, the South Korean government encourages private firms to establish research facilities to promote industrial restructuring and technological development, and in Taiwan scientists are encouraged to set up their own firms to commercialize the results of their R&D (OECD 1992, 268).

The provision of adequate funding for innovation is obviously critical for building technological capabilities (Segal 1987, 28), which makes it an important focus of state intervention in many industrial countries. State supports, which include the provision of matching funds and the co-financing of R&D through technology funds where loans are only repaid if projects succeed (UNDP 2001, 83), can encourage firms to make risky R&D investments. Such measures, however, are increasingly contested, as the 'standard' view claims that discretionary subsidies are necessarily inefficient and undesirable. They are therefore strongly discouraged by new international agreements, while being treated as anathema in most mainstream economic discussions. Moreover, many economists and policymakers argue that such direct supports give national firms an unfair advantage over rivals in other countries (Ostry and Nelson 1995, 30) and violate the concept of national treatment. From this standpoint, support for universities and public research institutes that have direct links to industry seems more attractive, if only because they are less visible politically (Nelson 1996, 289).

Many governments have been active in creating or reforming financial structures and services to better serve innovative enterprises (Nelson 1996, 287). 'The role played by national banking systems in the financing of R&D and intangible investments is now considered an important factor in shaping structural competition in each country' (OECD 1992, 20). Some governments have even played an important role in establishing venture capital industries to stimulate innovation. Most developing countries, however, lack the sophisticated financial systems that are a prerequisite for attracting large volumes of venture funds (UNDP 2001, 84).

Another way that national authorities can enhance the diffusion and adoption of new technologies is by designing and enforcing regulations that ensure effective technology transfer. Several countries, including many from the developing world, have specific regulations for the control and facilitation of technology transfer agreements. For many developing countries these regulations were put on the agenda by the failed negotiations over an International Code of Conduct for the Transfer of Technology in the 1970s under the auspices of UNCTAD. Before they collapsed, these negotiations had identified certain practices as unacceptable, given the technological needs of developing countries. These practices included the charging of excessive royalties, the inappropriate charging of other costs, and the imposition of restrictions on research or on the commercial and industrial activities of the licensee, including export restrictions, price, quantity, or geographical limits on operations. Unfortunately, 'many of such laws [in the developing countries] were substantially modified or repealed during the 1990s, as part of a process of liberalization of economies' (Correa 2000, 13). The problem is that, while these regimes were gradually being dismantled, competition policies were not being formulated to regulate the resulting restrictive practices and technology transfer abuses (ibid.). In this regard, TRIPS claims to encourage the transfer of technology from the developed to the developing countries and explicitly allows for national legislation that aims to control undesirable technology transfer practices. The agreement cites exclusive grant-back provisions, obligations not to challenge the validity of licensed rights, and coercive package licensing as examples of possible abuse. The agreement leaves the direction and rate of technology transfers up to the negotiating abilities of the parties involved and makes no recommendation on how such transfers should take place, nor does it define clearly when the spirit of this requirement is being violated. Developing countries must therefore press for adequate commitments from the developed countries to ensure the flow of technology.

Other policies that may affect innovation and technology transfer include those related to trade, education and training, and government procurement policies. Export subsidies or protection from imports may enhance local production and technological capabilities and give local firms an advantage over foreign rivals (Stoneman and Vickers 1988; x). Education and training policies help ensure the quality and availability of scientific personnel both for industry and for the domestic science and technology complex. Finally, procurement policies may act as a hidden form of protection for the purpose of technological advancement (ibid.).

This discussion highlights the importance for developing country policymakers to realize, as they embark on the design of policies to accommodate TRIPS, that arguments to adopt laissez faire/laissez 'innover' approaches to technology development are not well supported by the evidence. The creation of good framework regulations that include well-defined property rights, effective contract enforcement, the rule of law, and reasonable equality of application (Lipsey 1991, 5) are very important, but not enough. In promoting their high technology industries, the developed countries have complemented such measures by a diverse array of interventions including policies that deal with science and technology, industrial competitiveness, and exports (Malecki 1997, 239; Ostry 1990, 53; Ostry and Nelson 1995, 61).

Policies and Regulations Specific to the Pharmaceutical Industry

In addition to the above policies that can help to determine the implications of stronger global pharmaceutical patents for developing countries, it is necessary to consider specific policies designed to impact the pharmaceutical industry in particular. This includes all those measures that governments use to rationalize drug expenditures in accordance with their health care needs and their current level of development. Such measures are important for various reasons. Not only do they influence the supply and demand of pharmaceutical products, which in turn, affect the profitability of firms and their strategies regarding innovation, but they also aim to ensure that the pharmaceutical industry plays a constructive role in the achievement of national health goals. This, once again, draws attention to the fact that the intellectual property rights regime is only one of many regulatory measures that determine the behaviour of the pharmaceutical industry. Moreover, it serves as a reminder that it is necessary to go beyond strict definitions of national systems of innovation when studying the pharmaceutical sector because that industry is also distinguished by its primary role in national health care systems.

Regulation of the pharmaceutical market is very complex, and it differs country to country. There are, however, several policies that seem to be prevalent, irrespective of the country's level of income or industrialization (Saxenian 1994, 1). These include essential drug lists or formularies, rules on competitive procurement or bulk purchasing, rules governing generic drug substitution, various forms of price control, user fees, and the provision of better information for health care workers and patients. All such regulations have a significant impact on competitiveness, efficiency, and innovation in the pharmaceutical industry. Nevertheless, it is important to bear in mind that their primary goal is to enhance the welfare of those who are ill.

In all countries, governments are responsible to some degree for designing and administering public health systems and health insurance schemes, and in regulating private health care firms. In doing so, one of their concerns is to ensure that the costs of medical treatments, including the cost of drugs, remain affordable for most individuals and groups of citizens. As a result, governments invariably end up being heavy, if not the main, purchasers of drugs, as they seek to obtain the best possible prices for off-patent medicines, by restricting the monopoly rents accruing to patented drug owners (Jacobzone 2000, 9).

Formulating appropriate pharmaceutical policies requires a lot of detailed information, which may often be challenging for developing countries to acquire and to update on a continuous basis. It also requires policymakers who are knowledgeable about factors that influence demand, like user fees and physician prescribing behaviour, and supply, like R&D, marketing, patent protection, and changing production costs (Jacobzone 2000, 15). Regulating demand first involves 'defining' the market, that is, determining the rules for market authorization and eligibility for reimbursement. All countries have specific market authorization guidelines; however, 'most developing countries lack well-functioning drug regulatory systems, backed up by a quality control laboratory, that can keep nonsensical drugs, ineffective drugs, and poorly made products out of the market' (Saxenian 1994, 2). On account of such difficulties some developing countries rely on the safety and efficacy procedures of advanced industrial countries. Strict regulatory regimes that serve to ensure the safety and efficacy of pharmaceutical products have often been the subject of intense criticism by the industry, whether in developed or developing countries. Procedures to gain market approval for products tend to be both costly and time-consuming. This is why some industrial countries, under pressure from their pharmaceutical industries, have agreed to grant patent term extensions or patent term restoration for alleged 'time lost' in the regulatory process.

In addition to market authorization policies, most countries have a universal system of drug coverage or insurance. It is common to find health authorities in developing countries using essential drug lists or formularies to guide the selection of products and to determine the quantities that should be kept in stock in various institutions or for which patients can be reimbursed. In some developed countries, like Canada, private insurance bodies are permitted to define their own drug lists. Laing (in Saxenian 1994) observed that, when combined with education, essential drug lists or formularies can contribute to a significant decrease in drug expenditures.

Because demand tends to be price inelastic for many drugs, it can be influenced by physician-prescribing behaviour, government procurement, and price controls. Public policies and guidelines that influence physician-prescribing behaviour include information provision and even financial penalties on providers prescribing too many drugs or overly expensive drugs (Saxenian 1994, 3). In developing countries these efforts may be of limited value since a high proportion of drugs consumed are self-prescribed. Nevertheless, the brand name pharmaceutical industry tends to expend large sums in its efforts to influence physician-prescribing behaviour.

Governments and large purchasers can also influence the demand and the availability of drugs through competitive procurement methods and bulk purchasing which enables them to obtain drugs at low cost. Through these mechanisms, organizations can often obtain deep discounts on brand name and patented drugs. Competitive procurement systems require specialized technical skills, as well as access to comprehensive pharmaceutical information, and these requirements may be challenging for many developing countries which may be why so few of them take advantage of international competition or international agencies, like the International Dispensary Association and UNICEF, in pharmaceutical purchasing. For some the main problem may be short-term liquidity constraints (Saxenian 1994, 7–8).

Many countries, in both the developed and developing worlds, have regulations that control the prices of pharmaceutical products directly. Price controls are largely designed to counter the monopoly power of firms enjoying patent protection, although they may also be applied to generic drug substitutes. The two main methods used to control prices are profit control or 'cost-plus' regulations, which are based on production costs while allowing for a certain profit margin, and 'fixed' price systems, which involve fixing prices and allowing for free supply behaviour (Jacobzone 2000, 33). In the case of Egypt, limits are also generally placed on the number of allowable substitutes on the market at any given point in time. In most OECD countries, with the exception of the United States, Germany, and Denmark, governments usually combine systems of free and fixed pricing. Several factors are considered when fixing the price of a drug, including its therapeutic value, reference to existing products, reference to international comparisons, and the contribution of the pharmaceutical industry to the economy (ibid., 34). In contrast, many developing countries base their price control regimes on 'cost-plus' formulations despite the method's numerous problems (Saxenian 1994, 12), including the need for extensive data review to verify the true costs of production. Multinational enterprises often use transfer pricing to manipulate the calculation of production costs, or they attempt to continuously reintroduce the same product with minor variations to get price increments approved. If price controls do not take adequate account of inflation or of changes in production costs, products may be discontinued or quality may suffer. Finally, there are problems of transparency in the application of such price controls, with negotiations always being vulnerable to corruption.

Supply and demand in pharmaceutical products is also influenced by generic drug substitution policies, which substitute less expensive drugs with similar or identical therapeutic effects for expensive brand name or on patent drugs. Many countries are active in fostering the use of generic drugs to curb health care expenditures despite strong opposition from the brand name pharmaceutical industry. Generic substitution can have a significant impact on the profitability of brand name firms, particularly when their best-selling products go off patent. Governments usually rely on the dissemination of information and economic incentives to promote the use of lower-priced generic drug substitutes. They may also pass regulations, as in the United States, that allow pharmacists to fill prescriptions with generics and/or that require both the brand and generic names of a product to be included on the packaging to facilitate substitution.

Although not strictly considered part of a national system of innovation, these aspects of health policy, through their impact on supply and demand in the pharmaceutical sector, can have a significant influence on the innovation strategies of pharmaceutical firms. As such, these policies may impact or mitigate the implications of stronger IPRs in particular national settings. It is important to recognize, however, that these efforts can only be as effective as a country's institutional enforcement mechanisms. They are also dependent on a country's 'health care finance and delivery system, its level of trained manpower, including pharmacists and physicians, the capacity of the drug regulatory agency, features of the pharmaceutical distribution system, and pharmaceutical spending levels' (Saxenian 1994, 3). All of these factors are likely to influence the outcomes of TRIPS as they relate to the pharmaceutical industries of developing countries and particularly as they relate to public health in these countries.

Conclusion

This chapter developed a national system of innovation approach to assessing the implications of stronger IPRs for the pharmaceutical sectors of developing countries. A national system of innovation was defined to include all aspects of a national economy that interact to influence innovation including history, language, and culture, which are considered to have an important impact on the dynamics of policy change. Inevitably, the diversity of such an approach makes generalizations regarding the specific implications of TRIPS very difficult; however, it does permit a contextualization of patent policy reform and offers a realistic view of the complexity of the innovation process.

Our discussion of innovation brought to light two major issues. First, the linear view of technical change that is implicit in most mainstream intellectual property analyses fails to distinguish clearly enough between patent theory and patent policy. Although the theoretical foundation of mainstream intellectual property rights theory is essentially designed to deal with the circumstances surrounding basic research, intellectual property policy is mainly used to encourage more applied research activities in which risk and uncertainty tend to be much lower. This confusion may easily lead to inappropriate patent policies that do not adequately disentangle private and public rights. Second, our discussion has revealed that this misleading conceptualization of the innovation process as a linear one obscures the very important fact that it is actually an evolutionary process based on a complex and interactive process of learning, searching, exploring, and utilizing existing knowledge. From such a perspective diffusion is not something separate that happens after innovation has occurred, but something that tends to play a significant role in innovation itself. The international diffusion of technology is almost certainly closely related to innovation, technological progress, and economic growth, especially in developing countries where innovation is initially generally based on imitation facilitated by the existence of lax patent regimes, among other things.

To understand the full implications of TRIPS for developing countries, we must look beyond the resulting changes in intellectual property regimes to consider other national factors that will influence the process of innovation and the operations of the pharmaceutical industry more generally. To this end, this chapter considered three key elements of national systems of innovation including the innovative strength of firms, the scientific and technological infrastructure of a particular country, and the coherence of government policies that deal with innovation or the operations of the pharmaceutical industry in the interests of public health. Although these three key elements were discussed separately, it is critical to recognize that their harmonious interaction is central to economic and technological development. Indeed, innovation depends on the quality and number of components in a national system of innovation, as well as on the relationships between firms, suppliers, markets, public institutions, financial and banking institutions, education and training, and infrastructure (OECD 1992, 22).

In the remainder of this study we will be applying the framework developed in this chapter to assess the likely implications of TRIPS on the pharmaceutical and health sectors of Egypt. Although some commentators have argued that it is too early for such assessments, since many developing countries, including Egypt, have only recently applied the agreement, the NSI approach outlined here should give us a reasonable idea of what to expect with regard to pharmaceuticals and public health in the coming years and beyond. The NSI approach will also enable us to identify the complementary policy changes that might allow this policy shift to yield significant net benefits for the developing world.

5 Patent Policy and the Evolution of Egyptian Pharmaceuticals[1]

This case study will seek to assess the implications of TRIPS on Egypt's pharmaceutical industry, and on its health sector, from the perspective of a national system of innovation.[1] This requires some understanding of key aspects of the evolution of Egypt's pharmaceutical industry, since that has shaped the context for contemporary responses and outcomes of TRIPS-related patent policy reforms. There are basically five phases that characterize the evolution of Egypt's pharmaceutical industry as identified by the Egyptian Academy of Scientific Research. An examination of each phase shows that Egypt's domestic industry has undergone quite revolutionary changes as it sought to cope with the radically different policies of three different military regimes, ranging from state-led import substitution policies to market-led export promotion policies. Yet, in spite of these dramatic policy shifts, successive governments have remained focused on the need to avoid excessive reliance on foreign manufacturers in order to more effectively manage society's public health needs.

There are three basic aims of this brief historical and contextual account. First, it aims to demonstrate that a relatively weak pharmaceutical patent policy has been instrumental in fostering the emergence of a vigorous domestic industry that has come to satisfy a great proportion of domestic demand; however, it was only during a brief episode in the 1960s, when this patent policy was complemented by a comprehensive pharmaceutical plan, that the innovative potential of the industry was revealed. Second, it aims to show that the industry that did emerge through this process achieved this approximate national self-sufficiency in ways that were desirable from a public health point of view, in the sense that the industry supplied needed drugs relatively reliably and at affordable prices. And finally, it aims to prove that the industry that emerged in this way had relatively limited innovative capacities, which is not surprising given the strategy that was adopted starting with the 'open door' policies of the Sadat regime. These historical realities have conditioned the most likely domestic response to a strengthened patent regime today.

Phase 1 (1933–1961): Establishing the Domestic Industry

The first phase begins with the birth of the domestic pharmaceutical industry, which occurred when the coming of the Second World War triggered the growth of Egyptian financial capital by reducing the exporting capabilities of multinational firms based in the industrial countries (Galal 1983, 237). As a direct result, two specialized pharmaceutical plants were quickly established in Egypt: Misr Company (Misr Bank) in 1939 and C.I.D. Company (Industrial Bank) in 1940. Soon other private companies sprang up, with Memphis Pharmaceuticals joining the two original ones to become one of the three largest locally owned firms. By the end of this phase, sixteen medium-sized enterprises and twenty-two small drug laboratories had joined these three companies. The state's role during this initial phase was limited. Weaknesses in the system of drug registration, inspection, and testing by laboratories run by the Ministry of Health reinforced the state's laissez-faire approach. No special protectionist measures were introduced to foster this emerging local industry, which faced intense competition from foreign-owned firms that constituted the primary source of domestic supply (around 90 per cent).

To make matters more challenging for the local industry, in 1949 the Egyptian government adopted a new patent law as part of its preparations to become a member of the Paris Convention for the Protection of Industrial Property two years later. Law No. 132, Concerning Letters Patent and Industrial Drawings, Models and Inventions, provided patent protection only for pharmaceutical processes for a period of ten years from the date of filing. To its supporters, the law was designed to fulfil four main objectives. First, it was a necessary measure for Egypt to fulfil its pending obligations under the Paris Convention. Second, it was hoped that the availability of this form of protection would stimulate the search for new methods of production, which would encourage R&D efforts that were thought to be commensurate with local capabilities and resources. Third, it sought to promote effective competition between drugs with the same therapeutic effect, which could be expected to lower market prices. Finally, because the law only provided process as opposed to product protection, local technology importers could avoid certain licensing restrictions that dictated raw material and intermediate goods supply sources, allowing them to keep their costs down. Critics of Law No. 132 claimed that it was nothing more than a measure aimed at inhibiting the industry's development since it restricted the previously free use of foreign technologies.

Until the time of Gamal Abdel Nasser's 1952 revolution the development of the domestic pharmaceutical industry remained relatively limited, especially in comparison with its foreign counterparts. Market structures, in which multinational interests were still heavily entrenched, significantly restricted the growth of local producers by discouraging many of them from investing in much needed expansion of their own facilities (Galal 1983, 237). Thus, the domestic industry remained primarily a collection of small laboratories 'formulating' imported raw ingredients into pills, syrups, and vitamins, based on products developed elsewhere by MNEs. Quality levels remained low, as there was no effective mechanism for monitoring or enforcement, and incentives for indigenous research and development remained woefully inadequate. By 1956 this sluggish performance was set to change, again under the impetus of war. In this case, the economic blockade of Egypt by England and France during the Suez Crisis demonstrated the urgent need for Egypt to develop a significant local pharmaceutical industry by highlighting the risks of being totally dependent on external suppliers for critical drugs. At the time the only company manufacturing a treatment for schistosomiasis, commonly known as bilharzia and endemic to Egypt, was a British-owned one, and it ceased production during the blockade, allegedly because of poor sales. Although the health authorities attempted to persuade the company to continue production by agreeing to a higher price, the firm remained unrelenting, leaving Egyptian authorities no choice but to find ways to manufacture the drug locally. Ironically, those local efforts eventually resulted in a drug that was 80 per cent purer than the original British version.

This incident was significant in shaping the future course of Egyptian pharmaceutical policy for two main reasons. First, it demonstrated that in an uncertain world it was very dangerous for Egypt to rely too heavily on foreign suppliers for its key pharmaceutical needs. Second, the success of this attempt suggested to Egyptian policymakers that

Egypt probably had the capability to greatly expand and improve its home-grown industry, even within the framework of the new intellectual property law. As a result, the market share of local firms began to grow steadily even as local consumption increased, so that by 1962 the domestic industry was supplying some 29 per cent of domestic consumption.

This era introduced many far-reaching changes in the structure and operation of the industry – a legacy that has not fully dissipated even today. The first significant measure of the Nasser regime was to place a ceiling on the profits of distributors, although according to Galal (1983, 237), this was quickly neutralized by false export prices which, in turn, led the state to take action to regulate import purchasing and transfer pricing. Specifically, the state concluded that the high cost of the raw materials imported by small individual firms was a major problem, largely due to their inability to obtain more favourable terms through concerted action. To remedy this, the state established government monopolies for the importation and distribution of drug ingredients and products in an effort to negotiate more favourable prices and improve quality control. The Supreme Organization for Drug Planning and Control, established by Law No. 290 of 1960, was to rationalize importation to the local formularies. In retrospect, it seems that this decision did strengthen Egypt's capacity to make good pharmaceutical policy, partly by enhancing local knowledge of the international pharmaceutical market, including different supply sources and price opportunities. Furthermore, it allowed health regulators to become more familiar with the generally accepted quality standards for the materials required in the drug production process and to learn about the formal standards used in other countries, as well as the industry's standards used by firms to establish the relative quality of materials obtained from different sources of supply.

Phase 2 (1962–1975): Nationalization

The second phase of the industry's evolution is generally considered the most significant one in the development of the pharmaceutical sector. During this period the state made no changes to its pharmaceuticals patent policy but rather complemented its IP regime with the introduction of a comprehensive plan for the development of the industry as a whole. Indeed, it is widely accepted, even among leading mainstream economists like Eggertson, that the thrust of Egypt's phar-

maceutical policies during this era was 'well suited for the mobilization of resources, forced industrialization, and for taking advantage of
economies of scale in various basic industries,' as was the case in many
Soviet-type economies at the time (1990, 334). The resulting short-lived
golden age of pharmaceutical development began in 1962, when the
state intervened dramatically to reorganize the trade and production of
drugs. This took the form of a comprehensive nationalization program
introduced partly in response to the disintegration of Egypt's relations
with its traditional drug suppliers. For this purpose, the government
created a General Organization for Drugs, Chemicals, and Medical
Appliances (the DCMA) and fostered and encouraged the merger of
smaller enterprises into larger, more viable, economic units.

The DCMA, under the auspices of the Ministry of Health (MOH)
monopolized the importation, production, distribution, and planning
of pharmaceuticals. Its primary goal was to achieve national self-sufficiency in drug production. To achieve this goal the state began a program of import substitution seeking to develop local production to the
point where it would account for the greatest possible share of local
consumption. To this end it established a domestic company, El Nasr
Chemicals Company, for the manufacture of the main raw materials
needed for local pharmaceuticals production. The DCMA also allowed
for the local production of drugs that were not categorized as essential,
like vitamins and painkillers, after full consideration of their socioeconomic importance. Imports were to be based on necessity only. This
meant that if local production of a drug was possible, it would not be
imported, and that in all cases imports would be limited to essential
drugs only. To control transfer pricing by MNEs, all imports were
henceforth to be approved by the DCMA. In the event that a multinational company refused to lower its prices when requested to do
so, and this was common because of fears that other countries would
follow Egypt's lead, the DCMA frequently resorted to importing the
needed products from cheaper markets.

As critical as these policies were, Dr Essam Galal, the organization's
second director, insisted that the most significant role of the DCMA
was its emphasis on the importance of R&D for industrial development. Under Galal's directorship, the organization created a major
research centre that was financed through mandatory contributions
(1 per cent of sales) from local and foreign companies. Researchers
were sent to train in MNEs in both Egypt and abroad and needed
equipment was readily purchased from these companies. Soon

research projects were initiated to find treatments for schistosomiasis, rheumatism, and certain infectious diseases endemic to Egypt. According to Galal, every pharmaceutical firm at the time had an active research and development facility. Local firms were actively encouraged to approach researchers in the DCMA before resorting to MNEs for licences. In many cases, research teams proved capable of developing drugs based on foreign technologies by using different processes in conformity with Egypt's intellectual property law. This not only had the effect of saving the local industry unnecessary licensing costs and much needed foreign exchange, but also of greatly enhancing learning opportunities for local researchers.

The very success of these policies ensured strong opposition from those producers who were threatened with potentially being displaced by this growing industry. Soon after the 1967 war with Israel, many projects in the Egypt's pharmaceutical sector came to an abrupt halt, as various economic sanctions were imposed on the country. The main multinational companies showed their displeasure by refusing to contribute to the training of personnel or to the R&D operations of the DCMA. They also refused to make their technologies available under licence or to sell needed equipment to locals, while increasing the price of their raw materials and refusing to extend normal trade credit for the drugs that Egypt still needed to import, so that all such imports had to be paid in cash. These sanctions had a great impact on the DCMA, which was forced to slow its expansion and to discontinue some of its research projects. Although the golden age was brought to a close by these events, they nevertheless served to heighten the state's determination to achieve greater domestic self-sufficiency in pharmaceutical production. But the resulting excessive and growing preoccupation with political objectives diverted attention away from scientific and economic exigencies, and this soon took its toll.

The Sadat government took power in 1971 and succeeded in expanding local production of pharmaceuticals dramatically by developing a complete pharmaceutical industry based on seven public sector firms: two for the production of raw materials and packaging; two for   handling all imports, storage, and distribution; and three joint ownership firms (Egyptian and foreign)[2] to expand local production. By 1975 the local industry was supplying 84 per cent of domestic consumption, when just two decades earlier it had been supplying less than 10 per cent. However, there were many problems associated with this spectacular growth. First, under wartime conditions, concerns about quality were simply overwhelmed by the demand for quantity, as pharmaceutical production was increased dramatically within a very short period to achieve self-sufficiency. In this context, a general lapse in drug quality occurred partly because the state did not want effective quality controls to impede growth and therefore allowed the industry to treat such controls as voluntary. Second, pricing policies were largely driven by the desire to make drugs affordable given the country's social realities, but this resulted in an almost total neglect of commercial realities. As a result, although high subsidies ensured a level of pricing that was commensurate with social needs, they also tended to eliminate much needed competitive pressures that might have promoted more indigenous R&D and that, in turn, might eventually have diminished the industry's heavy focus on duplicate drug provision (Galal 1983, 239).

Added to this were the growing problems associated with the state's national policy of guaranteed employment or its 'graduates policy.' Initially, this had facilitated the rapid growth of a local industry, but it soon began placing significant pressures on the public sector, which had to absorb an excessive number of graduates relative to its ability to utilize such labour. These problems were exacerbated by the fact that the links between university research and potential commercial users of this knowledge were very weak, partly because the state tended to be overly concerned about the unpredictability of professors and students whose views were considered suspect if only because they often failed to take 'adequate' account of the 'realities' within which the state's policy decisions had to be made. This fundamental lack of trust undermined the contribution that academia could have made to industrial and technological development. Indeed, within the prevailing political climate, the government seemed to prefer to treat the pay of faculty and students as sinecures, actively discouraging them from making effective connections off-campus. This same basic lack of trust was also pervasive between academia and industry.

Finally, and related to the former point, the integration of the various elements of this national innovation system was very weak. As just noted, linkages between industry and academia were highly inadequate with both operating in almost exclusively separate spheres. Even 'the [local pharmaceutical industry's] coordination with supportive industries and services was always laborious and often ineffective,' observed Galal (1983, 239). In addition, transfers of technology, know-how, and experience were limited between both public sector and joint-ownership firms. In the public sector annual competitive assessments of individual companies hindered cooperation of this sort and prevented the harmonization of production lines, which led to the frequent duplication of popular over-the-counter drugs and serious shortages of less-rewarding, more specialized drugs (ibid.). Meanwhile the behaviour of the international firms, as noted above, was largely influenced by wartime loyalties and a general disapproval of Egypt's pharmaceutical development plan.

These problems combined with financial constraints stemming from the industry's high levels of indebtedness and low profitability, partly because of the government's pricing policies, contributed to a notable decline in pharmaceutical R&D and a weakening of the national system of innovation more generally. The waning drive of the Sadat government to effectively implement the pharmaceutical policy, developed by Galal under the Nasser regime, meant that the further spectacular expansion of the industry was based on increasingly fragile foundations. One of the greatest problems was that the government no longer tied industrial development to research, so that the promise of institutions like the General Organization for Drugs, Chemicals, and Medical Appliances could not be realized. Under these conditions, the ability of the local industry to continue to benefit from Egypt's relatively lax intellectual property regime was greatly compromised.

Phase 3 (1976–1983): Opening the Pharmaceutical Market

The sweeping economic changes that launched Egypt's transformation into a market-based economy began in the mid-1970s. The goals of Sadat's so-called open-door policies, which characterized the third phase of Egypt's pharmaceutical industry's development, were to liberalize the economy and to attach primary importance to attracting foreign capital to stimulate growth and technological progress. Within this broad strategy the pharmaceutical sector attracted the particular interest of foreign investors, no doubt encouraged by the international pharmaceutical lobby. Soon various foreign actors, including some heads of state, were actively pressuring the new government to prioritize the 'opening' of this sector to greater foreign investments and competition. These pressures were welcomed by the government which was already committed to the very same policy changes that were being advocated from outside.

In a dramatic departure from the previous policy of import substitution, the government began by significantly liberalizing drug imports. MNEs eagerly submitted a list of the drugs that they wanted to import into Egypt. Approximately 90 per cent of them were considered not essential for the country's needs and as such authorization for their importation was initially denied. It was not long, however, before this decision was overridden by the minister of health. This political manoeuvre, in addition to the restriction of the role of the DCMA to one of simple monitoring, led staunch nationalists to conclude that the government was undermining the local industry. According to the government, however, the purpose of all of these changes was to increase competition, improve quality, and increase efficiency.

Initially, these hopes appeared to be fulfilled since, starting in the late 1970s, these market reforms led to massive investments in the pharmaceutical industry by both foreign and local industrialists.[3] The competition that emerged between these new players and the existing public sector producers did not serve to strengthen the latter or to make them more efficient. In fact, Sadat's liberalization policies produced economic and technological changes that undermined the local industry, ultimately rendering it highly inefficient. The foreign firms had some overwhelming advantages. Their massive advertising budgets allowed them to win market share by focusing on promotional activities, which local industry leaders could not afford or unwisely dismissed as a waste of resources. The foreign firms were able to introduce new products not produced in Egypt and to become monopolists in certain drug categories as a result. The domestic industry was unable to overcome these obstacles, especially since the linkages between local firms, raw material suppliers, and domestic research institutes were so very weak. In the absence of effective cooperation and government support, the level of R&D carried out by the industry remained negligible, despite a growing realization of the importance of such activities for their future ability to compete. Individual companies acting alone found most R&D ventures too risky and therefore opted for licensing arrangements with MNEs, instead – a preference that still exists today.

These tendencies were reinforced by the government's introduction of a de facto increase in patent protection for foreign firms in an attempt to attract even more foreign investments, while avoiding confrontation with local industry leaders who would have strongly rejected formal changes to the law. The government was already acutely aware that there was discontent with its broad development approach, but protests had largely remained fragmented as some industry leaders found lucrative opportunities in the newborn private sector. Open and formal changes in Egypt's patent regime would surely have given rise to a strong and unified political opposition, which was something the government did not want to risk, given that many of the leaders of the local industry had been soldiers in Egypt's liberation movement just two decades earlier and still had strong ties to certain elements in the state apparatus. Thus, enhanced patent protection could only be achieved by informal administrative means, whereby the minister of health simply slowed down the registration of generic drugs by delaying or denying market authorization. Unfortunately, this served to further undermine the potential benefits that the local industry could have derived from Egypt's ostensibly weak patent law.

Phase 4 (1983–1992): Expansion without Foundations

The fourth phase of the pharmaceutical industry's evolution is characterized by the declining policy autonomy of the Egyptian government as a result of the economic crisis that it faced during the 1980s, which facilitated the heavy intervention of its major creditors in domestic affairs. Even though there was a growing realization among policymakers that the competition that had emerged between foreign and local pharmaceutical firms was premised on the latter's increasing dependence on technology licensing and vulnerability to adverse terms of trade, the government's ability to design or to implement an effective technology policy had become very limited. Indeed, the only area where it still seemed possible to tip the competitive balance in favour of the local industry was pharmaceutical patent policy. By reverting back to the previous policy of facilitating rapid generic approvals, Egypt's MOH guaranteed the renewed expansion of the locally owned private sector. This growth created the illusion that all was well, when in reality the underlying foundations were quite problematic because they encouraged an even heavier reliance on foreign technology licensing, without a comparative strengthening of autonomous technological capabilities. This particular dilemma was characteristic of many developing countries at the time. Indeed, concerns over the inability of developing countries to promote endogenous and autonomous technological development on account of abusive market behaviour related to the transfer of technology were at the centre of international negotiations during the 1970s and early 1980s, with Egypt playing an active role in the lead taken by developing countries in pressing for the creation of a code of conduct to regulate such transfers and for revisions of the Paris Convention. These countries argued that technology tended to be overpriced and that technology owners 'engaged in unfair practices that limited the recipients' control over the process' (Sell 1998, 29). They believed that government intervention was necessary to ensure that the best possible terms and the fairest conditions were obtained from technology suppliers. In response, the developed countries insisted that the creation of an international legal framework governing technology transfers was not only impossible but that the market was the *only* and most efficient mechanism for the acquisition of technology. As these negotiations proceeded, the United States became increasingly uncompromising and hostile to the code's rationale (Sell 1998, 97), especially as the U.S. economy was experiencing a decline in its international competitiveness and a growing trade deficit during this period (see chapter 2). In the end, U.S. pressures brought the negotiations to an unsuccessful close in 1985.

Negotiations in the World Intellectual Property Organization (WIPO) concerning the Paris Convention (1980–1984) similarly ended with disappointment. In this instance, the developing countries had feverishly argued that since the 1930s the Paris Convention had been gradually changed to favour technology owners to the detriment of the collective goals of the developing world (Costa 1988, 62). But before the formal negotiations started, many industrial countries had already adopted a 'no compromise' approach, dooming the enterprise to failure from the very beginning. By the end of these negotiations the United States was militantly demanding stronger intellectual property protection (Sell 1998, 139), a matter that it would henceforth pursue unilaterally and in the context of the GATT negotiations.

Perhaps the single most important factor that weakened the negotiating power of developing countries during this period, and that undermined their ability to translate the knowledge gained during these earlier negotiations into policy initiatives at home, was the onset of the debt crisis of the early 1980s. As explained in chapter 2, much of the blame for the economic ills that befell the developing countries at this time was attributed to domestic policy failures by the World Bank and the International Monetary Fund as a justification for their standard policy packages that called for an increased role of free markets and private enterprise and a reduction in the role of the state. As a direct result, the ability of developing countries to formulate effective technology policies that would necessarily require significant degrees of government intervention, was further limited. Within this context, a strategic science and technology plan formulated by policymakers in Egypt's Academy of Scientific Research, following the momentum created by international negotiations in the U.N.'s Conference on Trade and Development (UNCTAD), did not find a receptive audience among the country's politicians. Heavy reliance on World Bank and IMF financing, and the urgent desire to seek relief and aid from the United States, conditioned the government's rejection of the proposed plan. Indeed, according to one source, who was highly positioned in the academy at the time, it was U.S. pressure that ultimately induced the government to reject the plan altogether. After this, the one bright option that remained open to Egyptian policymakers wishing to promote the development of the local pharmaceutical industry in the time leading to TRIPS was the informal readjustment of its intellectual property regime. The severe pressure to reduce public spending, including that on health care and drugs, highlighted the desirability of such a policy shift.

By 1985 the de facto increase in patent protection that foreign-owned firms had enjoyed in Egypt due to the ministry of health's 'go slow on generic drug approvals' policy came to an abrupt halt. According to one MNE executive (interviewee) this shift occurred after the German-owned pharmaceutical company Bayer demanded a very high price for a drug for schistosomiasis. Faced with this potentially serious threat to the country's public health, the minister of health was forced to reconsider the issue of generic drug approvals. Accordingly, the ministry not only rejected the price proposal, but also arranged for the drug to be manufactured locally and supplied at one-fifth the price being demanded by Bayer, using active ingredients imported from South Korea rather than from the parent company. This experience encouraged the Ministry of Health to return to its earlier policy of promoting the manufacture of generic substitutes for the benefit of Egyptians. This change in MOH policy, combined with the relative profitability of the industry, gave impetus to the renewed rapid growth of locally owned private sector firms. In the absence of incentives to behave otherwise, these firms focused on short-term goals, which were most readily achieved by licensing foreign technologies. In-house R&D was not given much priority and there were no longer any mechanisms in place to encourage these new companies to turn to local technology suppliers.

The lack of in-house research capacity led to the industry's preoccupation with reformulations of the same pharmaceutical substances into different preparations. This meant that much of the industry's resources went into the production of different versions of the same drug that only occasionally involved minor improvements. Although this behaviour is characteristic of the early stages of development in the pharmaceutical industry and does produce important learning effects, it also led to the neglect of serious research on drugs to deal with the diseases of greatest national relevance. Yet without the concurrent development of the country's scientific and technological support structure, domestic firms were unlikely to change their strategy. This problem remained invisible since success was not measured from an innovation perspective but rather from that of public health. The economic crisis of the 1980s resulted in severe pressures on the state's budget and in significant cutbacks in social spending, so that the ability to maintain services in education and health greatly suffered. As the government's health spending decreased, it became increasingly important for essential drugs to remain affordable, not only to enable continued government provision but also to reduce the burden on the poor, who were having to spend more of their very limited personal resources on health. An ability to respond to health crises and to produce affordable drug alternatives in sufficient quantities were clearly the main concerns of the government.

By 1991 there were thirty drug producers in Egypt: eleven public sector firms, fourteen locally owned firms, and five joint venture firms. Collectively, these were satisfying 90 per cent of local consumption. During this (and well into the next) period, the market share of foreign-owned and public sector firms continued to decline, while that of the locally owned private sector continued to increase (see chapter 6). The fragile foundations on which the local industry's growth depended would soon be exposed when Egypt's accession to the WTO-TRIPS altered the competitive balance between local and foreign firms.

Phase 5 (1992 to the Present): Altering the Balance

As with the previous phase of the pharmaceutical industry's development, the fifth phase has seen public policy being overwhelmed by increasing external pressures, which have impeded the state's ability to establish Egypt as a fully fledged export-led market economy. Initially, the government's desire to privatize and deregulate the pharmaceutical industry was strongly reinforced by pressures from the World Bank and the IMF, and this was soon followed by even stronger pressures linked to new obligations accepted by Egypt when it agreed to join the World Trade Organization. The economic reforms that Egypt has had to adopt to comply with the rules of the WTO, including those related to TRIPS, have drawn intense criticism from many quarters, including local industry leaders and concerned public health officials. In the short term, this has led to a number of compromises as to the speed with which these new obligations could and should be met by the government.

Although the formal end to state-led industrialization could be traced back to 1974 when Sadat's 'open door' policies were introduced, it was not until after the Gulf War in 1991 that significant restructuring of the Egyptian economy took place, as a result of the implementation of a comprehensive economic reform program at the behest of the World Bank and the IMF. With the passing of the Public Business Sector Law (Law No. 203) in 1991, the gradual privatization of state-owned enterprises (SOEs), including all pharmaceutical firms, was mandated. In the first instance, the law sought to equalize the treatment of public and private sector firms. To accomplish this objective, the government adopted a two-pronged approach (UNCTAD 1999, 25). First, SOEs were to be given greater managerial autonomy, that is, they were to be separated from their ministries and reorganized into separate, financially independent holding companies. The pharmaceutical SOEs were to be placed under the directorship of a newly created Pharmaceuticals Holding Company, which was, however, still to operate under the authority of the Ministry of Public Enterprise. New regulatory measures were to be introduced to govern both these 'new' SOEs and private sector firms, equally.

Clearly, the initial focus of these reforms was on the terms and conditions under which these public enterprises were to be run and managed. The question of ownership, as such, was addressed rather carefully, especially in the pharmaceutical sector. In practice the proportion of private ownership of SOEs was determined on a case-by-case basis by the government. In the pharmaceutical sector the government has insisted on retaining a 60 per cent public interest so that it can continue to influence production and pricing decisions in accordance with social and public health objectives and so that it can respond expediently to potential public health crises. The government thus set a 40 per cent limit on the privatization of these firms, with 10 per cent reserved for employee stock options.

Not surprisingly, there are some who believe that the Egyptian government's cautious policy on the ownership question is erroneous. According to these critics, the poor profitability, the relative inefficiency, and the low labour productivity of most public companies show that the government should not remain actively involved in drug production (Subramanian and Abdel-Latif 1997, 23). These critics can point to data that suggest that public sector pharmaceutical companies receive LE150 million per year in subsidies and carry a potentially unserviceable debt of up to LE350 million. However, it is important to recognize that these public sector firms satisfy approximately 30 per cent of local drug consumption needs by supplying essential drugs at affordable prices. In other words, some of these companies may be unprofitable because they ensure that drugs like insulin remain accessible to most Egyptians who need them. These needs would not likely be more effectively, or efficiently, met by either the private sector producers in Egypt or expanded imports. The discussion in chapter 6 will highlight other significant contributions of public sector firms, which among other things include the fact that they account for one-third of the country's exports in this sector.

In the course of the 1990s the government's initially cautious approach to reform was gradually set aside, again with strong external support – or maybe even direction. In 1997 the government passed Investment Law No. 8, which was to clarify and extend the provisions contained in Law No. 230 of 1989. Among the extensive changes introduced, two were of particular significance for the pharmaceutical industry: namely, the legalization of 100 per cent foreign participation in all types of businesses in the country and the gradual elimination of price controls and profit margin limitations. This policy shift appears to have had the intended effect since several wholly owned subsidiaries were established in Egypt soon after Investment Law No. 8 came into force. Egypt now has approximately one-quarter of the world's one hundred largest MNEs operating within its borders, including Bayer, Glaxo Wellcome, Novartis, Du Pont, and Rhone Poulenc in the field of pharmaceuticals.[4] Despite this positive reaction, foreign pharmaceutical firms remained unimpressed by the speed at which the Egyptian government was going to allow the prices of pharmaceuticals to rise to market-determined levels (Ministry of Economy 1998, 8). They were especially incensed because exceptions were to be allowed in utilities and pharmaceuticals, so that price controls could remain in place at least for the short to medium term. The government's decision to maintain pharmaceutical price controls was formally challenged by foreign firms that approached the Ministry of Health demanding equal treatment with other industries. The ministry's rejection led the case to be brought before the State Assembly (the country's highest legal authority in such matters) where the MOH's decision was upheld – allowing drug prices to remain under the effective control of the state, for the protection of society.

The state's insistence on retaining its power to influence drug prices in accordance with public health objectives shows that its adherence to the market-oriented policies being so strongly promoted by the World Bank and the IMF remained pragmatic, to a degree. The government's 'managed open door' policies did facilitate the development of a rather vigorous, if technologically limited, pharmaceutical industry. As the 1990s progressed the MNEs operating in Egypt were faced with increasing competition and loss of market share to locally owned firms, which in many cases produced lower-cost generic drugs. In response the foreign firms focused on two issues to enhance their position and their profitability. First, they sought to take full advantage of the discretionary nature of the price control regime. Second, with the backing of the U.S. government, they intensified their efforts to force Egypt to reform its lax IPRs regime in order to curb the ability of local firms to compete with their most profitable drugs with lower priced, therapeutically equivalent alternatives. These efforts were given special impetus after Egypt's 1994 accession to the WTO with its TRIPS.

The shadow of TRIPS altered the context within which pharmaceutical policy was made, especially as the Egyptian government came under intense pressures from abroad to forgo the transition period provided for in TRIPS and to implement its provisions more or less immediately. This led to the complete abrogation of the 'unwritten rules,' which had protected the interests of the multinationals to a significant degree. It became obvious that full enforcement of TRIPS would raise the prices of patent-protected drugs by prohibiting or delaying their imitation, thereby forcing the government to either import or accept foreign firms as the sole source of domestic supply. In response the Egyptian minister of health began to expedite the registration of drugs patented outside of Egypt, for which an application had not yet been made in Egypt. In so doing, the MOH was clearly and strongly encouraging the registration of new generic drugs during the transition period. This policy brought the government under intense pressure from the Pharmaceutical Research and Manufacturers of America (PhRMA), and from U.S. diplomatic personnel, to restore the earlier system of de facto patent protection by delaying approvals for new generic drugs while expediting the approval of brand name products. Before long the impact of such pressures was evident in the generic drugs approval process. Domestic firms accused the Ministry of Health of unjustly curtailing their legitimate rights during the transition period, including their right to manufacture existing patented drugs so long as they were using different production processes, in which case they were not infringing on the intellectual property rights of the originator under current Egyptian law. The apparent acquiescence of the Ministry of Health to foreign demands was reflected in the large number of generic drugs that were denied registration in the late 1990s and in the speed with which market authorization was granted to foreign firms both for locally produced and imported drugs during this period (Abdelghaffar 2001, 10). In addition, the government was pressured into granting exclusive marketing rights and increased protection for the confidential data of MNEs, as required in the drug approval process.[5] These provisions were incumbent upon countries seeking to make use of the transition period granted in TRIPs, and they effectively limited the significance of the transition period.

Within this context the Egyptian government drafted its new IPRs law in 2000. Although it was soon approved by the Cabinet, it was passed by the People's Assembly only two years later, after intense national debate. The new law fully conforms to TRIPS and closely reflects U.S. interests, since both WIPO and USAID had a considerable say in its final shape; however, it also contains some controversial provisions designed to promote industrial development and protect public health, as will be discussed later. Although the long-term implications of the new IPRs law remain to be seen, the purpose of this study is to offer some guidance on what we can reasonably expect from it, given the key pharmaceutical/health aspects of Egypt's national system of innovation.

Conclusion

This chapter outlined the main features of the evolution of Egypt's pharmaceutical industry before the arrival of the 'TRIPS challenge' in 1995. It described the emergence of a strong national industry, which eventually came to satisfy 93 per cent of Egypt's domestic demand for pharmaceuticals. The growth of this industry was first stimulated by war, and at one stage – in the second phase under Nasser – it was part of a comprehensive nationalist strategy in which the public sector took the leading role and the potential for the country to develop an innovation-based industry was revealed. Unfortunately, this soon gave way to a model that prematurely shifted the government's focus to the need to attract foreign investment and to use that as a vehicle for acquiring foreign technology and developing R&D capabilities. In the absence of a comprehensive science and technology plan, including suitable incentives to foster local innovation, neither foreign nor local firms were motivated to invest adequately in research and development.

Nevertheless, the maintenance of a lax patent regime, and a certain (though inconsistent) emphasis on the promotion of generic drug substitutes, did stimulate the growth of a national industry that was able to satisfy the bulk of the country's demand for pharmaceuticals. This growth was heavily based on the production of 'foreign drugs' under licence or on the production of generic substitutes; nevertheless, the local industry undoubtedly gained technical and business skills through this process. Historically, the maintenance of a lax patent regime had enabled the state to effectively deal with supply shortages and high prices resulting from volatile relations with major foreign drug suppliers. Even in the 1980s and 1990s, when such threats had become less real, Egypt's lax patent law continued to stimulate growth and promote domestic competition, thereby helping to keep prices in check.

The combination of Egypt's market-liberalizing policies and its lax patent regime encouraged the growth of a locally owned private pharmaceutical industry to such a degree that international firms intensified their efforts to curb the growing market power of these domestic firms. They focused their attention on Egypt's lax patent regime, since the state was clearly unwilling, or politically unable, to deregulate pharmaceutical prices in the short or medium term. With Egypt's accession to the WTO, and especially with the promulgation of a new IPRs law that is fully consistent with the provisions of TRIPS, it seems that the MNEs have essentially succeeded, with the strong support of the U.S. government, the World Bank, and the IMF, and of course, the pharmaceutical lobby. A formidable struggle on the part of locally owned and public sector firms and some concerned health officials, however, continues to delay full implementation of TRIPS, thereby giving local firms a little time to better prepare for the situation that they are about to face when the new intellectual property law drastically curtails their ability to compete with the MNEs.

Adopting the strong patent regime embodied in TRIPS early is likely to pose a major and potentially critical challenge to Egypt's nascent national system of innovation. Locally owned firms, both private and public, will undoubtedly find their position threatened by this policy shift, while the foreign-owned firms will benefit significantly from the stronger patent regime, which will ceteris paribus improve their market power, their profitability, and their dominance of R&D. Egypt's domestic pharmaceutical industry is not yet ready to participate in reaping the potential benefits of this new regime. It has grown impressively, and it has 'learned by doing' to some degree, but its development has been hampered by the government's need to give some priority to the necessity of managing the impact of its economic liberalization policies on Egypt's public health. In these circumstances the maintenance of a lax patent regime provided opportunities for the emergence of a national industry and for strong domestic competition, but in the short term this did not provide for the kind of development of autonomous technological capabilities required for a robust pharmaceutical industry that could derive significant benefits from the full implementation of TRIPS.

In the following chapter we will consider these issues in greater detail. In particular, we will consider the innovative capacity that has emerged in the local pharmaceutical industry, the strength of the supportive scientific and technological infrastructure, and the adequacy and coherence of complementary government policies. These three key factors are critical if Egypt's pharmaceutical firms are to reap net benefits from a stronger patent regime and thereby continue to contribute to the health of Egypt's people and economy.

6 Stronger IPRs and Egypt's (Bio)Pharmaceutical Innovation System

In this chapter I discuss how in Egypt the pharmaceutical industry was affected by the country's traditional IP policy, given some of the key pharmaceutical/health aspects of its national system of innovation, from here on referred to as its biopharmaceutical system of innovation. As discussed in chapter 4, the maintenance of a relatively weak IP system had promoted the rapid development of the pharmaceutical sector in industrial countries by enabling them to draw freely on existing knowledge and technologies. It was also emphasized that IP policy represents but one element in a complex system of institutions and incentives that collectively shape a country's technological and economic performance. Here, I show the achievements of the Egyptian pharmaceutical industry and the challenges facing it, which come not only from foreign sources but also from weaknesses in the scientific and technological support structure and from the development of the pharmaceutical industry itself. The central purpose of the discussion is twofold: first, to assess the plausibility of the claims being made by the proponents of stronger IPRs, as discussed in chapter 3, and to offer explanations as to why certain outcomes are deemed more or less likely; second, to identify those aspects of Egypt's biopharmaceutical innovation system that require improvement or transformation in light of these circumstances.

To restate, the NSI approach is appropriate for an assessment of the implications of TRIPS for the pharmaceutical needs of developing countries because the ultimate justification for this global IP regime is based on the concept of dynamic efficiency to enhance public welfare. The argument is that restrictions on technological diffusion and higher prices should be accepted now, in order to promote long-term innovation and development. However, for developing countries the validity of this argument depends on whether they have the technological and institutional capabilities to respond to stronger IPRs by undertaking more effective and successful R&D, which depends on the strength of their NSI. This agreement is not likely to promote dynamic efficiency or welfare at the national level in those parts of the world where national systems of innovation are too weak to meet this challenge. Even the World Bank acknowledges that 'because the overwhelming majority of intellectual property – new inventions, proprietary commercial information, digital entertainment products, software, trade names, and the like – is created in the industrialized countries, TRIPS decidedly shifted the global rules of the game in favour of those countries' (2001, 129).

This chapter has four main parts. The first part discusses the development of the domestic industry in terms of an overall appraisal of growth, investments, and trade. The second examines the challenges facing the industry in relation to the way the industry developed in Egypt. In the third part I examine key aspects of Egypt's biopharmaceutical system of innovation by considering elements in the scientific and technological infrastructure and the coherence of government policies. As discussed in chapter 4, all of these issues need to be considered in order to assess the chances of a beneficial and successful transition to a TRIPS-compliant regime. The fourth part presents the conclusion of the chapter.

The Development of Egypt's Pharmaceutical Industry

Production in the Egyptian pharmaceutical industry has been growing rapidly since the opening of the market to private investment in the late 1970s. Combined pharmaceutical production of the locally owned, foreign-owned, and public sector firms was estimated to be at U.S. $1.27 billion in 2004, a figure over three times as great as at the beginning of the decade and over sixteen times as great as at the beginning of the 1980s. Yet this is probably a gross underestimation of the true valuation of the sector because of Egypt's price controls. Pharmaceutical production is expected to keep growing in the double-digit range in the foreseeable future (UNCTAD 1999, 62). In 2000 total domestic production satisfied 93 per cent of domestic consumption by value. The past two decades have seen the locally owned private sector exhibit the most spectacular growth which by the end of this period had come to supply close to half the industry's total output. Although the value of output by foreign-owned and public sector firms has also increased during this period, their share of the total market diminished, with the public sector exhibiting the most shrinkage.[1]

Throughout the past three decades, the industry has been one of the most competitive and profitable in Egyptian manufacturing. Gross profit margins currently hover around 20 per cent (Orabi and Nour el Din 1999, 2), while in 1995 it was reported that the most profitable locally owned firm had a gross margin upon sales of approximately 44 per cent compared with 43 per cent for the best-performing multinational firm and 18 per cent for the best two public sector firms. The figure for the foreign-owned portion of the industry, however, may be misleading since subsidiaries are obliged to import raw materials from their parent companies at high prices, so that reported costs usually incorporate a margin of profit (Subramanian and Abdel-Latif 1997, 12).

The high levels of capital investment in the industry have been reflected in both greater productivity and enhanced manufacturing capacity with commensurate advances in local learning that accompany the production of generics and off-patent drugs and the training of personnel to operate state-of-the-art technologies. Capital investments by locally owned firms have increased at an average annual rate of 30 per cent during the 1990s, allowing many of these firms to reach world class standards.[2] Amoun, a locally owned firm acquired by Glaxo Wellcome in 1997, employs state-of-the-art technologies. The former owner of the company has since started up another local pharmaceutical giant that also implements the latest technologies. Some fifteen locally owned firms are among the most successful in the manufacture of drugs in finished dosage forms, and they 'employ the most advanced manufacturing systems in the country' (Fayez 1997, 4).

Capital investments by the foreign sector during the 1990s increased by an average annual rate of 14 per cent,[3] largely due to an increase in the number of firms operating in Egypt but also due to investments in upgrading local operations. Glaxo Wellcome Egypt was the first company in the Middle East and Africa to introduce ISO standards into its manufacturing practice. According to an UNCTAD publication (1999, 68), other MNEs have since followed suit and are improving quality standards to achieve ISO 9000 certification and eventually full U.S. Food and Drug Administration approval or are meeting EU Good Manufacturing Practice (GMP) standards. But while foreign subsidiaries have been largely credited with introducing new management styles that prioritize productivity and quality, they have also been heavily criticized for the slow pace at which they have generally upgraded their operations.

In contrast to the private sector, capital investment in the public sector actually decreased by an average annual rate of 2.4 per cent during the 1990s.[4] This has generally been attributed to the fact that the government turned away from the idea of expanding the public sector to strongly promoting privatization. However, according to Dr Galal Ghorab, chairman of the Pharmaceuticals Holding Company, it is also due to the fact that the Ministry of Health 'discriminated' against public sector firms by withholding payments in the order of LE 350 million for drugs purchased to cover the needs of its affiliated hospitals and the national Health Insurance Plan (Essam El-Din 2000). Even so, the government has put tremendous efforts into renovating and upgrading existing production facilities in an attempt to improve profitability and exports. Indeed, many public sector companies have achieved ISO certification and have expanded their product ranges to include higher margin products like vitamins, veterinary products, and cosmetics.

Despite the broad success of the pharmaceutical sector in terms of growth in domestic production and investment over the past couple of decades, the industry continues to generate heavy net foreign exchange costs because imported inputs make up a significant share of the total cost of production at the same time as industry exports remain at a mere 5 per cent of total domestic output, even though exports have grown rapidly over the past decade, at an annual average rate of 28 per cent (Subramanian and Abdel-Latif 1997, 7). Thus, while the 1999 UNCTAD investment review of Egypt identified pharmaceutical products among Egypt's competitive exports, or 'rising stars,' it also identified the sector as an 'underachiever' in terms of exports relative to the high growth in world imports between 1992 and 1996 (UNCTAD 1999, 17). Locally owned firms account for about two-thirds of Egypt's pharmaceutical exports, with the remainder in the public sector.[5] According to Ghorab, the latter group of firms has the goal of gradually increasing exports from the current level of slightly less than 2 per cent to 15 per cent of their annual output. At this stage, exports are largely composed of generic products including aspirin, antibiotics, dermatologicals, geriatrics, cough syrups, and vitamins that are primarily bound for markets in Russia, Eastern Europe, and some Arab countries, where quality standards and regulatory requirements are not as strict as they are in key markets in industrial countries.

That the multinationals have chosen not to export from Egypt is clearly a matter of concern. At this point these foreign subsidiaries are not exporting because of parent company restrictions (N. Galal 1999, 12; Orabi and Nour El Din 1999, 2; Subramanian and Abdel-Latif 1997, 11). The MNEs claim that Egypt's price controls create 'artificial' or 'unfair' export opportunities, so that they prefer to export from locations where there is greater price discretion. Defending the position of these firms, one MNE chairman explained that parent companies just want to avoid the possibility of their own subsidiaries (based in different countries) engaging in price competition in third-country markets.

The situation in Egypt's domestic market is likely to change dramatically when the WTO rules are more fully applied. At present, imports of finished pharmaceutical products account for only 7 per cent of domestic pharmaceutical consumption, and they are essentially limited to high technology products,[6] milk formula, disposable syringes, and gauze. This largely reflects the success of past import substitution policies in building a strong domestic industry and in persuading foreign firms to establish production facilities in Egypt. It is also, however, the result of import controls that limit the number of drug substitutes to six versions or to drugs that have no local equivalents. Such control is critical in the pharmaceutical sector where in the global marketplace there are approximately 100,000 different pharmaceutical products, developed from about 5,000 active substances, and produced by thousands of manufacturers (Saxenian 1994). The vast number of products has given rise to 'information problems relating to the quality of specific drug products and their cost-effectiveness' (ibid.). Limiting the number of available products with similar therapeutic value to six versions at any point in time has helped the Egyptian government to deal with this problem. Unfortunately, the removal of import quotas in accordance with WTO rules will have a dramatic effect on the government's ability to continue to do so with the consequent proliferation of brand name drugs with similar therapeutic effects competing in the domestic market.

A final reason the Egyptian industry continues to incur a substantial foreign exchange deficit, despite its apparent success, is the fact that it remains highly reliant on imported raw materials. At present Egypt imports over 85 per cent of these requirements, mainly from India, China, Japan, South Korea, Europe, and the United States. Only 15 per cent of these requirements are produced locally, by two firms: El Nasr, a public sector firm, and Gist Brocades, which is foreign owned. The industry's relative inability to produce a greater proportion of its raw material requirements domestically distinguishes it from its more mature counterparts in other developing countries like India, Argentina, Mexico, China, and Korea, which have the capabilities to manufacture the bulk of their raw material requirements locally (Oxfam 2001).

Unfortunately, pledges made since the 1960s by foreign subsidiaries to introduce technologies for the domestic manufacture of key pharmaceutical chemicals remain unfulfilled (Fayez 1997, 4), which may not be so surprising since it is well known that MNEs use the trade in intermediate chemicals to transfer profits from one jurisdiction to another (Lall 1974, 156). Indeed, MNE records in Egypt show that the share of imported raw materials relative to total operating costs has been particularly high, inviting the strong suspicion that this trade is used for transfer pricing (N. Galal 1999, 12; Orabi and Nour El Din 1999, 10; Subramanian and Abdel-Latif 1997, 13).

Although the strong performance of Egypt's pharmaceutical industry is attributable to a number of factors, including the opening of the market to private investment in the late 1970s and the implementation of Investment Law No. 8 in the early 1990s, which encouraged foreign investment by allowing full ownership, the country's pharmaceutical patent policy, with its limited scope and duration, has probably been decisive in allowing and fostering the establishment of strong domestic production capabilities oriented to the supply of domestic pharmaceutical needs. This view is supported by the 1999 UNCTAD investment review of Egypt which states: 'Owing to the nature of the governing patent law in Egypt (Law No. 132 of 1949) which allows patents to expire after ten years, the Egyptian pharmaceutical industry has excelled in terms of manufacturing generics' (UNCTAD 1999, 61). The manufacturing capacity that emerged mainly took the form of the formulation and packaging of imported raw materials based on technologies that were almost entirely adopted and adapted from the developed countries. In this situation, the maintenance of a relatively lax patent regime has been necessary to minimize the costs associated with this type of industrial development, as is more fully discussed in chapter 4. Egypt's traditional pharmaceutical patent policy allowed local firms to invent around a patent relatively easily to produce generic equivalents, and when that proved impossible due to a lack of know-how, the limited patent term reduced the time before the product could be legitimately imitated. These conditions allowed the growth of a vigorous domestic pharmaceutical industry and encouraged the rapid emergence of multiple suppliers of most new drugs, which in turn, encouraged effective price competition.

The industry derived a wide variety of benefits from Egypt's relatively lax patent regime. As noted above, foremost among these was the fact that it gave local firms the right to produce 'frontier' drugs using alternative processes while they were still under patent protection, or to copy them within a short time after the patent expired. It has been estimated by several local industry leaders that such activities accounted for approximately 25 per cent of their profits. Profitability was further augmented by the fact that this weak patent regime only protected pharmaceutical processes, so that local firms could import raw materials from the lowest cost suppliers without fear of infringing the intellectual property rights of the multinational enterprises who often owned the patents on such products and their components. The ability of local firms to reduce production costs in this way not only increased the competitiveness of their products in the domestic market, but also facilitated the steady growth of their generic pharmaceutical exports. From a public health perspective, local industrial leaders have argued that their ability to enhance profitability as such allowed them to continue to produce less profitable products that were needed by society.

One might expect that a lax IPR regime would have discouraged foreign investments in the pharmaceutical sector, at least until the government had agreed to accelerate the implementation of TRIPS. However, this does not seem to have been the case. The presence of a significant and growing market and the desire to counter each other's presence has tended to attract foreign investments in this sector, which tends to confirm the argument (made in chapter 4 of this study) that investment decisions are largely made to maintain technological leadership and market position irrespective of the availability of patent protection. According to Glaxo Wellcome's chairman in Egypt, Dr Negad Shaarawi, 'if Egypt has no meaningful IPRs then we have to find other ways to gain a competitive edge. For me the answer is to increase resources, that is, to have properly supported operations regardless of IPRs.' Thus, Glaxo Wellcome purchased Amoun Pharmaceuticals, a local company, for U.S.$117 million in 1999, the largest cross-border acquisition in Egyptian history, which gave Glaxo Wellcome a 4 per cent share in the booming generic drug market. In reality, this event was only the latest in a series of similar investment decisions made by other multinationals during the 1990s. In 1994 Eli Lilly and its local agent Alkan acquired the plant of Roussel Uclaf Egypt, and in 1995 a decision was taken to invest LE 45 million to establish a new facility to produce human insulin, the first of its kind in the Middle East (UNCTAD 1999, 64). In the late 1990s, Scherer, a global leader in the production of soft gels, built a new plant introducing the latest technologies and training techniques (UNCTAD 1999, 64). During the same period Rhone Poulenc acquired Amereya, a local pharmaceutical firm, and subsequently merged operations; and Bristol Myers Squibb expanded their operations to double production by 2000. It would appear as though the existence of a lax patent regime has actually attracted foreign investment, rather than deterred it, as some would have expected. These investment decisions served to effectively undermine the foreign industry's efforts to pressure the Egyptian government to forego the grace period permitted by TRIPS. Indeed, one frustrated IPR analyst working for a leading multinational in the region was led to declare that rather than 'punish' the government, 'MNEs continue to introduce almost all of their latest medicines which are vulnerable to imitation and perhaps even more problematic export piracy; they continue to increase spending on marketing and employment; they persist in licensing manufacturing to companies that engage in the piracy of other MNE products; and worse yet they continue to invest in local companies that pirate the products of other MNEs even after knowledge of the problem.'[7]

Based on this experience, some have expressed a real concern that as pharmaceutical patent policy is strengthened in Egypt as a result of TRIPS, foreign firms may have less incentive to invest in the country because they will have profit guarantees that do not depend on such investment. Of course, supporters of TRIPS argue that the introduction of stronger IPRs can be expected to stimulate investment in more innovative activities by both local and foreign firms; however, this is unlikely to happen on a significant scale because of the way in which the domestic industry has developed and the absence of key pharmaceutical/health aspects of the national system of innovation to provide a conducive environment for such investments.

Challenges Emanating from the Development of the Industry

As discussed in chapter 4, in-house R&D is an important feature of modern pharmaceutical firms because it augments their capacity to adopt and adapt existing technologies. Even though an important amount of learning, and even of innovation, does occur simply as a result of being engaged in the process of production, inadequate levels of R&D are generally associated with relatively weak learning effects. This tends to reinforce continuing dependence on foreign technology licensing and to block the path to the endogenous development of more autonomous technological capabilities. Without such capabilities, an industry cannot hope to benefit significantly from the introduction of stronger IPRs, since its ability to generate patentable innovations will be relatively limited. According to the director of the Patent and Trademark Office, Dr Fawzie El Rifaie, Egyptian nationals submitted only three of the approximately sixty pharmaceutical patent applications made in July and August 2001. Under these circumstances, one can only agree with Subramanian and Abdel-Latif (1997, 4) when they contend that increases in patent protection will only serve to 'displace local producers and render the market less competitive, leading to a rise in prices and consequent rent transfer from local consumers and producers to foreign title-holders. The absence of an appreciable R&D effect will mean the country will not derive any dynamic benefits in the form of reduced costs and prices, so that in welfare terms the country will be worse off.'

The lack of adequate investment in R&D, and the consequent weakness of the learning effects associated with the type of production investment that was established, were undoubtedly the most serious shortcomings of the Egyptian pharmaceutical industry as it faced the new world of TRIPS. In the Egyptian industry, firms spend less than 2 per cent of their revenues on R&D, as compared with the 12 to 18 per cent spent by firms in more advanced industrial countries. Although some original research does take place, much of this research activity is restricted to 'searching' for drugs that have been developed elsewhere and that can be adopted or adapted for the Egyptian market. When a local firm identifies a potentially interesting product, it normally asks its research partners to determine whether it is suitable for the local market. If it is, and the company has the required production capabilities, then it arranges for its local development and production, either by using an alternative production process or by obtaining a licence from the technology owner.

Critics of the industry's development path argue that this simple process of searching, developing, and producing has not led to a sufficient understanding of the underlying knowledge and technology involved in drug innovation. According to Dr Mohamed Baha El Din Fayez, Professor Emeritus at the National Research Centre in Cairo, 'the business of imitation has not been taken with adequate seriousness. There exists a misguided belief that imitation is not an economically dynamic enterprise. Thus, reverse engineering is considered of limited use and leads to a "bad reputation" for those who practise it.' Fayez contends that this is largely why the industry has been unable to reduce its heavy reliance on licensing arrangements with foreign firms.

At the end of the 1990s, locally owned and public sector firms produced approximately 40 to 50 per cent of their products under licence from foreign technology owners, with the remainder being generic copies. However, even this does not fully reflect the weakness of the industry's present capacity to innovate. To appreciate this one has to understand that the majority of these product licences are for products whose patents have actually expired but which are still produced under licence due to a lack of know-how or because of the need to obtain raw material ingredients from the original technology owner. It goes without saying that this situation has both financial and developmental costs for the industry and the economy. The direct financial costs stem from the need to pay unnecessary royalties, which put further strain on scarce foreign currency reserves. The developmental costs are linked to the lack of genuine learning that is associated with the majority of these licensing arrangements.

These problems are exacerbated because such production licences are often obtained by individuals who do not, themselves, have any manufacturing capacity, but who will sell or lease the licence to any available and willing manufacturer. The manufacturer will then produce, package, and market the product in Egypt. In this process there is ultimately very little technology transfer and no real investments or R&D. There is little learning apart from that which inevitably occurs as a result of the production process itself. In the case of pharmaceuticals even this learning is particularly limited since the production process often consists of little more than the mixing of several purchased inputs. In other words, most of the technology transfer agreements in this industry in Egypt have relatively little substance and transfer very little technology.

Unfortunately, few observers expect the industry's development path to change significantly in the near future, especially since stronger patents and intensified competition will further constrain the capacity of firms to undertake long-term oriented activities like R&D. Of course, because of the relatively small size of the plants, the firms, and the market in Egypt, it would not be easy to develop a capacity for fundamental innovation. Indeed, if one accepted the industry's oft-repeated claims that it costs upwards of between U.S.$250 and U.S.$400 million or between LE 850 and LE 1360 (almost half the revenue generated by the entire pharmaceutical industry) to develop a patentable drug, it would be impossible. But such estimates have been widely – and rightly – questioned. There are several factors that make the calculation of such costs questionable including the refusal by pharmaceutical companies to allow independent verification of their R&D figures, accounting assumptions, and the arbitrary inclusion of risk (Story 2000, 4–5). Correa (2001, 4) notes that 'figure[s] on R&D provided by industry (about $500 million per drug) does not correspond to actual expenditures, but to expenditures adjusted for costs of capital and to compensate for R&D failures. The assumptions made for these calculations are very controversial.' It is also important to keep in mind that these estimates are based on U.S. practices. In Japan, for instance, companies take approximately 25 per cent less time and spend about 50 per cent less money than do companies in the United States to develop and commercialize new products *whose essential features have largely been previously discovered*, or so-called me-too drugs (Mansfield 1988, 19).

Indeed, those who focus on breakthrough innovations or 'blockbuster' drugs, which involve the development of new molecular entities, neglect that the early stages of development are largely characterized by minor continuous innovations that lead to important learning effects. To take advantage of these learning opportunities, Fayez suggests that pharmaceutical research in Egypt can be directed towards following the advances of competitors who have the capabilities and resources to develop breakthrough drugs (1997, 4). He contends that local research can successfully focus on developing compounds that result from incremental structural improvements or composition modifications to the pioneer product, which only involves trailing-edge research and generates 'me-too' drugs (ibid.). Many observers believe that Egypt can become a good base for the performance of low to intermediate R&D activities, which in addition to those mentioned above could also involve the local performance of clinical trials and testing. 'In general because industrial R&D can be conducted in developing countries at a much lower cost, there is potential for the Egyptian pharmaceutical sector to capture a portion of this expenditure' (UNCTAD 1999, 65).

The focus on the capabilities and resources required for fundamental innovation in order to be able to significantly benefit from a stronger patent regime, however, has led others to conclude that 'the prospects of developing a genuine R&D based industry in Egypt in the medium term are not very bright' (Subramanian and Abdel-Latif 1997, 19). Whether based on realistic or applicable estimates of drug development costs, many local firms believe that they cannot afford to undertake research into new pharmaceutical preparations (*Al Alam Al Yom* 1999, 3). It is also unlikely, even with the full implementation of TRIPS, that foreign subsidiaries will perform significant R&D or innovation in Egypt. According to one MNE chairman, 'no efforts are being taken to build R&D in Egypt by the foreign industry ... R&D will not likely be improved in Egypt under any conditions in the foreseeable future, even with the passing of the draft [IPRs] law.' For the leaders of these firms the problem in Egypt is only partly due to inadequate patent protection. It has much more to do with expected financial returns and a weak scientific and technological support structure. As they see it, in Egypt the limited purchasing power of consumers, government price controls, and intense competition in most therapeutic categories tends to limit R&D incentives. A recent U.K. study reported that large pharmaceutical firms were 'unwilling to pursue a line of research unless the potential outcome is a product with annual sales of the order of $1 billion' (CIPR 2002, 37), which effectively excludes research into diseases of national relevance to many poor countries. In any case, according to several MNE chairmen more than 'adequate' financial returns are required. In effect what is needed is a strong NSI, according to the chairman of Gist Brocades, Derek Hennecke, who explained, 'IPRs are only beneficial in the long run. Companies will likely wait and see that the laws are consistent before investing in new technologies. In pharmaceuticals the short term will not offer much change. Egypt offers a low cost haven but a poor institutional structure. For pharmaceuticals it is easier to operate where the costs are much higher but where institutions are reliable.'

For countries like Egypt, with a significant market and the potential to develop a significant technological capacity, the unwillingness of MNEs to undertake significant research and development activities is particularly problematic because these firms exercise control over the great majority of the existing patents. Although they may not patent all of their products in all developing countries, they tend to do so in countries like Egypt where there is some risk of local imitation (CIPR 2002, 41). Strong patent protection in such countries not only curbs local competition, but also limits competition internationally since it can inhibit exports through the control of distribution channels (ibid., 42). Hence, in Egypt, the enforcement of strong IPRs is likely to mean more patenting by the MNEs as they try to limit competition both at home and abroad. For local firms, the gravity of this situation is heightened by the aggressive marketing strategies of MNEs, which are often successful in maintaining the market dominance of their products well beyond the expiration of their patents. The combination of strong IPRs with the extensive power that can be exercised through marketing allows the MNEs to consolidate their market power and secure their high profits. At least this appears to be the view of industry itself since it has not only been relentless in its pursuit of stronger IPRs, but it also has one of the highest ratios of promotion and advertising costs to sales among all major industries. Indeed, international pharmaceutical companies spend approximately 35 per cent of their sales revenues on marketing, which is double what they spend on research and development (Hemsley 1997, 12). In Egypt the disparity is even greater since the foreign sector's R&D costs are approximately equal to just 1 to 2 per cent of annual sales, while marketing expenditures hover around 35 per cent. More recently it seems that these companies have supplemented their aggressive marketing campaigns with predatory pricing strategies that frequently discount drug prices by up to 30 to 40 per cent in order to undercut local competition (Zein el Abedien 2001, 3).

In the absence of effective government regulation of pharmaceutical marketing practices, local firms have been largely unable to provide an effective counter-balance to the marketing power of the multinational firms. Historically, local producers have tended to neglect marketing partly because they could not afford to invest heavily enough in such promotional activities and partly because they saw it as a waste of resources, not realizing quite how powerful it could be. Today the inability of local firms to compete in the marketing arena is undermining their position in the marketplace and compromising their relations with physicians, other health care providers, and consumers, in comparison with foreign firms. Thus, the current marketing advantage of MNEs with the introduction of strong IPRs will greatly challenge the future ability of the local industry to develop and expand.

Challenges Emanating from the Biopharmaceutical Innovation System

The ability of the pharmaceutical industry to cope with changes in its competitive environment on account of the imposition of a strong IPRs regime will depend on the support it can derive from the key pharmaceutical/health elements in Egypt's national system of innovation. As discussed in chapter 4, technological advance occurs through a community of actors that includes firms engaged in production and research, public research institutes and universities, government departments, and financial institutions. Over the past four decades Egypt has developed an extensive scientific and technological infrastructure. Some of the key strengths of the system include the availability of educated and specialized personnel, a network of R&D institutes, some well-focused R&D, and a tradition of government support for S&T institutions (UNCTAD 1999, 18). Nevertheless, the system has, for various reasons, remained relatively immature and highly diffuse and thus tends to underperform relative to its potential capacity. Among its key weaknesses are inefficient management structures characterized by inadequate resources and weak quality control, design, and standardization protocols; poor financial support services; and a marked isolation of S&T institutions from the broader socioeconomic context (UNCTAD 1999, 19). Weak communication networks and a lack of trust have also greatly inhibited the potential of the country's extensive infrastructure and have reinforced dependence on foreign technology suppliers. The following section considers the characteristics of the major actors in Egypt's biopharmaceutical innovation system in order to demonstrate how these are likely to affect that sector's ability to benefit from the imposition of stronger IPRs.

Universities and Public Research Institutes

Egypt has thirty-three universities, most of which are publicly controlled and funded but which also engage in projects sponsored by international donors. The thirteen largest universities have faculties that include most fields of science such as medicine, pharmacology, dentistry, agriculture, and engineering. There are twenty-two institutes and research centres affiliated with these universities, and eighty-one research centres affiliated with sixteen ministries, including the Ministry of Health, Ministry of Scientific Research (MOSR), and the Ministry of Agriculture. These universities and institutes are home to a number of distinguished scientists with strong education, skills, and experience.

There is little doubt as to the contribution that Egypt's higher education policies have made to the advancement of science in that country, particularly in the production of highly educated and specialized personnel. New graduates generally have a strong knowledge base as a result of their university studies. In 1997 there were 114,137 individuals engaged in national S&T activities. The distribution of researchers was as follows: natural sciences (22.8 per cent), engineering and technology (15.7 per cent), medical sciences (22.8 per cent), agricultural sciences (14.7 per cent), and social sciences and humanities (24 per cent) (MOSR 1997). Selective elements of this strong human resource base have contributed to the emergence of several centres of research excellence that are conducting successful and well-focused research in biopharmaceuticals.

The most significant player by far in the Egyptian biopharmaceutical innovation system is the National Research Centre (NRC), formed in 1956. Initially established to fuel the transformation of industry in Egypt, the NRC today possesses an extensive scientific and technological infrastructure with thirteen divisions and sixty-six departments that cover the major areas of industry, agriculture, health, environment, basic science, and engineering. Its human resources exceed 2,000 researchers, making it the largest national R&D institution affiliated with the Ministry of Scientific Research. The centre is devoted to both basic and applied research. Its primary objective remains to respond to the country's key production and service sectors through the research it conducts in different areas of S&T, scientific consultation, and training.

A close second to the NRC in terms of national importance for the development of health biotechnology is the newly established Genetic Engineering and Biotechnology Research Institute (GEBRI) of the Mubarak City for Scientific Research and Technology Applications (MUCSAT). Egypt's first major technopole, MUCSAT was established as a centre of research excellence in advanced biotechnology with the goals of introducing valuable biotechnology products and services to the market through R&D and technology transfer. Of the twelve institutes to be created within MUCSAT, four are now complete, including GEBRI. It is located on 80 hectares in the Bourg El Arab Industrial Complex just west of Alexandria. GEBRI's mission 'is to establish a regional and national centre of excellence in advanced molecular biotechnology and create a lasting partnership between itself as a governmental research institute and industry, based on a relationship of sustained mutual benefit.' Its goals are to develop 'products' of high economic value through molecular biotechnology and genetic engineering to strengthen Egyptian industries; improve and develop the expertise in and market value of molecular biotechnology; develop international collaborations to secure a place in the international biotechnology revolution; and finally, achieve financial independence. To this end, it has established several specialized departments including proteins research, nucleic acid research, medical biotechnology, environmental biotechnology, and bioprocess development.

Overall the strength of Egypt's science base is evident in the number of papers published in peer-reviewed journals. Egypt's record in this regard far outstrips other countries in the Middle East region despite being modest in comparison with other more advanced developing countries. Nevertheless, this suggests that Egyptian scientists publish far more frequently than their regional neighbours but also that Egypt has notable potential to produce new scientific knowledge and to communicate it to the international scientific community. The strong drive to publish within the Egyptian academic community is driven by considerations related primarily to promotion within the academic hierarchy, as it is in many higher education systems around the world. Several critics, however, have expressed concern with the narrowness of this incentive, arguing that a lack of planning and coordination of research priorities means that only a limited number of projects upon which these publications are often based are actually concerned with fulfilling social and market needs. As a result, science generally tends to be isolated from society.

Another problem appears to be the S&T complex's relative weakness in developing applied sciences and technologies. This is partially a result of the fact that the higher education sector encompasses 70 per cent of all S&T institutions and 75 per cent of all scientists and engineers working in Egypt. Thus, only 25 per cent of scientists and engineers are working in the various productive sectors of the economy. This is not considered an optimal situation for a country striving to apply new technologies for the fulfilment of social goals (MOSR, 1997).

The S&T system's imbalance in favour of academia is further exacerbated by the manner in which most public research institutes function. In general, these institutes tend to place greater emphasis on academic achievements rather than on technological advancement. Thus, it is not uncommon to find that senior researchers spend much time supervising theses for young researchers who are in the process of preparing master's and doctoral degrees. Because of this, research topics found in national research institutes tend to be similar to those undertaken in universities with a heavy emphasis on low-level rudimentary science and the production of papers. Applied research tends to be marginalized in such an environment. This predicament is reinforced by a lack of appropriate infrastructure, which includes proper equipment and state-of-the-art technology (Ibrahim 1996). 'Much of the equipment is either far behind the state-of-the-art or obsolete. Some institutions constructed mostly with foreign funds have better equipment, but local capabilities for repair and maintenance remain severely limited' (MOSR 1997, 13).

In addition to unsuitable physical conditions, several other factors appear to be having a negative impact on the advancement of research in the biopharmaceutical sector. The first of these is the 'failure' of policy to create critical masses of professionals in designated areas in order to heighten their effectiveness. The excessive number of individuals employed in public research institutes on account of Egypt's guaranteed employment policy for new graduates who have attained outstanding academic achievement tends to dilute the effectiveness of those few high-calibre individuals who work among them. One expert noted that in many cases the latter, who have usually completed graduate studies abroad, find themselves incapable of making similar contributions at home as they did in the host country of study. 'He [the graduate] cannot continue this [advanced research] because he is put with people who were not exposed to the same environment, or because his department is not equipped or ready to help him continue.' A couple of exceptions do exist, however, where these critical masses have been formed, including in the NRC, especially its Biomedical Research Department, and GEBRI in MUCSAT. These institutions are staffed by young graduates who were educated in distinguished institutions around the world and who can consequently 'speak the same language.'

A second and related problem is the lack of consideration for how graduates who are sent abroad to obtain advanced degrees are to transfer the knowledge acquired to colleagues and their home institutions once they have returned to Egypt. There is often doubt that the home institution is even equipped for this knowledge transfer. Unfortunately, in some cases the graduate ends up employed in a field other than his specialty because of a lack of a 'technological' match within the national science and technology system. This not only deprives the 'system' of the potential knowledge it could have acquired but also results in a waste of resources. The country does not benefit sufficiently from having sponsored this person, and that individual may abandon the system altogether by choosing to work abroad where work conditions and remuneration are more suitable.

'Brain drain' is a major concern, not only for Egypt but for all the Arab countries. According to Dr Samia Salah, chairwoman of the Drug Policy and Planning Centre, 'we cannot maintain our brain power and nurture it so that it remains, grows, and contributes. These people go abroad because they cannot fulfil their personal and professional needs.' Indeed, the *Arab Human Development Report* of 2003 stated that emigration of highly qualified Arabs to the West is perhaps among the most serious factors undermining knowledge acquisition in Arab countries. 'The Arab brain drain constitutes a form of reverse development aid, they note, since receiving countries clearly benefit from Arab investments in training and educating their citizens. More significant, however, is the lost potential contribution of the emigrants to their countries of origin' (UNDP 2003).

Linkages

Egypt's pharmaceutical sector is not geographically clustered.[8] Pharmaceutical firms are located in several cities and industrial zones, and research centres are found all over the country. Although Cairo may be considered the main hub of industry and research, the recent establishment of MUCSAT, just outside Alexandria, in addition to the existence of several strong firms and research centres in Alexandria is challenging the traditional dominance of the capital. The pharmaceutical system is widely described as one of dispersed 'dynamic individuals,' 'isolated islands,' or 'successful nuclei.' Yet the absence of major geographical clusters in industry and research does not seem to be a significant reason for the notable weakness or complete absence of robust local linkages among the key players. Rather, it is an acute lack of critical relationships and cooperation due to the general absence of trust, the need for individual recognition, and the pervasiveness of unqualified partnerships[9] that are stunting the sector's potential. Although this problem has not gone unnoticed by the government, efforts to remedy it through workshops that encourage local cooperation, the support of national research networks, and the establishment of a specialized centre to coordinate national research activities are only in their preliminary stages. Also, some private actors have been actively attempting to improve local linkages either through the establishment of consulting firms or simply through personal efforts.

Linkages between Individuals and within Singular Institutions

In Egypt major actors in the pharmaceutical sector are almost always identified as individuals rather than as organizations, whether in academia, government, or business. One expert noted that the more successful schools of pharmacology were comprised of 'outstanding individuals but not teams, or even schools, but rather specialized personnel.' It is also not uncommon to hear that a certain leader *is* the organization or *is* the position. Although there are some benefits associated with this system including positive individual influence on the advancement of policy, research, and the development of a number of critical technologies associated with endemic diseases, there is little doubt that there are also some serious disadvantages.

In the absence of established institutional relationships individual personalities and preferences tend to unduly influence cooperation within and among institutions. 'The actors [in the pharmaceutical sector] are fragmented and there are few mechanisms for cooperation unless people are pushed to work together,' one expert noted. As a result, integrative efforts are as difficult within institutions, that is, between specialized personnel in different departments, as they are among different institutions. This undoubtedly makes the initiation and completion of projects at the institutional level very challenging.

Emphasis on the individual also means undue and undemocratic influence on the future of entire organizations and inevitably the pharmaceutical sector. Generally, if the incumbent is well connected and reasonably intelligent then the organization is likely to succeed, that is, attract funds, do good research, and find partners for further development, and if he or she is not, then the organization is likely to be marginalized. As a result, the retirement or relocation of key personnel tends to have profound effects on the continued success of an organization. Many local leaders acknowledged the need for creating institutional systems where individual roles and relationships are well defined so that a system's operations, and in some cases existence, no longer revolve exclusively around key personnel, but few have taken concrete steps to establish such systems.

Those organizations that have attempted to do so have mainly begun the implementation of information and documentation systems that not only enable key individuals to move in and out of organizations more smoothly, but that also encourage cooperation between an organization's personnel. For some organizations this requirement has been imposed, while for others it has been a voluntary choice in recognition of the benefits that could potentially result from recording the activities and accomplishments of staff and researchers. Thus, for the National Organization for Drug Control and Research (NODCAR) the World Health Organization (WHO) demanded the implementation of standard operating procedures. Initially, it took several years for personnel to agree to document their activities and to share their work with colleagues and other interested partners. There was a fear that making such information 'freely' available would somehow diminish the incumbent's importance in the organization. Although the attitude at NODCAR has gradually changed, new staff has to be continually retrained because the tendency to hoard valuable information is, as the management put it, a national problem. The challenge, restated by another expert, is to re-educate people to operate in a wholly new manner so that they can cooperate for mutually beneficial outcomes.

Linkages between Different Research Institutions

Naturally, the problem at the individual level extends itself to the institutional level but for different reasons. According to one expert, '[research] institutions are mostly stand-alone and doing individual work.' A ministerial decree was recently issued that called for the formation of a high-level committee for the coordination of research between research institutes and universities in all disciplines at the national level; however, such an attempt seems misplaced. In fact, dozens of collaboration protocols exist between different institutes and universities. The problem seems to emerge in practice and implementation rather than in the actual identification of partners and the drafting of cooperative arrangements. Two explanations may clarify why this is the case. The first is that groups of scientists in different centres prefer to work on their own, and they remain protective of their outcomes until something concrete can be made public. The team is then credited with all the effort if a project succeeds or spared criticism if it fails. The second is that most institutes have weak monitoring and follow-up procedures so that there is no way to ensure that a collaborative project is pursued to the end. Partners tend to be enthusiastic at the beginning of the collaboration but as this excitement wanes, so does the drive to complete the project. As a result, many projects whose final outcome may have been to develop a product end instead with simply a publication or two.

It is not intended by these observations to state unequivocally that no cooperative arrangements are fruitful. But there is little doubt, as one expert made clear, that such challenges diminish the potential of even those arrangements that do in the end work out. Dr Maha El Demellawy of GEBRI at MUCSAT, among several others, spoke of how important it was for the various local institutes to work together to complement each other with their diverse expertise and resource bases. She noted how her department was establishing strong connections with the University of Alexandria and its affiliated research institutes. To her, the key to sustaining momentum is good planning and a clear division of responsibilities and deliverables from the very beginning of the project, but in the end she warned, 'it all depends on the people in the arrangement.'

Industry Linkages

The weakness of linkages between pharmaceutical companies and between these companies and national research centres and universities is deeply embedded in a complex history of industrial development. Galal observed that signs of serious problems were evident in the early 1970s when firms were finding coordination with supportive industries laborious and ineffective. The transfer of technology, know-how, and experience were limited between both public sector and joint-ownership firms. In the public sector annual competitive assessments of individual companies hindered cooperation of this sort and prevented harmonization of production lines, which led to the frequent duplications of popular over-the-counter drugs, and serious shortages in less rewarding specialized drugs (Galal 1983, 239) – problems that appear to persist to date.

It was also clear back then that the relationship between industry and academia was seriously inadequate. One incident in particular seems to stand out historically. In the early 1970s the National Academy of Sciences developed a drug called Proximol for the relief of urinary tract colic resulting from the presence of stones. The drug was also effective in dissolving the stones and expelling them from the urinary tract. Researchers had obtained the principle ingredient, a herb, from its original locality in Luxor (southern Egypt) where natives had been using it for millennia for the treatment of urinary tract problems. Back in the laboratory the researchers succeeded in extracting and isolating the herb's chemical constituents and subjected them to pharmacological examinations – a process that led to the identification of the active chemical ingredient with the reputed biological effect. Several clinical trials by urologists in the Faculty of Medicine at Cairo University confirmed these findings.

The results of this research were then taken to the Cairo Pharmaceuticals Company for commercialization. In their excitement the researchers had neither obtained a patent nor had they signed a contract. One researcher confided: 'We were young. We thought we were going to be rich ... We were so overwhelmed with joy that an industrialist was interested in our research that we were content that our work was market worthy and commercializable on a national scale. We were content that our drug would heal people. It was a great moral reward!' The company demanded more information about the technological know-how involved in the production of the drug after having been impressed with the initial laboratory results that the researchers had provided. This information was readily turned over, and the company began to manufacture the drug for domestic use. As the drug gained popularity, the researchers thought it wise to obtain patent protection; however, upon approaching the chairman of the company for royalties their request was denied. There was no contract, and the company insisted that the researchers should be content with the 'moral' gratification. With the help of the media this incident came to be highly publicized within the research community. Aside from feelings of betrayal and mistrust, the incident fostered a feverish attitude of self-interest as researchers began to turn their attention to research for academic rather than commercial purposes. But as the research community turned inward, the domestic industry increasingly turned to foreign technology suppliers. Eventually industry was not turning to or supporting local research institutes at all. Instead, local industrialists kept their attention focused on licensing the technologies of foreign brand name companies. Irrespective of whether the significance of this incident has been greatly exaggerated, it is clear that a legacy of mistrust persists. According to Dr Venice Gouda, former minister of science and technology, 'trust between the actors in the biotech sector is limited, there is no trust between business and the research community.' The statements of several other local experts confirmed this assertion.

Despite the genuine existence of a problem related to trust, experts also emphasized that the current lack of robust linkages is more likely due to the inability of universities and public research institutes to train qualified personnel, perform relevant research, and sustain links with industry and society at large. One interviewee observed that many academicians knew how to explain scientific concepts very well but were largely incapable of solving practical problems. Therefore resorting to these centres for technical support was not very useful. Similarly, other experts contended that 'these institutions are for academic promotion not technical advancement.' They suggested that an administrative system be established to facilitate the progression of research from idea to market. Nevertheless, there are attempts particularly between public sector firms and research centres to forge collaborative relationships. According to Dr Kadria Abdel Motaal of VACSERA, 'we are trying hard to collaborate because we really believe that unless we complement each other regarding research, instruments, labs, human resources, we are not going to go to far. We are trying to approach, and we are approached by, all our counterparts in different research institutes, and we try to reach agreements whereby we exchange confidential information about staff and equipment to see where complementarities can arise, so as to not repeat the same research.' In the same vein, Dr Galal Ghorab, chairman of the Pharmaceuticals Holding Company, stated that they had signed a contract with the NRC to start preparing diagnostic tests for hepatitis B and C. He also noted that his company and its affiliates were initiating cooperation with several national universities and the National Cancer Institute. The willingness of public sector firms as opposed to private actors to cooperate with national research centres was confirmed by other experts. For instance, one interviewee stated that 'it is supposed to be the private sector that has more courage to assume conjoint risk with a local scientist but in reality it is not ... they do not take risks. They adopt projects that have minimal science, like a natural product. They will contract a local scientist to perform the extraction of the natural substance that has certain pharmaceutical properties. They do not take risks with novel drugs ... but of course there are exceptions.'

International Linkages

International linkages are abundant in the health biotechnology sector in Egypt. Two very interesting observations appear to emerge in this regard. First, unlike in conventional pharmaceuticals where highly desirable linkages with the multinational industry are based primarily on licensing arrangements, in the health biotechnology sector there appears to be an explicit preference for strong linkages with international research institutes and universities. Local experts generally believe that 'dealing with multinational companies in the area of health biotechnology is not very fruitful' largely because multinationals were not willing to transfer know-how but rather may agree to license a product for local filling and packaging. For many this did not satisfy the goal of national self-sufficiency in the health sector. Despite this understanding relations with the multinational industry are indispensable primarily because of the sector's reliance on raw material and equipment imports, but also because of some important training arrangements. Thus, most international linkages in the health biotechnology sector are in the form of educational exchanges, research, and training. Perhaps one of the primary determinants of the nature of these linkages is the extent to which the Egyptian education system as a whole encourages young graduates to complete their studies abroad. The result of this dependence on foreign education and training, primarily in the advanced industrial countries, has led to the formation of a web of networks both with foreign experts and with those Egyptian scientists who choose to remain abroad.

All of the interviewees who had travelled abroad to complete their studies or training commented that they continued to communicate with former colleagues including to request information or to collaborate on specific research questions. According to Dr El Sayed of the Egyptian International Pharmaceutical Industries Company, his unit's connection with the International Organization for Genetic Engineering allows for cooperation to solve specific problems or to skip certain stages of the research process entirely. He also noted that corresponding with friends in foreign universities and institutes to achieve the same aim was common.

The second interesting observation, and perhaps because of the situation just described, was that key players in the health biotechnology sector were relying on educational and research institutions mostly in the advanced industrial countries for education, training, and research support, but they were relying on the more advanced *developing* countries for technology transfer arrangements. The three countries that were most commonly mentioned in this regard were China, India, and Cuba. Some interviewees mentioned security issues and economic protectionism as reasons for limited cooperation with the advanced industrial countries in this area. Others, however, mostly stated that in the end it was a matter of cost. According to one interviewee, buying technology from countries like Germany was too expensive, particularly in the early stages of cooperation. He noted that, although cooperation with the Chinese was also costly and the technologies generally more 'rough,' it was still the most affordable alternative for a cash-strapped industry.

At the national level the Academy of Scientific Research is active in maintaining Egypt's presence in a variety of international S&T unions and associations. According to Dr Fawzie El Refaie, the academy's president, most international unions or associations have mirror committees in Egypt that cooperate. There are thirty-three such committees that correspond to thirty-three international bodies. While these local counterparts exist, El Rafaie said that the government has been trying to activate local participation and involvement in international S&T unions not only through sending local representatives to international meetings, but also through encouraging 'scientific tourism' in Egypt. He noted, however, that the former would likely be challenging on account of limited funds. The best opportunity therefore lay in attracting some associations to convene meetings and carry out research projects in Egypt, as some have already agreed to do.

Complementary Policies

Egypt's drive to integrate rapidly with the global economy, and its acceptance of a market-driven economic development strategy has led to a 'laissez faire, laissez innover' orientation. In line with a certain kind of economic thinking, government officials increasingly believe that the role of government is merely to construct a national environment in which the efficient allocation of resources can be effected by market forces. From this perspective governments are not supposed to discriminate between industries, and this thinking has governed Egypt's economic reforms over the past decade. Reforms have aimed at establishing a general and consistent set of incentives for the entire industrial base while eliminating targeted incentives for specific sectors including pharmaceuticals. This approach is now widely accepted, but it continues to be the subject of controversy, if only because the most successful developing countries of East Asia clearly did not heed this advice. Even within the World Bank there are those who disagree strongly with this view, suggesting that the most appropriate policies for the evolution of any industrial sector must be derived from the technological conditions prevailing within that sector, because it is these that will determine the steepness of the learning curve and the need for 'special support' during the industry's formative years. Thus, it is argued that 'market incentives may not provide correct signals for resource allocation or capability building if there are valid infant industry arguments for intervention' (World Bank 1992, 2).

In the case of pharmaceuticals, these arguments can be buttressed by another argument, namely, that a nation's basic pharmaceutical supplies are of sufficient strategic importance that a substantial domestic production capacity can be justified on those grounds alone. This, too, turns into an argument to justify a degree of targeting in the case of this industry. The fact of the matter is that without targeting of some kind for the pharmaceutical sector it is unlikely that this industry would thrive, and even less likely that it would develop a greater capacity to innovate.

In most OECD countries comprehensive pharmaceutical policies are aimed at promoting innovation and diffusion in existing technologies. Among the diverse measures used by governments in this respect are the enforcement of regulations to ensure effective technology transfer, the provision of subsidies and tax incentives, and the participation in jointly funded R&D consortia with the private sector, in addition to extensive direct involvement in R&D activities (Freeman and Soete 1997, 378; Correa 2001, 2). It is noteworthy that the discovery of drugs with significant therapeutic gain has often been made by public institutions, which then licence their development to private actors (Correa 2001, 2). At least 70 per cent of such drugs were developed with some form of government support (UNDP 1999, 69). In contrast, Egypt does not have a comprehensive pharmaceutical policy nor does it have a coherent technology policy, although President Mubarak did announce on several public occasions that a technology policy would be formulated soon. At present Law No. 43/1974, which gave the government the right to authorize technology transfers through joint ventures on a case-by-case basis, forms the basic legal framework in this respect. Egypt's increasing openness to foreign investment, however, has meant that recourse to Law No. 43 is diminishing while dependence on market forces to regulate technology transfer is increasing.

Yet concern over the likelihood of market abuse regarding technology transfers, especially considering the asymmetric bargaining power between the technology owner and the technology purchaser, which will be further augmented with the introduction of a stronger IPRs regime, has prompted the government to include provisions in its new trade law to govern such arrangements. The law, therefore, establishes the rights and obligations of both the technology importer and the technology owner. Accordingly, the transfer agreement must include all the relevant know-how, including sufficient information about the S&T capabilities required for the importer to make optimum use of the technology. In addition, the law stipulates the conditions under which a technology transfer contract can be nullified including any attempt by the technology owner to restrict the freedom of the importer to use, adapt, or fully exploit the potential of the technology. These provisions are particularly critical in the area of pharmaceuticals, where it has long been acknowledged that most of the value of a drug is found in its active components, so that one can argue that if the industry is to advance it needs to acquire the knowledge to produce many of these components. Indeed, the domestic industry's weakness in this regard clearly exacerbates its dependence on foreign technology suppliers and heightens the need for strong policies regarding technology transfer particularly in the face of TRIPS.

Unfortunately, the ability of the Egyptian government to enforce these new technology transfer regulations is questionable. The new trade law does not include provisions to deal with violators of technology transfer agreements, which greatly compromises the ability of the law to act as a deterrent of abusive behaviour. It is also likely that enforcement of the law will meet with strong opposition from technology owners who will use their asymmetric information and bargaining power to exploit the limited expertise of government regulators in order to undermine the law's effective implementation. In any event, even if such measures are effectively implemented, they remain highly insufficient to address the diverse challenges facing the pharmaceutical industry. What is needed here is a strategic plan aimed specifically at guiding the development of the sector towards higher value added research-based production (UNCTAD 1999, 69; Subramanian and Abdel-Latif 1997, 23). In the absence of this plan, efforts to encourage local innovation and to address weaknesses in the pharmaceutical/health aspects of the NSI will likely remain inadequate and fragmented.

To bring Egypt's pharmaceuticals sector to the point where it could derive significant benefits from TRIPS, Subramanian and Abdel-Latif

(1997, 23–4) suggested that the government and the industry adopt a 'graduated approach' to the development of the industry. According to their strategy, the first phase would involve the local industry's acquisition of capabilities to manufacture bulk generic drugs, perhaps in collaboration with foreign partners. In the second phase the industry would begin to invest in various R&D activities starting with improvements in drug quality and eventually leading to research in tropical diseases. In the third phase Egyptian companies would be well placed to establish research partnerships and other strategic alliances with foreign companies. It is argued that this is considered one of the later stages in industrial development because it does not depend simply on firm behaviour but on 'national virtues' that create cross-border opportunities (Freeman and Soete 1997, 346). In this regard, it is interesting to note that over 90 per cent of technology transfer arrangements and alliances are made among companies based in the United States, Europe, and Japan (Hagedoorn and Schakenraad 1991; Freeman and Hagedoorn 1992, in Freeman and Soete 1997, 348). It is clear that all the stages in this graduated approach are dependent on 'national virtues' to a greater or lesser extent.

As the full implementation of TRIPS moves closer there has been much talk about the development of a more comprehensive pharmaceuticals strategy. Recently, an expert committee was established under the chairmanship of Dr Atef Sidqui (former prime minister of Egypt) for this purpose. The goal of the committee's efforts will be to improve the competitiveness of the pharmaceutical industry, to protect local production and to expand export markets. The committee will also consider the various factors that threaten the development of the local industry, particularly those that emanate from international pressures and obligations. It is already anticipated that the committee will call for significantly increased supports for national research institutes, public sector firms, and raw materials production; improved linkages between national and regional players; and participation in global strategic alliances. Yet identifying such possibilities is only the first step. The greater challenge will be to find effective ways of implementing them, particularly given the complex nature of the interests involved and the new circumstances in which they have to be brought into existence. Of course, any plan to guide the development of the pharmaceutical industry must be complemented by an appropriate and effective competition policy that takes due account of the recent restructuring of the industry and of the evolving marketing strategies of multinational

firms combined with the imminent danger associated with the introduction of a strong IPRs regime. Indeed, it is the latter that has given
impetus to the formulation of an explicit competition policy in Egypt,
which had traditionally relied on the presence of a dominant public
sector, the ability to control prices, and the ability to direct resources to
achieve social goals. The biggest danger is that this new IPRs regime
may be used in a manner that undermines the Egyptian industry and
inhibits technology transfer with consequent adverse effects on public
health, as has been widely recognized: 'Though the patent system was
devised in order to reward inventiveness, encourage technological
progress and foster dissemination of innovations, patents are used in
many cases as commercial tools in order to restrict or delay legitimate
competition' (Correa 2001, 7). In the pharmaceutical sector this will
primarily mean a rollback of generic manufacturing, and that will
compromise a key tool now used by governments worldwide to limit
the costs of the patent system; there is ample evidence to suggest that
even in the industrial countries generic competition sharply reduces
prices after a patent expires (CIPR 2002, 43). This is even truer in the
developing countries, where generic producers usually supply most
drugs (World Bank 2001, 137).

Even in the absence of deliberate attempts to eliminate legitimate
competition, the provision of stronger patent protection in the field of
pharmaceuticals has definitive outcomes that result in the monopolization of certain markets by foreign firms in developing countries
(Harmsen and Subramanian 1994, 12). Indeed, both the World Bank
(2001, 137) and CIPR[10] (2002, 43) concur that the resulting increased
market power of multinational firms will result in a consolidation and
restructuring of domestic industries. Thus, according the World Bank
(2001, 137), 'in most cases ... local enterprises will come under pressure
to close down or form alliances with larger firms, resulting in a concentration of the industry.' TRIPS acknowledges the possibility of such
anticompetitive outcomes and grants states certain rights to minimize
these dangers.

Developing countries, including Egypt, require competition policies
that address their respective developmental needs and that complement their development strategies. In this respect there is much to
learn from the Japanese model, particularly for the years 1950–1973,
when that country was 'catching-up' so effectively to the leading
industrial countries (Singh and Dhumale 1999, 10). During that period
Japanese competition policy was an integral part of its industrial pol-

icy, which in turn was a central pillar of its development strategy. The main concern of Japan's industrial policy was to sustain high levels of private investment in building a strong, competitive, and technologically sophisticated national industrial base. To this end, some restrictions were imposed on product market competition. Indeed, the explicit goal of competition policy was to attain an 'optimal,' as opposed to a 'maximum,' level of competition, where optimum was defined in terms of effectiveness in promoting the country's broader strategic objectives. In practice this frequently involved encouraging cooperation between certain firms or ensuring that competition did not become destabilizing and destructive.

Unfortunately, Egypt's efforts to establish a viable competition policy are still in their formative stages. Although the country has had significant international assistance in this regard, weaknesses in the country's institutional environment and in some cases political will are inhibiting the derivation of expected benefits from the implementation of a competition regime. Both national authorities and private sector actors have resisted or challenged the development of a competition policy at certain times and implementation continues to be marred by personal interests. Ali El Din and Mohieldin (2001, 22) noted that initial resistance from state officials was based on the fact that a competition policy would necessarily force discipline on its own activities. In doing so it might lead to the cessation of uncompetitive activities and enterprises which nevertheless served social purposes, including the provision of employment. On the part of private actors, these authors noted that the implementation of a competition policy was resisted on the grounds that it may lead to greater government intervention and more charges of unfair trade practices. The government also made no attempt to incorporate activities in the informal sector and offered little guarantees regarding consistent and just enforcement (ibid., 26).

In light of these circumstances, weaknesses in the institutional structure supporting the pharmaceutical industry and the absence of key policies needed to guide and to strengthen its future development make the introduction of stronger patent protection particularly problematic in Egypt. Without efforts to address the weaknesses in the S&T system, the industry will likely continue to increase its reliance on foreign technology licensing on terms that may ultimately hinder its ability to develop autonomous technological capabilities that would allow it to derive significant benefits from TRIPS in due course. With the introduction of stronger patent rights, this situation is likely to become more costly to Egypt because the bargaining power of the technology owners will be augmented as a result. The absence of an effective competition policy will allow them to use that power to undermine many of the positive features of the present situation. Thus, the MNEs are currently instigating price wars to drive out smaller competitors by means of retailer rebates, while pursuing a range of mergers and acquisitions that will diminish competition in the domestic industry. These outcomes raise special concerns regarding the local industry's ability to continue to contribute to public health by providing reasonably priced pharmaceutical products in a reliable manner.

Indeed, the impact of stronger IPRs on the prices of pharmaceuticals is one of the most serious outcomes expected to result from the imposition of TRIPS in the current context. This agreement increases the monopoly privileges of MNEs, and this will almost certainly lead to an increase in prices and an unnecessary lag between the appearance of the original drug and the introduction of cheaper therapeutic equivalents. Even the proponents of stronger intellectual property regimes admit that 'with IPP firms may expect to gain more control over prices and price changes for the products covered by patents once price regulation is relaxed. Firms may attempt to set introductory prices at a higher level than would be the case absent IPP ... High prices may still represent cost savings versus the next-best-alternative such as surgery, but not compared to generic competition in the absence of IPP' (Rozek and Berkowitz 1998, 26).

According to Ministry of Health officials, generic drugs are on average 33 per cent cheaper than brand name products. This is why changes to the country's patent regime have been intensely resisted by those officials who are primarily concerned with public health who point to the apparently paradoxical fact that, in this case, protection has generally led to lower prices. In the words of one official, 'in addition to being the near-exclusive supplier of inexpensive drugs for the poor, and perhaps chiefly because of this fact, the pharmaceutical industry in Egypt has traditionally been a protected sector' (Fayez 1997, 2). This is particularly significant when one considers that 85 per cent of expenditures on pharmaceutical products come directly out of household budgets, with only 15 per cent being covered by the National Health Insurance Plan, which benefits only a small portion of the population. As in most developing countries, drug prices in the marketplace have a disproportionate impact on the welfare of poor people, who are estimated by the Ministry of Health to include 22 per cent of the Egyptian population (or as high as 40 per cent by other sources), and who would be forced to delay or forgo treatments because of high drug prices.

This is the context in which Egypt's former Minister of Health Dr Ismail Sallam has repeatedly warned of the dangers posed by enhanced intellectual property rights for the human right to health, which requires that drugs be accessible.[11] Although he acknowledges that drug policies must ultimately conform to political and economic realities, he has insisted that these competing claims have to be balanced in such a way that adequate access to drugs is ensured for the population at large (Salama 1997, 3). Sallam has been clear in his position that TRIPS would impede drug access primarily because of its negative impact on the domestic industry with serious consequences for Egyptian consumers who are reliant on its relatively affordable drugs (ibid.). These sentiments are echoed by Médecins Sans Frontières, the Nobel Prize–winning humanitarian and medical agency, which believes that implementation of TRIPS will reduce reasonable access to medicines in developing countries because it will raise drug prices and impair local manufacturing capacity (Banta 2000).

The global pharmaceutical lobby continues to argue that stronger IPRs will ultimately benefit everyone; local MNE executives in Egypt, however, were remarkably frank in admitting that for the time being their product and pricing policies totally exclude large parts of the population. But they did not see this as a problem since they simply assumed that it was the job of the government to deal with it. Of course, what this ignores is that the government's ability to do that job is increasingly constrained by budgetary constraints, rising drug prices in the market, and the increasing hostility to 'government subsidies' in the official international policy debate. Representatives and leaders of MNEs in Egypt were therefore surprisingly forthcoming in their discussions of their prices and their pricing policies. Pfizer's director of external affairs and health policy set the tone of the discussion when he suggested that the majority of Egyptians could not afford MNE drug prices in any event, so that the industry contributes minimally to the health of the majority of the population. Glaxo Wellcome's communications manager for Egypt estimated that only 1 to 3 per cent of the population can afford their drugs: 'We target the elites. The government can continue to target the have-nots. They can continue to provide low price, low quality drugs to support state run medical facilities.' To illustrate the scale of the disparity she noted that when Zantac

(a popular antacid) came off patent protection in Egypt, generic companies provided a therapeutic equivalent for one-tenth of the original
price. Indeed many of the MNE leaders interviewed for this study
stated that they have not been 'good national citizens' in this regard,
although they would also argue that it was not their responsibility to
deal with the special problems created by the fact that so many Egyptian people lack adequate purchasing power.

The pervasiveness of premium pricing for patented products is an
inescapable fact. To suggest otherwise would be to have misunder-
stood what the fuss over pharmaceutical patents is all about. High
price/low volume strategies for the introduction of new brand name
drugs (whether or not they are therapeutically distinct) are common in
the pharmaceutical industry, even when cheaper and equally effective
alternatives are available. That is one of the reasons for the very high
expenditures on advertising and marketing. In this case the link
between stronger IPRs and their 'premium pricing policies' is not
merely an abstract concern; it is a matter of explicit and active planning
by the MNEs. Thus, according to an internal document provided by
one of the MNEs, a strong emphasis on premium pricing for patented
drugs will follow the full application of the new IPRs legislation in
Egypt.[12] Indeed, MNE leaders were quite candid about their intention
to press for higher prices with the change to Egypt's patent regime,
and the fact that many people could not afford their products was simply taken as a given and not their concern. A chairman of one MNE
subsidiary stated that 'if someone poor cannot afford the drug then
that's life, it's too bad. We are an industry not a charity. Just because
the average Egyptian is poor does not mean that prices should vary
very much. I mean what is the government's role?'[13]

By implication it is therefore one of the government's roles to control
drug prices, either in general or for certain segments of the market. As
noted in chapter 4, price control regimes for pharmaceuticals are found
all over the world, and in many cases they coexist with strong patent
regimes helping to mitigate their impact on prices. In Egypt it is estimated that price controls keep drug prices at one-fourth of those in the
United States, and at one-half those in other developing countries
(Rozek and Berkowitz 1998, 13). As part of Egypt's reform program in
the 1990s a new pricing method was implemented called the 'cost-
plus' formula. According to this method a company is asked to submit
the price at which it desires to sell a product to a committee headed by
the Ministry of Health and comprised of members from the Ministry of

Economy, the Ministry of Finance, and industrial representatives. Companies are permitted to factor in a 15 per cent profit margin on essential drugs (classified by the WHO), 25 per cent on non-essential drugs (for non–life-threatening diseases), and a 40 per cent margin for over-the-counter drugs (mostly vitamins and painkillers). The pricing committee has databases on the costs of raw materials and other processes involved in the manufacture of drugs in order to be able to review and verify company submissions and to exact the lowest prices.

When the product is therapeutically distinct there is greater price discretion. In such cases the price eventually agreed on covers costs plus a handsome profit. In most other cases, however, the committee will push down the price irrespective of the company's demands after technical considerations have been taken into account. If a drug is categorized for the treatment of a chronic or life-threatening disease it is exempt from the value-added tax. According to one MNE chairman, companies often attempt to demonstrate this for all their drugs since approval is discretionary. The system also encourages companies to register drug variations in order to be eligible for price reviews. In the case where a company does not accept the price reached through negotiation the product is not given market authorization.

Egypt's price control system is coming under pressure by both domestic and foreign sources. Both locally owned and foreign firms complain that the government's pricing policy does not take account of the rising costs of production. They argue that as products realize losses over time it becomes increasingly difficult to allocate resources to such activities as R&D. MNEs also complain that this system encourages imitative behaviour, as local firms choose to copy new and more lucrative products, developed by MNEs, until the financial rewards dwindle and the cycle is repeated with newer products. As a result, MNEs have been continually pressuring Egyptian authorities to eliminate price controls by threatening to move operations elsewhere, particularly to the Gulf countries (Al Bassil et al 2002, 20–1). Yet, despite these complaints, it appears as though foreign firms enjoy the greatest price discretion; this has sparked a bitter national debate and led to demands by local industry leaders for greater transparency in the pricing process.

Internationally, the global pharmaceutical industry has been active in attacking and threatening governments that continue to have price control regimes for pharmaceuticals, and it has gone to great lengths to prevent governments from introducing new price cuts. In November 2001 a group of the world's largest multinational companies contributed U.S.$189 million to Germany's state-sponsored health plan in order to prevent the Ministry of Health from imposing a 4 per cent price cut on prescription drugs, because they feared that this would have set a precedent for other European governments (Fuhrmans and Naik 2002). Even so, Italy imposed a 5 per cent price cut in May 2002, and the French government cut the prices of a hundred drugs by as much as 15 per cent while making it clear that it was willing to impose more cuts if drug price increases continued to put unreasonable pressure on health expenditures (ibid.). It is notable that these rather surprising government interventions were aimed at some of the industry's costliest drugs, successfully promoted by massive marketing efforts which led to widespread use of new and more expensive drugs, despite their limited therapeutic benefits over older versions (ibid.).

The arrangement reached with the German government turned out to be the exception rather than the rule because it did not stop other governments from doing what the German government had threatened to do. In most other cases, the industry has therefore responded to unacceptable price controls by threatening to deprive the country in question of new drugs that are developed. In 2001, Hank McKinnel, the CEO of Pfizer, attacked the pricing policies of many European Union countries and indicated that such misguided policies could lead to 'a denial of access to new treatments' (Pollard 2001). Other MNEs concur with this view and add the standard argument that price control policies are ultimately self-defeating because they undermine research in these countries and encourage its relocation to more profitable countries like the United States (ibid.). Similar threats are also echoed in the developing countries, as in one regional symposium, where Mohammad Salah Roushdie, the chairman of Pfizer Egypt, signalled the industry's willingness to withhold the introduction of new treatments until IPRs were strengthened and prices raised. To emphasize the point he noted that the entire Middle East and North Africa region represented a mere 1 per cent of the global market, so that it would cost Pfizer next to nothing to wait for intellectual property and price reforms (Al Alam Al Yom 1999, 3).

Conclusion

This chapter examined the achievements and weaknesses of the Egyptian pharmaceutical industry in order to assess the likelihood of it benefiting from the imposition of the stronger IPRs implied by the full application of TRIPS. It demonstrated that Egypt's traditionally lax pharmaceutical patent policy was partially responsible for fostering a domestic pharmaceutical industry with significant participation of locally owned private and public sector firms. The lax patent regime enhanced the ability of these firms to imitate foreign pharmaceutical products and processes and to benefit from important learning effects as a result. Over time this contributed to domestic competition and to public health. Initially, the industry was able to develop very success-fully. Indeed, by the late 1990s it supplied 93 per cent of domestic needs at relatively low prices while remaining one of the more profit-able industries in the country. However, although these firms had been among the greatest beneficiaries of Egypt's lax patent regime, together with the consumers of pharmaceuticals, their longer-term prospects were limited by major weaknesses in the country's scientific and tech-nological support structure, including weak local linkages and the absence of key government policies. Today, those weaknesses have become more visible and more critical because they will prevent the local industry from being able to benefit significantly from the new TRIPS-related IPRs regime or from being able to protect the public health system from adverse effects.

It is evident from this analysis that, in order to give effect to the declared objective of TRIPS (Article 7), to ensure that intellectual prop-erty rights 'contribute to the promotion of technological innovation and to the transfer and dissemination of technology, to the mutual advantage of producers and users of technological knowledge and in a manner conducive to social and economic welfare, and to a balance of rights and obligations,' developing countries will need more than just longer grace periods to reform their legal systems. Continued improvements in the level and nature of innovation in these countries are unlikely to occur in the presence of stronger, internationally harmo-nized patent rights, unless they are able to strengthen the pharmaceuti-cal/health aspects of their national systems of innovation. Reforming and establishing such systems will necessitate a concerted effort on the part of government, research institutes, universities, industry and its federations or associations, the medical profession, pharmacists, and other relevant parties. Unfortunately, the introduction of a stronger IPRs regime will make this very challenging.

Recently, even the World Bank has suggested that the level of IPRs should vary in accordance with a country's income level (2001, 129).

More accurately, it should vary by the strength of their NSI, difficult though that is to define. In this regard, CIPR (2002, 10) has concluded: 'It is our contention that intellectual property systems may, if we are not careful, introduce distortions that are detrimental to the interests of developing countries. Very 'high' standards of protection may be in the public interest in developed countries with highly sophisticated scientific and technological infrastructures (although we note, as above, that this is controversial in several respects), but this does not mean the same standards are appropriate in all developing countries. In fact we consider that developed countries should pay more attention to reconciling their own perceived commercial self-interest, with their own interest in the reduction of poverty in developing countries.'

Egypt is a lower-middle-income country with a relatively weak national system of innovation.[14] The capabilities of its pharmaceutical firms to innovate have evolved over time through learning by doing, but they remain weak in R&D, one of the key indicators of innovative capacity. The entire industry continues to rely heavily, and in many cases unnecessarily, on production under licence, with significant financial and development costs for the industry and the economy. A significant improvement in this performance will depend on the industry's ability to create a viable scientific and technological complex, or NSI, that provides a sufficiently positive environment to allow the industry and the country to benefit from stronger IPRs. However, the problem is not only that the present structure is weak. The future does not look much more encouraging since Egypt has no comprehensive or effective strategy for the development of its pharmaceutical industry or for the attraction of more knowledge-intensive investments by foreign firms in this sector. Egypt's past policies can be said to have paid inadequate attention to the real long-term needs of the pharmaceutical industry, having been more concerned with short-term concerns. There were good reasons for this and the results have been rather positive to date, but the new TRIPS regime will pose a challenge that could undermine many of these gains because of the serious weaknesses in the national system of innovation that now exists in the country. Against this background, it appears that the substance and speed with which government policies are being implemented in the new era of TRIPS neglect many important aspects of the economic and institutional infrastructure that affect processes involved with the acquisition, diffusion, and utilization of knowledge. In this environment a continued 'laissez innover' strategy coupled with stronger IPRs is likely to stifle and reverse the early gains that have been made in allowing foreign technologies to be mastered and improved. This in turn will place limits on the industry's and the country's long-term development (Freeman and Soete 1997; Romer 1994; Freeman and Perez 1988) and the improvement of living standards – and public health in particular.

The conclusions of this chapter are particularly disturbing for Egypt's fragile public health system, which is currently undergoing significant reforms. Reliance on pharmaceutical products is expected to grow in the coming years, and much of this expenditure will continue to come directly out of household budgets. Because of its expected negative impact on the prices of pharmaceutical products, the implementation of TRIPS is likely to make the challenge of obtaining medical treatments even more desperate for the poor. Unfortunately, it is not likely that these costs will be offset by significant improvements in research on local diseases or that technology transfer will accelerate or that the country will be able to strengthen the pharmaceutical/health aspects of its NSI. For the moment, Egypt continues to maintain a strict price control regime; however, it is uncertain how long it will be able to resist growing pressures and threats to dismantle this system.

TRIPS essentially deprives developing countries of the opportunity to chart their own technological course in accordance with their own national needs and priorities. Many developing countries are reforming or adjusting their development plans to reflect the unrelenting, and largely inappropriate demands of this new IPRs regimes, and the global trade regime of which it is a part. The potential adverse implications of stronger pharmaceutical patent protection for public health have, however, struck a sensitive chord with developing country governments and with public health advocates worldwide. In fact, international concern over TRIPS has been mainly focused on its likely impact on access to health-related treatments for the poor, rather than on its likely impact on innovation and industry. The next chapter shows how and why these two dimensions, industrial development and public health, are inseparable, and takes a closer look at the continuing controversy surrounding TRIPS.

7 Policy Options under TRIPS: Reality or Illusion?

In the preceding chapter conclusions were drawn that suggested a need to broaden economic analysis of the impact of TRIPS on the pharmaceuticals industries of developing countries to include critical pharmaceutical/health aspects of their national systems of innovation. Indeed, the main purpose of this study is to emphasize the importance of understanding the role of historical, social, cultural, and political factors even when attempting to assess the specifically economic implications of that agreement. So far the study has demonstrated that the short-term costs of this agreement for the developing world are clear and substantial, while the long-term gains are ambiguous and uncertain. The purpose of this chapter is twofold: (1) to analyse recent international events that have transpired as a result of the continuing disagreement between the developing and the developed countries over the impact of TRIPS on national pharmaceuticals industries and public health systems, and (2) to examine key changes in Egypt's new patent law. My central argument rests on four main points:

1 It is evident that the developing countries have come a long way since the Uruguay Round negotiations, when they were largely pressured and threatened into accepting TRIPS, even though neither their local pharmaceuticals industries nor their public health systems were adequately prepared to deal with the implications. Their increasingly sophisticated understanding of TRIPS and its implications for their economies and their future technological development, combined with a better understanding of the international negotiation process, is evident in the policy process that led to the creation of the Declaration on TRIPS and Public Health at the

Fourth WTO Ministerial Conference, in Doha (Qatar) in November 2001.[1]

2 Nevertheless, Doha also showed that despite this strengthening of the position of developing countries, the industrial countries largely delineated the scope and substance of these negotiations. Indeed, although the developing countries were said by some to have made substantial gains, in reality the industrial countries conceded nothing in the Doha Declaration that TRIPS did not already permit, with the resolution of those contentious issues that were not already clearly stipulated in the agreement postponed to future negotiations.

3 From the perspective of this study, the most important outcome of this latest phase in the policy process was that it implied a problematic fundamental reaffirmation of the core requirements of TRIPS by the developing countries. The success of the industrial countries in limiting the negotiations to a discussion of the so-called flexibilities already embedded within TRIPS with respect to public health effectively obscured the need for a more critical discussion of the impact of the core TRIPS requirements on innovation and technological diffusion in the developing world. In effect, the industrial countries insisted that the developing countries must accept that these negotiations could proceed only on condition that TRIPS was accepted as part of the solution to any public health problems, so that, under no circumstances, would discussion of the desirability of TRIPS be reopened.

4 Given this reality, it is likely that the implementation of key provisions in Egypt's new patent law that were designed to protect and promote the development of the local pharmaceutical industry and public health will continue to be challenged by the global pharmaceutical industry and by Egypt's stronger trading partners despite the conformance of these provisions with the policy options permitted under TRIPS and confirmed at Doha.

This chapter deals with the events that began in the latter half of the 1990s when there was growing confusion over the flexibilities embedded within TRIPS, and that ended in November 2001 when ministers of the WTO member states adopted the Doha Declaration at the fourth WTO ministerial session. Beyond this, a brief discussion is included concerning the General Council's decision in August 2003 regarding the resolution of a key issue that had been postponed during the Doha meeting. It also examines key changes in Egypt's new patent law that was passed soon after the Doha meeting. The discussion is presented in four main parts. The first deals with how the demand for clarification of TRIPS emerged within the WTO TRIPS Council. The second deals with the events that unfolded during the latter half of 2001 as the developed and developing countries struggled to ensure that the text of the Doha Declaration would reflect their respective needs and priorities. The third part considers the practical implications of these events. The fourth and final part examines key changes in Egypt's new patent law and interprets them in connection with the issues dealt with in this study.

The Demand for Clarification of TRIPS

TRIPS includes various provisions that in principle allow WTO members to take various measures to protect public health. As discussed in chapter 4, the most significant provisions are those related to parallel imports, exceptions to exclusive rights, and compulsory licensing. Yet, despite the existence of these provisions in TRIPS, developing countries have found it exceedingly difficult to make use of them to address serious public health concerns, even in the case of genuine national health emergencies. This has been so because the United States government, responding to a strong pharmaceutical lobby, has led the industrial countries in pressuring them not to take advantage of these provisions, but to adopt a particular interpretation of TRIPS, one that primarily serves its interests and those of its large multinational pharmaceutical firms.

The international pharmaceutical lobby has been relentless in its efforts to ensure that most of the concessions, which had been made to the developing countries in persuading them to sign TRIPS, should not be utilized by them in actual practice. As a result, countries that attempted to invoke these legitimate provisions of the agreement have quickly found themselves in conflict with the U.S. government. Thus, when the Thai government sought to make use of parallel imports and the compulsory licensing of certain drugs to fight a raging AIDS epidemic, the United States signalled its strong disapproval and threatened economic sanctions, until the government of Thailand abandoned these policy instruments in 1999 (Moreau 1999, 24). The government's hands were further tied when it was also forced to terminate the operations of its Pharmaceutical Patent Review Board, which had the power to compel companies to divulge sensitive cost data, thereby providing some protection against anticompetitive behaviour and limiting the extent of transfer pricing (ibid.).

By early 2000 the Pharmaceutical Research and Manufacturers of America (PhRMA) was heavily lobbying the U.S. government to intervene actively on its behalf in other countries where it considered IP protection to be insufficient. Thus, in its February 2000 submission to the U.S. Trade Representative, PhRMA specifically demanded that Argentina, Egypt, and India be placed on the US's Priority Watch List because 'all three countries are out of compliance with WTO TRIPS obligations and all three adversely affect our industry's ability to market our products, and weaken efforts to carry out research and development into vital new therapies with adverse impacts worldwide. Furthermore, these countries have taken aggressive postures in international trade fora adverse to U.S. government and industry interests' (PhRMA 2000).

These three countries were the primary targets, but not the only ones. The submission proceeded to identify thirty other countries for inclusion in the slightly less-threatening USTR Watch List.[2]

In August 2000 sixteen of these thirty countries, including Egypt, were moved up to the Priority Watch List, while thirty-nine others were placed on the less serious Watch List. Meanwhile, between 1996 and 2000 the United States filed fourteen WTO complaints relating to an alleged inadequacy of foreign IP regimes (USTR 2000, 1). On this score, it appeared to be willing to do 'whatever it takes' to achieve its objectives. Thus, one American official told me in Cairo that if necessary the U.S. government would be willing to set up a separate agency to keep up with these proliferating 'global indictments.' It was only when the issue of the inaccessibility of patented HIV/AIDS treatments for the poor in the developing world exploded on the global stage that the United States was forced to re-examine these callous policies, at least for a time.

It is by now well known that the developing world is facing a startling HIV/AIDS epidemic. Of the 33 million people infected with HIV/AIDS worldwide, 90 per cent live in poverty-stricken regions of Africa, Latin America, and Asia where AIDS is a fatal, rather than a chronic, disease largely because HIV/AIDS treatments are priced well out of most people's reach. This stark reality revealed the unacceptability of the demands by the U.S. government and the global pharmaceutical industry for the accelerated implementation of TRIPS in these poor countries. The issue was soon brought to a head in two international cases in South Africa and Brazil.

The Case of South Africa

In an effort to improve access to HIV/AIDS treatments for its 4.2 million infected citizens, the South African government passed the 1997 Medicines and Related Substances Control Amendment Act, authorizing parallel imports and encouraging generic substitution of branded pharmaceutical products. In response, the multinational pharmaceuticals industry immediately began pressuring the South African government to rescind this law, while urging Washington to reinforce its demands. It was not long before the U.S. government did inform the South African government that it considered the law in question to be 'unacceptable' and then proceeded to impose some minor economic sanctions while threatening more severe reprisals by placing the country on its Priority Watch List (Mabry 1999, 25). Initially the position of the South African government remained firm in spite of these threats, which led the South African Pharmaceutical Manufacturers Association (PMA) to take the South African government to court in March 2001. The PMA argued that the provisions in the law concerning parallel imports and generic substitution granted excessive powers to the health minister, discriminated against the industry, and violated TRIPS. But these allegations had little basis in reality. The fact of the matter was that parallel imports were routinely used in many countries, particularly in Europe, while generic substitution had been a mainstay of U.S. drug policy for two decades. Moreover, there could be no doubt that South Africa's AIDS crisis qualified as a national emergency under TRIPS, which meant that the use of strong measures including parallel importing, generic substitution, and even compulsory licensing of certain drugs would not constitute violations of that agreement. Indeed, this is why the South African act had been carefully drafted to give the minister of health only the power to 'prescribe conditions for the supply of more affordable medicines in certain circumstances so as to protect the health of the public' (ibid., 22).

As this court case proceeded, international criticism of the United States and of the global pharmaceutical industry intensified, and many observers came to feel that the industry was doing irreparable damage to its already troubled image. But it was only when worldwide protests from HIV/AIDS and human rights activists threatened to disrupt Vice-President Al Gore's presidential campaign that the United States appeared to soften its stance (Abbott 2002, 471). Accordingly, President Clinton issued an executive order in March 2000, which declared that the United States would not put pressure on developing countries that

took measures to provide cheaper HIV/AIDS drugs to their populations, so long as they adhered to TRIPS. The Bush administration subsequently announced that it would not rescind this policy. With its
major ally partially withdrawing support, intensifying public criticism,
and no real basis for its lawsuit, the PMA was essentially forced to
announce on 18 April 2001 that it was withdrawing the suit. The South
African government subsequently announced its intentions to move
quickly to implement the law.

The Case of Brazil

On 1 February 2001 the WTO approved a U.S. request to establish a
dispute settlement panel to judge the compatibility of Article 68 of
Brazil's 1996 industrial property law with the provisions of TRIPS.
The focus of the dispute was the stipulation that an IP holder is
obliged to work his patent locally within three years of the issuance of
the patent or else risk being forced to license the invention to others
wanting to do so. The article also stipulates that if the IP holder
should choose to utilize his patent through importation, rather than
working it locally, then others would also be permitted to import the
invention from other 'legal' sources as well. The United States, in its
complaint, argued that this provision discriminated between imported
and locally produced products and was therefore illegal under TRIPS.
According to U.S. officials, exclusive patent rights could not be made
conditional on the way in which a right holder chooses to service the
local market, by working the patent in the country or by importing the
product.

The Brazilians insisted that the law was fully compliant with TRIPS
and that the article provided a necessary tool for the government to
increase access to essential treatments, particularly those related to
HIV/AIDS. Indeed, Brazil had initiated a highly successful program
providing for the universal distribution of HIV/AIDS medicines,
which the Brazilians believed to be dependent on the local production
of HIV/AIDS drugs and on their ability to negotiate favourable terms
with the industry. The strong provisions for compulsory licensing in its
patent law were rightly considered an important asset in their negotiations with the global pharmaceutical industry. Indeed, the threat to use
the provisions of this law against the pharmaceutical companies per-
suaded those companies to lower their prices on several occasions. In
addition, the Brazilians countered Washington's complaint with a

complaint of their own by arguing that Articles 204 and 209 of Title 35 of the U.S. Patent Code violated the non-discrimination principle under TRIPS. These articles stipulate that patents obtained for inventions backed by government subsidies or goods covered by federally owned patents respectively, must be 'substantially' produced in the United States in order to ensure patent protection (Yerkey and Pruzin 2001a). However, this dispute was not pursued when the two countries reached an agreement concerning the Brazilian law.

Faced with another international public relations disaster when the 'Brazilian' dispute came to be widely perceived as yet another U.S. attack on a country struggling to meet its public health needs in the context of a severe humanitarian crisis, the United States withdrew its case in June 2001. In a bilateral settlement, Brazil agreed to give advance notice to American authorities before issuing compulsory licences in any industry. A joint communication issued by the two countries on 25 June 2001 states: 'without prejudice of the U.S. and Brazil's different interpretations of the consistency of Article 68 with the TRIPS, the U.S. Government will withdraw the WTO panel against Brazil concerning the issue, and the Brazilian Government will agree, in the event it deems necessary to apply Article 68 to grant compulsory license on patents held by U.S. companies, to hold prior talks on the matter with the U.S. These talks would be held within the scope of the U.S.-Brazil Consultative Mechanism, in a special session scheduled to discuss the subject.'[3] However, in an effort to stem possible emulation of the Brazilian law by other developing countries, the USTR issued a clear statement that it viewed 'local manufacturing requirements as being inimical to the principles of free trade and inconsistent with various WTO rules, including the TRIPS' (Yerkey and Pruzin 2001a). It went on to warn that 'the U.S. government will aggressively engage other countries that impose or maintain such requirements and, if appropriate, pursue WTO dispute settlement.'

Demanding Change

These unfortunate experiences, when added to the growing disappointment due to the slow progress in implementing the WTO-related agreements on textiles and agriculture, had a decisive impact on the perception of the WTO and TRIPS in many developing countries. In essence, these countries came to believe that the industrial countries were reneging on the fundamental trade-off on which their acceptance of the WTO and TRIPS had been based. That trade-off involved their acceptance of stronger patent regimes and more liberalization of trade in services in return for more liberal trade regimes for textiles and agriculture. But it seemed that the developing countries were not achieving any of the promised concessions. In fact, the United States and Europe continued their protectionist agricultural policies and even increased farm subsidies since the Uruguay Round, while demanding that developing countries should continue to eliminate all such barriers to trade. Similarly, very little progress had been made in opening up northern markets to developing country textiles, with only a few products taken off quota lists. Thus, it appeared that the stronger WTO members had scarcely implemented their end of the bargain, while they were actively insisting that the developing countries should not only implement stronger IPRs through TRIPS, but that they should do so in an accelerated manner with little technical and financial support because that suited industrial country interests.

As a result, many frustrated developing countries came to the conclusion that a renegotiation of the WTO agreement and its various constituent elements was needed to address these various implementation issues. Unfortunately, the stronger industrial powers and the WTO bureaucracy considered this demand unacceptable, undoubtedly in part because the industrial countries feared that the substantial gains that they had made during the Uruguay Round negotiations would likely be compromised. 'It is impossible to re-negotiate the Uruguay Round. It will lead to an unraveling of the whole process, for you cannot re-negotiate parts of it,' declared Paul-Henri Ravier, deputy director general of the WTO (Macan-Markar 2001). However, such intransigence only strengthened the resolve of the developing countries to create a strong common policy position, despite the significant differences in their interests and circumstances. In the debates that followed, it was common to find India, Pakistan, Egypt, or Brazil taking the lead and trying to speak on behalf of the group as a whole.

The unified front that emerged among the developing (and least developed) countries was most evident at the TRIPS Council meeting in April 2001 when they demanded a special session to clarify the 'room for maneuver' within TRIPS, and especially the nature of the relationship between TRIPS rules and a country's access to drugs. These had become pressing issues because many developing countries felt that recent international pressures to enforce stronger global IPRs had called into question the effectiveness and the usefulness of many of the concessions and safeguards that they had negotiated originally. The constant demands for accelerated implementation and the threat of retaliation from their stronger trading partners, particularly the United States, whenever they tried to make use of the flexibilities in TRIPS had led this group of countries to conclude that a clarification of the rights and obligations conferred by that agreement was urgently needed.

The fact that the WTO acceded to this demand was largely the result of three factors: increased unity in the developing country ranks, as a result of the disappointing results to date; the unifying effect of the South African AIDS experience, which served to highlight certain fundamental conflicts between the owners and users of today's technology, especially in the pharmaceutical field; and the desire of some of the strongest members of the WTO to launch a new round of trade negotiations. The formation of a more coherent and stable developing country coalition has complementary explanations.[4] The first is that experience was teaching the developing countries that institutional objectives could not be achieved without a degree of political unity and the ability to articulate a clear and coherent policy position. Abbott (2002, 480) argued that this realization emerged in part out of the controversial process that resulted in Supatchi Panitchpakdi succeeding Michael Moore as director general of the WTO. It seems that the developing countries had entered those negotiations with a clear awareness that efforts would be made to weaken their coalition and that they had to resolve to resist them if they wished to succeed (ibid.). However, in part, this realization had begun to emerge even earlier, as it became increasingly clear that TRIPS had been created primarily as a result of the concerted efforts of global corporations. In any event, whatever the reasons may have been, the united front that was established and maintained by these countries throughout the negotiations that led to Doha was an outstanding achievement which sent the unambiguous message that they were serious about finding a collective solution to the potential threat posed by TRIPS to public health. Their task was made easier by the fact that TRIPS had rather similar implications for public health in almost all developing countries. These did vary somewhat from country to country, depending on the country's domestic pharmaceutical manufacturing capacities; however, ultimately all of them were experiencing difficulties with rapidly rising health care costs, struggling and beleaguered local industries, and unrelenting foreign pressures to strengthen their IPR regimes and to expedite full implementation of TRIPS. Finally, the emergence of an effective coalition among the developing countries was also due to their realization that individually they would not have been able to defend their interests due to their limited human and financial resources. 'For many developing country delegations in Geneva, a few individuals (if that) may be called upon to attend not only to all WTO matters, but to matters at various other international institutions' (Abbott 2002, 479). Indeed, in some cases it is only because of funds provided through technical assistance from industrial countries that developing countries are even able to send delegations to attend meetings of the WTO and of other international organizations. Under these conditions the unified front that emerged among the developing countries was a remarkable achievement. However, it was not the only reason why the industrial countries acceded to the demand for the Doha discussions of TRIPS.

The second significant reason for the WTO's acceptance of the developing countries' demand for a review TRIPS stemmed from the international concern raised by the dispute over South African access to anti-AIDS drugs. This case had triggered the mobilization of activist organizations worldwide in support of developing country efforts to increase drug accessibility to the chronically ill. Non-governmental organizations (NGOs) like Oxfam, Médecins Sans Frontières (MSF), Health GAP Coalition, Consumer Project on Technology (CPT), Third World Network (TWN), and Treatment Action Campaign (TAC) made tremendous efforts to use the South African case to focus the world's attention on the pain that could be inflicted by the strict application of TRIPS on the poorer countries of the world.

The activities of these NGOs were not limited to raising public awareness. MSF was successful in influencing the European Commission to adopt a more moderate approach to the problem of access to patented medicines in the developing world (Abbott 2002, 478). Both MSF and TAC played a role in facilitating the importation of 'cheaper' anti-AIDS treatments into South Africa from Brazil (ibid.). Others, including CPT, Oxfam, and TWN, assisted in the production and distribution of influential position and policy papers and offered advice to developing country officials on their rights and obligations under TRIPS. These efforts helped to subject the WTO to extreme public scrutiny and led many to wonder whether the organization could be relied on to fairly serve the interests of all of its members, and not just the rich and powerful ones. This was the context within which the WTO agreed to address the possible links between stronger patents and access to drugs within the WTO TRIPS Council. To have rejected the developing countries' request under these conditions would undoubtedly have damaged the organization's credibility in the eyes of many.

The third reason why the WTO agreed to the Doha discussions was that several of its strongest members, including the United States, the European Union countries, Canada, and China, whose accession to the WTO was soon to be announced, were keenly interested in launching a new round of trade negotiations at the next ministerial conference because they were anxious to further expand international market access for agricultural products, manufactured goods, and commercial services. A willingness to discuss concerns over TRIPS and its implications for public health appeared to be a necessary concession to achieve agreement on this demand, given the strength of the developing countries' coalition, which could otherwise have blocked the effort to launch a new round of trade talks. In fact, the serious disappointment of most of the developing countries with the early results of the Uruguay Round suggested that the industrial countries needed to show a willingness to go far beyond a mere review of TRIPS. Mike Moore, the director general of the WTO, was among those who began calling for a 'development round' or a 'development friendly round,' which basically meant a round that encouraged and facilitated the full participation of the developing countries and that would yield outcomes that take their needs and their demands more fully into account. Of course, only time will tell if this was rhetoric or reality, although the tough line taken by the industrial countries and the WTO until that time did not augur well. It should be noted, however, that by agreeing to the need for a 'development friendly' round, the leaders of the WTO were implicitly acknowledging that the original negotiations and outcomes had not been 'development friendly,' which is essentially the thrust of the argument presented in this book. Of course, the fact that these leaders were acknowledging the need for a wide-ranging reassessment meant that a review of TRIPS and its links to public health had to be accepted as part of those discussions. After all, it would have been impossible to talk of a 'development friendly' round without addressing one of the key concerns of the developing countries.

Not surprisingly, it quickly became apparent that the willingness to search for 'development friendly' alternatives would have to be confined rather narrowly since there was agreement from the very start among the most influential WTO members that TRIPS could not be reopened at these proposed talks, so that discussions would be limited to a clarification of the flexibility provided for in the existing agreement. The constraints that this imposed on the Doha discussions ensured that the discourse that emerged with regard to the implications of a stronger global IPRs regime differed markedly from that which had emerged during the Uruguay Round. At that time the main concerns revolved around the broader implications of stronger global IPRs for technological and economic development, and by association, for public health. The discussion had concluded that the impact would be positive, but that developing countries would need significant grace periods for phasing in the new rules if they were to be able to take advantage of the opportunities potentially afforded by stronger IPRs. Alternatively, the discourse around Doha was largely concerned with the interpretation and implementation of TRIPS and on the extent to which 'exceptions' could be invoked to safeguard public health. As a result, fundamental questions regarding the suitability of stronger IPRs for development were explicitly ruled out of these talks.

When the developing countries sought to raise more fundamental issues in discussing their public health concerns at Doha it was made clear by the industrial countries' representatives that these issues were not 'on the agenda.' Indeed, Brazil's attempt to link public health issues to its long-term need to develop a strong local pharmaceutical industry was immediately challenged by the pharmaceuticals industry representatives and by some industrial country governments, as evidence of an unacceptable 'hidden agenda.' In short, the agreement to review the implications of TRIPS at Doha was strictly on the condition that members must accept TRIPS as is and that the discussion must focus on its interpretation and its impact on access to medicines. This is the context in which the ensuing discussions and their outcomes must therefore be assessed.

Clarifying TRIPS

The attempt to clarify those provisions of TRIPS that allow members to take certain measures to protect public health led to an intense struggle between the developed and developing countries, with each side seeking to ensure that any resulting declaration would reflect its particular interpretation. The relative inexperience and weakness of the negotiating teams representing the developing countries during the WTO phase of the Uruguay Round had now changed dramatically, as evidenced by their ability to sustain a more or less united front and their success in using the threat to block the proposed new trade round, if the link between IP and health was not satisfactorily addressed. Of course, the narrow terms of reference imposed on the discussions meant that the developing countries ended up merely seeking a reaffirmation of things that TRIPS already permitted but that were being denied to them practice. In other words, there were no new demands to be negotiated; the focus was on interpreting the existing agreement.

The United States and its more militant allies were on rather shaky ground because they had insisted that fundamental issues were off-limits, and yet their position was in fact based on their rejection of a fundamental element of the original agreement, namely, its acceptance of the idea that 'special interventionist' policies could be adopted by members under certain conditions. This underlying contradiction in their position enabled most of the counter-proposals tabled by the industrial countries during these negotiations that were clearly meant to frustrate and prolong the negotiations, rather than to make meaningful contributions to the search for a mutually acceptable resolution. This is one reason why the industrial countries' coalition often appeared fragmented, with the more moderate EU position openly at odds with that of the United States and its more militant allies. Indeed, the 'hard line' adopted by the United States often made it easier for the European Union to present compromise proposals that allowed it to gain developing countries' support for its broader trade agenda. The following sections take a closer look at the negotiation process, after which an analysis of the resulting declaration is presented.

A Brief Overview of the Negotiation Process

The negotiations to clarify the flexibilities permitted under TRIPS and the relationship between TRIPS and access to medicines can be said to have formally started in June 2001, although internationally, concerns about these issues had been expressed much earlier. Between June and November 2001, the TRIPS Council convened a series of formal and informal meetings in an effort to reconcile the divergent views of the developed and developing countries on these matters. The magnitude of this challenge can be appreciated when one considers that initially the two sides struggled over whether there should even be a declaration and what form such a declaration should take.

It is important to recognize that the negotiations that followed were strongly influenced by the fact that there was a deep division within the developed countries' ranks. Indeed, it is more accurate to say that there were three broad voices at the table including the developing countries, a U.S.-led coalition of 'hard line' developed countries, including Canada, Switzerland, Australia, and Japan, and a more moderate European Union, which attempted to act as a 'broker' between the other two groups. On the whole, the developing countries put forward tightly argued proposals urging the need for greater flexibility in interpreting the existing TRIPS. The U.S.-led coalition, on the other hand, staked out a 'hard line' position that, at least implicitly, challenged things that TRIPS had explicitly permitted. While the EU position was closer to that of the developing countries, it remained unclear or silent on certain key issues. So divergent were these opening positions that, as the November ministerial session approached, many policymakers and analysts described the negotiations as having 'stalled' or being at an 'impasse.' Some even believed that they had 'collapsed,' making agreement at Doha impossible. Despite such pessimism, a declaration did emerge which dealt with many of the developing countries' concerns, although with some very important exceptions that would be addressed later.

The Developing Countries' Position

The position of the developing countries was clearly set out in a non-paper,[5] 'Ministerial Declaration on TRIPS and Public Health,' presented to the TRIPS Council meetings of 19–21 September.[6] The preamble asserted that the protection and promotion of public health and nutrition was a fundamental obligation of any state, and that measures to that end remained within the sovereign power of governments under the terms of TRIPS, as it now stood.[7] Moreover, it argued that states were not meeting that obligation when high drug prices prevented large segments of the population from access to needed treatments. Indeed, such a situation was said to violate fundamental human rights and could threaten the economic and social balance of states. Hence, if and when TRIPS impacted negatively on the availability and affordability of needed medicines, this raised legitimate national and international concerns and tended to give national governments the right to take corrective action.

Recent international events, however, had cast doubt on the freedom of governments to adopt corrective measures under such circumstances, even when these were formally consistent with their obligations under TRIPS. Thus, in accordance with the principles stated in the preamble of TRIPS, the developing countries sought to remind other WTO members that intellectual property rules should 'not themselves become barriers to legitimate trade.' To this end, the draft explicitly acknowledged the 'vulnerability of developing and least-developed country Members to the imposition or threat of imposition of sanctions and to the prospect of being deprived of incentives or other benefits ... beyond the framework of the WTO.' This statement was meant to highlight the fact that TRIPS was intended to 'reduce tensions by reaching strengthened commitments to resolve disputes on trade-related intellectual property issues through multilateral procedures' as stated in the agreement's preamble. Therefore, all actions beyond the framework of the WTO, for example, the use of Section 301 by the Americans, should be condemned as a clear violation of one of the key purposes of TRIPS. The submission therefore called upon members to 'refrain from imposing or threatening to impose sanctions and refrain from employing the grant of incentives or other benefits in a manner which could curtail the ability of developing and least developed country Members to avail themselves of every possible policy option to protect and promote public health.' Moreover, members were called upon to 'exercise utmost restraint in initiating and pursuing dispute settlement proceedings' with respect to measures taken by other members to address perceived public health needs.

The developing countries' proposal also sought a reaffirmation of the fundamental importance of the objectives and principles of TRIPS as set out in Articles 7 and 8. According to the objectives of TRIPS, the protection of IPRs 'should contribute to the promotion of technological innovation and to the transfer and dissemination of technology.' Yet the developing countries argued that there was a glaring deficiency in research and development with regard to diseases of primary relevance to them, in addition to low levels of technology transfer needed to develop their pharmaceutical manufacturing capacities. This was particularly essential in the short term as the availability and affordability of medicines could only be maximized if global R&D was complemented by local R&D and by sustained, or expanded, local production of generics.

According to the principles of TRIPS, members may 'adopt measures necessary to protect public health and nutrition ... provided that such measures are consistent with the provisions of this Agreement.' Based on this, the developing countries' draft suggested that 'nothing in the TRIPS shall prevent Members from taking measures to protect public health.' Specifically, every member should be understood to have the right to establish its own exhaustion regime (rules governing parallel imports) and complete freedom to determine when there was a need to grant compulsory licences.[8] However, the developing countries were deeply concerned with the question of how those members with little or no pharmaceutical manufacturing capacity could make use of the compulsory licensing provision under TRIPS, given the condition stipulated by Article 31(f) that 'any such use [of a compulsory license] shall be authorized predominantly for the supply of the domestic market of the Member authorizing such use,' which effectively meant that countries without production capabilities could not use compulsory licensing to address public heath needs. The developing countries thus suggested that provision be made for the possibility that a compulsory licence issued by one member could be given effect by another, if the issuing member was itself unable to manufacture the needed drug. The draft text also called for an extension of transition periods for the least-developed countries, as is consistent with Article 66.1 of TRIPS, where it is stated that 'the Council for the TRIPS shall, upon duly motivated request by a least-developed country Member, accord extensions of this [the initial ten-year grace period] period.' Therefore, as with its other proposals, the developing countries' draft remained largely within the framework of TRIPS.

On balance, the main goal of the developing countries' proposal was to ensure that TRIPS be interpreted in such a way that it did not obstruct the ability of members to address public health needs by means of suitable policies of their choosing both during and after the grace period provided. They were also to have the right to help each other in times of crisis. Unfortunately, the response of the U.S.-led coalition of industrial countries was very hostile to these interpretations, leaving the developing countries' negotiators frustrated and creating a rift between the United States and the European Union.

The Position of the U.S.-led Coalition

Faced with the relatively unified stance of the developing countries, the developed countries found it difficult to establish a common policy position in these negotiations; however, they did agree on a few key issues including limiting the scope of the negotiations to exclude public health/nutrition and the outright rejection of demands for a moratorium or even due restraint in disputes concerning public health.

Beyond these admittedly important points of agreement, it proved very difficult to find common ground, particularly between the United States and EU. The United States took a hard line from the outset, initially attempting to block support for a ministerial declaration altogether. Once it realized that this was probably unwise in the prevailing global environment, the United States made substantial efforts to achieve the same outcome at a lesser cost to its reputation, by seeking to persuade the EU, Canada, and Japan (also known as the QUAD) to sponsor its views. This proved difficult. Canada and Japan showed greater solidarity with the United States in the draft resolutions, but this support seemed inconsistent with their contributions in the discussion sessions, in which they showed a considerable understanding of the concerns raised by the developing countries. The EU insisted on taking a consistently more conciliatory line. The debate became even more difficult after the tragic events of 11 September 2001, when both Canada and the United States took swift measures to ensure that the TRIPS rules would not impede their access to needed drugs to deal with the anthrax scare that followed on its heels.

Not surprisingly, in the run up to Doha, the QUAD governments were intensively lobbied by the global pharmaceutical industry, as its representatives arranged for urgent meetings with senior government officials in all key QUAD countries, while holding numerous seminars and press conferences to warn officials and the public of the negative consequences that would result from a relatively liberal interpretation of TRIPS. They were particularly concerned that the coming negotiations might lead to a 'reopening' of the agreement, which could jeopardize the gains they had made during the WTO-TRIPS phase of the Uruguay Round. Harvey Bale, director general of the International Federation of Pharmaceutical Manufacturers Associations (IFPMA), set the tone of the ensuing debate when he declared that any 'easing up on the terms of the 1994 TRIPS accord could open the door for governments to abuse patents on all protected drugs by declaring national health emergencies when none existed' (Evans 2001). However, the industry's main substantive line of argument was articulated by Dr Rolf Krebs, chairman of the German pharmaceutical giant Boehringer Ingelheim, and president of the IFPMA, when he stated that 'more flexibility in TRIPS would be disastrous for continuing investment in research and development on AIDS' (ibid.). Both industry representatives and supporters claimed that stronger patents had little or nothing to do with the widespread lack of access to needed treatments. Instead, they claimed, this problem lay squarely with inadequate health care services and deficient health care infrastructure in the developing countries, as the U.S. Trade Representative emphasized repeatedly during the negotiations. Industry representatives were adamant in demanding that the flexibilities embedded in TRIPS had to be limited by interpreting the agreement in the narrowest possible way. They argued that it should not be possible to extend compulsory licences to a third country even if the country in need of certain medicines did not have the necessary manufacturing capacity. This argument was backed by a narrow interpretation of Article 31(f). On the question of exhaustion they went even further by suggesting that parallel imports should be generally regarded as counter-productive in that they interfered with the R&D funding plans of big firms. As it turned out, the pharmaceutical industry's demands and arguments were faithfully reflected in the draft proposal tabled by the United States at the 19–21 September 2001 TRIPS Council meetings.[9] Strenuous efforts to obtain the endorsement of its allies eventually led Australia, Canada, Switzerland, and Japan to add their names as signatories to this text. The proposal fell so far short of the developing countries' expectations that many feared agreement would prove impossible. Indeed, in some respects this proposal even seemed to restrict actions that were explicitly permitted by the existing agreement.

A major source of disappointment arose because both in its title and in the preamble the document insisted that discussion of the flexibilities under TRIPS should be limited to access to medicines for diseases like HIV/AIDS, tuberculosis, and malaria, that is, to cases of extreme human tragedies or pandemics. Yet, as just noted, TRIPS Article 8 unequivocally states that members are allowed to 'adopt measures necessary to protect public health and nutrition ... provided that such measures are consistent with the provision of this Agreement.' In essence, the United States and its co-signatories had little grounds on which to base their insistence that these discussions of the flexibilities embedded in the Agreement should be limited to 'access to medicines for HIV/AIDS and other pandemics.'

More generally, the document emphasized that drug prices were only one of several equally important determinants of access to treatments, while failing to acknowledge that stronger IP protection could have a significant impact on drug prices. Instead, it chose to focus on the alleged long-term benefits of the agreement by asking members to 'recognize that strong, effective and balanced protection for intellectual property is a necessary incentive for research and development of life-saving drugs and, therefore, recognize that intellectual property contributes to public health objectives globally.' Accordingly, members of the WTO were called upon to reaffirm the belief that TRIPS will ultimately contribute to greater availability of medicines and thereby to reaffirm their commitment to the existing agreement and its implementation. While it acknowledged that TRIPS did contain provisions that allowed members to introduce a number of special measures, it implied that this was legitimate only when dealing with pandemics. Moreover, it suggested that discussions within the council 'have clarified' members' views of such flexibilities, so that no further discussion was required beyond Doha.

The document also contained specific TRIPS clarifications regarding rules of interpretation, compulsory licensing, and parallel imports. It noted that TRIPS should be read in accordance with the customary rules of interpretation of public international law, but made no mention of the agreement being read in accordance with its own principles and objectives (Articles 7 and 8). Indeed, even in the discussions that followed, the United States was not prepared to acknowledge the paramount importance of these provisions even when other members of its coalition sought to do so in their interventions. For instance, a presentation by the Canadian delegation pointed out that 'both provisions [Articles 7 and 8] are important for recognizing and understanding the delicate balance and flexibility provided in the TRIPS. They may rightly be called upon in interpreting various provisions of the TRIPS.'

With regard to compulsory licensing, the draft text acknowledged that TRIPS did not establish grounds, but rather procedures, for their issuance. However, the draft implied that compulsory licences could only be used legitimately in cases of major pandemics. U.S. intransigence towards countries that sought to make use of compulsory licences under any other circumstances, even in times of national emergency, emphasized the highly restricted degree to which the United States was ready to respect the freedom of members to define national emergencies on their own. In its view, this was to be strictly limited to 'pandemics of life-threatening communicable diseases such as AIDS, tuberculosis and malaria.'

The remainder of the declaration was devoted to the issue of the exhaustion of rights. Here, the United States attempted to circumscribe the use of parallel imports by asserting the primacy of Article 28.1, which provides for exclusive importation rights for the IP holder, over

Article 6, which clearly leaves the choice of the exhaustion regime up to national authorities. In fact, in a footnote to Article 28.1 in TRIPS it is made clear that 'this right [exclusive importation], like all other rights conferred under this Agreement in respect of the use, sale, importation or other distribution of goods, is subject to the provision of Article 6.' Thus, Article 6 clearly takes precedence over Article 28. At the same time, the United States attempted to assert a very narrow definition of exhaustion by implying that intellectual property rights are exhausted in 'a market' as soon as the protected goods are sold in 'that market,' meaning that the purchasers are then free to dispose of the goods as they wish. Although U.S. trade officials claimed that such language was neutral since 'a market' could be read to mean global, regional, or national, the extent of the discussions that revolved around Washington's choice of words between QUAD negotiators reflected disagreement regarding the neutrality of such language, particularly since TRIPS imposed no such definitions.

Soon after the U.S.-led coalition had presented this draft declaration, MSF, Oxfam, and TWN felt compelled to issue the following joint press statement: 'The U.S.-sponsored paper presented yesterday, which was not even a complete draft, showed disdain for the concerns of the developing world, and risks bringing the TRIPS into further disrepute ... a unique opportunity to ensure that TRIPS does not prejudice public health in poor countries is being wasted' (MSF, Oxfam, and TWN 2001). It was indeed the case that the U.S.-led coalition's very narrow, interest-laden interpretations of TRIPS defeated the basic purpose of the Doha exercise, which was to discuss the concerns that had arisen internationally because, in practice, the relevant provisions of TRIPS were being interpreted so narrowly that members did not have sufficient leeway for addressing their legitimate public health concerns.

The Position of the European Union

In general the EU took a more moderate approach that was more sympathetic to the concerns of the developing countries. But its voice was less effective than it could have been because it had difficulty in presenting a clear, unified position. At the September meetings, the European Commission presented a non-paper in the form of a draft declaration that had not yet been approved by member states and that was later withdrawn. The draft appeared to be in line with the developing countries' proposals in major respects even though in some others it echoed those in the U.S. draft.

Of great significance for the developing countries was the fact that the preamble of the EU draft acknowledged explicitly that 'accessible price' is one of the important determining factors of access to medicines; that IP protection has a 'bearing' on the price of medicines; and that compulsory licensing and parallel imports could be used to ensure affordable access. In addition, the preamble also acknowledged that there was legitimate concern over inadequate research and development efforts concerning diseases of primary relevance to the developing world and that an IPR regime should encourage innovation and technology transfer in and to the developing world. More generally, it accepted that this was the intent of TRIPS, as stipulated under Article 7, as was the notion that IP protection should not be allowed to become a barrier to legitimate trade, nor should it neglect the special needs of the least developed countries for maximum flexibility in devising domestic laws to encourage technological development. In conformance with the developing countries' view, the EU proposal suggested that TRIPS should be implemented in ways that actively promoted wide access to affordable medicines in the context of national public health policies. Most importantly, it stated that TRIPS should be read in accordance with the objectives and principles as set out in its Articles 7 and 8. The text also affirmed that members had complete freedom to determine the grounds for granting compulsory licences and to choose the exhaustion regime that best suited their intellectual property objectives. Finally, it urged industrial country members to consider extending the transition periods for least-developed countries, consistent with Article 66.1 of TRIPS.

Not surprisingly, this document met with hostility from American trade officials and pharmaceutical industry critics. The senior vice-president for international affairs at PhRMA, Shannon Herzfeld, is reported to have said that the 'EU's "self-imposed" role as a mediator in the dispute ... was not particularly helpful as far as the U.S. pharmaceutical industry is concerned' (Yerkey and Pruzin 2001b). The draft had sought a reaffirmation of a commitment to TRIPS and its implementation and recognition that IPRs contribute to public health objectives that are globally in line with the U.S. proposal; however, this was not satisfactory given the overall thrust of the draft that tended to support the developing countries on key issues. Supporters and representatives of the pharmaceuticals industry immediately accused the commission of softening its stance on IPRs in order to gain the support of the developing countries on other issues, such as the environment, investment, and competition rules, which the EU wanted to include in a new trade round (Pruzin 2001).

The paper's hostile reception was soon followed by its withdrawal by the EU. There is no clear explanation as to precisely why it was withdrawn, yet it is safe to say that it was due to the combined opposition of the pharmaceuticals lobby, the U.S. government and the co-signatories of its draft, and several of the main European states, especially those with large pharmaceuticals industries. Indeed, an earlier proposal to facilitate the use of compulsory licences in developing countries was dashed by Germany and the United Kingdom, whose drug industries would have stood to lose the most as a result. U.S. opposition was naturally very strong given the hard line that the United States was taking in these discussions. In addition, Abbott (2002, 486) has suggested that it may also have been withdrawn because the developing countries felt that it 'did not incorporate some of the concepts more favorable to developing countries that had been floated in previous position papers.' However, that would make sense only if the developing countries saw the possibility that this might influence the EU to draft a new proposal more favourable to their concerns, which was not very likely.

Thus, as Doha neared, the differences between the major players seemed irreconcilable, even as the United States, Canada, and Japan intensified their negotiations with the EU, in a desperate attempt to develop a QUAD consensus on an acceptable wording for the declaration. Establishing such a consensus prior to the Doha meeting would have greatly bolstered the industrial countries' position and, the U.S.'s unrelenting hard line position, if the United States succeeded in having it accepted as the QUAD position.

The Anthrax/Cipro Affair

The continuous efforts of the U.S.-led coalition to deny the claims of the developing countries that TRIPS should give a relatively high degree of latitude to national governments in dealing with public health crises appeared to have been greatly compromised when both Canada and the United States took swift measures to deal with fears of bioterrorism in the aftermath of the September 11 attacks on the World

Trade Center in New York City. The issue arose when several enve-
lopes containing anthrax spores were sent through the U.S. mail,
infecting and killing a handful of people and triggering widespread
concern on both sides of the Canada–U.S. border. When it turned out
that the most popular antibiotic for the treatment of anthrax, ciproflox-
acin (cipro), was under patent to Bayer, both governments responded
immediately by threatening Bayer with the compulsory licensing of
cipro, if the company were not prepared to supply the needed amount
of the drug at a 'reasonable price,' even though there was no evidence
of a national emergency or even a situation of extreme urgency. One
might have thought that this graphic reminder of the fundamental
validity of the concerns of the developing countries might have softened the coalition's position in the countdown to Doha, but that was
not to be. The coalition maintained its obstinate hard line, thereby
greatly strengthening the perception, or the realization, that these
negotiations were primarily about power and self-interest.

Ultimately, the incident was useful in revealing the double standards
of the coalition. While denying developing countries the right to unilaterally invoke 'national health emergencies,' the Canadian government immediately entered into a contract with a local generics firm to
make generic copies of cipro to ensure adequate supplies of the drug in
case of an anthrax outbreak. This, despite the fact that not a single
Canadian had been infected and that only a few people had died in the
United States. Admittedly, the Canadian government later changed
that decision and agreed to purchase the drug from Bayer in exchange
for the company agreeing not to sue the government for patent
infringement. But the point had been clearly made. Faced with a threat,
or rather a perceived threat to public health, the Canadian government
had assumed that it had the power to override Bayer's patent rights.
That Ottawa reversed this decision because it would have found it
hard to justify its behaviour by claiming that anthrax constituted a
national emergency, or situation of extreme urgency, also indicated recognition that such power cannot be assumed arbitrarily.

The U.S. government's behaviour was even more sharply and more
clearly at odds with its hard-line position via-à-vis the developing
countries on this issue. It too immediately told Bayer that it would not
hesitate to override its patent on cipro if prices were not cut sharply.
U.S. Secretary of Health and Human Services Tommy Thomson,
warned that 'if Bayer did not cooperate, he would ask Congress for
new powers that would allow the U.S. to violate the patent without

paying damages to Bayer' (Alden et al. 2001). Yet 'cipro, it turned out, was not the only drug that could be used to treat anthrax; there was no epidemic of cases; and there was no shortage of cipro' (Waldmeir 2001, 14). Nevertheless, on 24 October 2001 Bayer reached a 'historic' agreement with the U.S. government whereby the company would supply up to 300 million tablets of cipro at a steeply discounted price (Bayer 2001).

Much of the world witnessed this affair in utter amazement. To many it was disturbing to see two of the countries that were playing such an obstructionist role during the TRIPS review so easily willing to take 'necessary' measures to protect the health of their citizens against a perceived, but rather hypothetical, threat. Meanwhile, they were continuing to prevent developing country governments from employing similar measures to protect and promote public health under more critical circumstances in which thousands of people were dying each day. Paulo Teixeira, director of the Brazilian government's AIDS program, observed that 'it smacks of one rule for the north, another for the south ... The anthrax outbreak is very distressing but I hope it will make them reflect more about our position that compulsory licensing is an entirely legitimate instrument if there is a problem of access to a crucial drug' (Dyer and Michaels 2001). Unfortunately, this was not the case.

The Doha Declaration

Differences between the developed and developing countries over clarification of TRIPS persisted up until the November meeting in Qatar. Informal discussions of the draft proposals circulated by the General Council chair in the last week of October, in a last ditch attempt to narrow the gap between the two sides, only revealed the extent of continuing disagreement. Even the title of the declaration, 'Elements for a Draft Declaration on Intellectual Property and [Access to Medicines] [Public Health],' remained bracketed, meaning that there was still no agreement as to the desired coverage of the declaration. Moreover, the fact that the title referred to intellectual property as opposed to TRIPS in particular reflected the reluctance of the U.S.-led coalition to deal with the specifics of TRIPS. Indeed, just days before the Doha ministerial conference, it seemed almost impossible to think that there could be agreement on a declaration by the end of it.

Intense negotiations, however, continued for the duration of the 9–14 November meeting and by the close a consensus text did emerge.

Some official sources suggested that a deal finally became possible when Brazil, one of the leading voices in the developing countries' camp, reached a key compromise with the United States in a closed-door session. The compromise largely involved the substitution of the legally binding language preferred by the developing countries that TRIPS 'shall not' prevent member states from protecting public health to TRIPS 'does not' and 'should not' prevent members from protecting public health, which merely constituted a political declaration. At this same meeting it was also agreed that the inability of countries with insufficient domestic manufacturing capacity to make effective use of compulsory licensing under TRIPS, should be postponed for future discussion.

Despite some concern that Brazil had breached the pact of solidarity maintained by the developing countries since the start of the negotiations, the compromise text received the support of all of the developing country members, and both the Canadian and international press gave very positive coverage to the resulting TRIPS declaration. Many analysts concluded that this document represented a significant breakthrough, which should be seen as a signal that WTO members could successfully reach consensus on controversial issues that were of vital importance to the developing world. According to one reporter writing from Doha, 'their [developing countries] biggest prize was U.S. backing for an assurance that WTO rules on trade-related aspects of intellectual property rights (TRIPS) would not enable patent laws to be used to block poor countries' access to essential medical supplies' (de Jonquières 2001, 6).

In reality, the Doha process left the developing countries in a position that was not very different from that in which they had found themselves when TRIPS was first negotiated. The concessions that had been made to them at that time were more or less reaffirmed, which was a victory of sorts since it meant that the attempt by the U.S.-led coalition to devalue many of those concessions by subjecting them to extremely narrow definitions, had largely failed. But it also meant that the developing countries did not make any significant progress in these discussions, and at the end of the day, they remain vulnerable to the same problem that bedevilled them the first time around, since they still have no enforcement mechanism to prevent the United States and its closest allies from devaluing those 'paper concessions' in practice.

Of course, the situation after Doha was different from that after the initial introduction of TRIPS, if only because a number of issues had now been more explicitly discussed so that the provisions of the agreement were necessarily somewhat less ambiguous as a result. This was a gain for the developing countries. Yet on a few issues one could argue that they had effectively lost some ground in the Doha process, since the interpretations that were most widely accepted as a result of these discussions, were rather narrower than they might have hoped for at the outset. A detailed look at the agreement reveals some pluses and some minuses, within the context of an overall situation that had not changed much. Unfortunately, the prognosis for the future looks rather discouraging if Washington's unilateralist tendencies continue to grow in an increasingly polarized and conflict-ridden world.

Possibly the greatest victory for the developing countries lay in the fact that the title of the declaration made reference to 'TRIPS and Public Health' because this meant that the attempt by the U.S.-led coalition to limit the declaration simply to a question of access to medicines for pandemics had largely failed. Since Article 8 of TRIPS explicitly allows members to 'adopt measures necessary to protect public health and nutrition,' these attempts by the U.S.-led coalition to restrict the rights given by TRIPS turned out to be a waste of resources which only served to cast an even deeper shadow over the reputation of the American government in these international debates. However, it is important to understand that what appeared as a hard-won victory for the developing countries was no more than a recognition of that which was already part of TRIPS. In accordance with this acknowledgment, members reaffirmed their commitment to TRIPS and agreed that it 'does not and should not prevent Members from taking measures to protect public health' and that it 'can and should be interpreted and implemented in a manner supportive of WTO Members' right to protect public health.' In truth, this rather simplistic assertion of the 'good intentions' that TRIPS does not and should not prevent members from taking measures to protect public health appears almost absurd given the circumstances that led to these negotiations. In this context, the reiteration of essentially unconditional, even thoughtless, allegiance to TRIPS appears incongruous at a meeting designed to assess its impact on public health and economic and technological development more broadly. Unfortunately, a closer look at the declaration reveals that much of it is little more than a legalistic paraphrase of the original TRIPS.

When the Declaration turns to consider the policy flexibility that is made available to member countries by TRIPS, it again appears to lend strong support to the developing countries' view. To this end, the declaration recognizes that (1) TRIPS should be read in accordance with its objectives and principles; (2) each member has the right to grant compulsory licences and the freedom to determine the grounds on which such licences are to be issued; (3) each member has the right to determine what constitutes a national emergency or situation of extreme urgency; and (4) each member is free to establish its own exhaustion regime without challenge. Although these interpretations conform closely to the proposals of the developing countries, they also essentially reiterate the original TRIPS. Yet perhaps the reaffirmation of these rights was important, if it can help to put an end to continued efforts by the global pharmaceutical industry backed by the U.S. government, to put pressure on developing country policymakers who wish to exercise these rights, as has clearly been the case for Egyptian and other health policymakers.

The Doha Declaration also reaffirmed the 'commitment of the developed country members to provide incentives to their enterprises and institutions to promote and encourage technology transfer to least developed country members pursuant to Article 66.2' of TRIPS and extended transition periods for this group of countries to the year 2016, without prejudice to their right to ask for further extensions as under Article 66.1. However, the value of such a commitment is questionable given the extremely limited capacity of this group of countries to absorb such transfers. Some would argue that the developed countries need to demonstrate their 'good faith' by being more forthcoming in their willingness to promote effective technology transfer to those developing countries that do actually have the capabilities to effectively absorb modern technologies in the short and medium terms. Indeed, one of the major demands of the developing countries in the negotiations following Doha was for the developed countries to encourage technology transfer to them in order to enable them to build stronger domestic research and manufacturing capabilities (ISCTD 2002a). Finally, as regards the extension of transition periods for the least-developed countries, this was a welcome gesture although it is, once again, something that is already clearly provided for in TRIPS (Article 66.1) because of 'their economic, financial and administrative constraints, and their need for flexibility to create a viable technological base.' Yet these are the provisions that can be considered as 'pluses' for the developing countries. If there was a victory at Doha, it merely consisted of successfully avoiding a rollback of rights.

Most of the issues that were ambiguous before continue to be so, although possibly to a slightly lesser degree. For the developing countries, it was important that the preamble of the declaration recognize that the developing and least-developed countries face grave public health problems which need to be addressed. However, by specifically naming HIV/AIDS, tuberculosis, and malaria, the U.S.-led coalition managed to keep open the possibility that the right to take certain actions should be triggered only by problems on a truly disastrous scale.

The declaration stresses the need for TRIPS to be part of a wider national and international program of action to address many of these problems. Once again the meaning of this passage is open to widely differing interpretations. Some analysts, like Abbott (2002, 491), believe that this statement declares that 'TRIPS should not stand as an obstacle to addressing public health concerns' and that there is an important role for key international organizations, like the WHO, in addressing international public health crises. I regard it as a reaffirmation of the developed countries' claim that TRIPS should be understood as being an important part of the solution to such public health concerns especially in the longer run. This provision would make it difficult to focus on the potentially negative impact of stronger IPRs on drug availability and affordability, particularly in the short to medium term. In other words, this formulation implies that in the absence of wider national and international action to address these public health issues in the developing countries, stronger IPRs cannot reasonably be singled out for blame.

This upbeat focus on the assumed long-term benefits of TRIPS is sustained in the declaration when IPRs are described as being critically important for the development of new medicines, while 'concerns about its effects on prices' are mentioned only in passing and without further specification. This passage was clearly a concession on the part of the developing countries to the U.S.-led coalition and the pharmaceutical industry since the developing countries had consistently argued that stronger IP protection does not appear to be encouraging R&D of relevance to them, while frequently being associated with significant price increases which reduce the ability of their populations to access much needed treatments. In the declaration these concerns are effectively marginalized because the positive impact of stronger IPRs on the development of new medicines is stated as a fact, while their *effect on prices* in the developing world, is mentioned only as a mere *concern*.

The most disappointing outcome of the Doha process for many developing countries was that no agreement was reached on the question of how members with insufficient manufacturing capacity can make effective use of compulsory licensing under TRIPS. Instead, the TRIPS Council was instructed to find an expeditious solution to this problem and to report to the General Council before the end of 2002. As noted earlier, the main problem is found in TRIPS Article 31(f) which states that 'any such use [of a compulsory license] shall be authorized predominantly for the supply of the domestic market of the Member authorizing such use,' which effectively places a limit on the export of medicines manufactured under a compulsory licence. Both the United States and European Union had blocked agreement to use the 'exceptions to exclusive rights' provided under TRIPS Article 30 to resolve the issue during the Doha meeting.

Although several proposals were put forward since that meeting with regard to this problem, an agreement was barely reached in August 2003. Initially, the United States had vehemently rejected the possibility of amending TRIPS by arguing that this 'might unhinge the balance of rights and obligations negotiated during the Uruguay Round' (ICTSD 2002a). Instead, the Americans had proposed that members accept a temporary moratorium on dispute settlement when a member grants a compulsory licence to export medicines to a country that is lacking manufacturing capacity (ibid.). Moreover, it had emphasized that this potential resolution be restricted to addressing diseases referred to in the Doha Declaration, such as HIV/AIDS, tuberculosis, and malaria and should further not apply to the developed countries or countries that choose not to manufacture a specific drug (Iibid.). The developing countries strongly rejected this proposal on the ground that it did not offer a 'sustainable or legally predictable solution' (ICTSD 2002b).

The Europeans had focused on the possibility of formulating an exception to Article 31(f), but in a similar vein to the United States, emphasized that this would only apply to products that were intended to deal with public health crises in the developing and least-developed countries that approximated the magnitude of the HIV/AIDS, tuberculosis, and malaria epidemics. Although the developing countries had shown some preference towards the European proposal, they nevertheless favoured establishing an authoritative interpretation of Article 30 'exceptions to patentability,' as they had suggested during the Doha meeting.

On 30 August 2003 the General Council decided that countries with insufficient or no manufacturing capacities in the pharmaceutical sector and those agreeing to supply the needed pharmaceutical products may waive obligations normally incumbent upon them in TRIPS Article 31(f). In other words, countries with weak or no pharmaceutical manufacturing capabilities could legally use compulsory licensing to seek and obtain the help of other capable WTO members in meeting their local health needs. The decision also acknowledged that some members will not use this system, while others would limit their use to situations of extreme urgency or emergencies. This decision spelled out the terms that members must adhere to should they decide to utilize the system and tasked the TRIPS Council with an annual review of the system to ensure that it was operating effectively.[10] At best, this agreement represents modest benefits for the developing countries; while at worst it legitimates protectionist measures by select developed countries, as is discussed in the next section.

In essence the Doha Declaration can be described as a document in which the developed countries say to the developing countries, 'we will admit you have a problem, if you admit the problem is best addressed by *business as usual.*' In other words, the developed countries agree to admit that the developing countries were facing tremendous health problems, even over and above the HIV/AIDS, tuberculosis, and malaria tragedies, and that national and international cooperation was required to address this situation. In return the developing countries were asked to agree that TRIPS, in its present form, is actually a major part of the solution, with the exception of the issue of compulsory licensing, which was addressed later. This is why they were asked to pay repeated homage to an agreement with which they had become extremely unhappy in the preceding years.

Realistic Expectations

When the immediate orchestrated euphoria surrounding the alleged victory of the developing countries at Doha had subsided, a few moments of sober reflection soon made painfully apparent to many analysts and activists that there had actually been little value added. 'Developing countries came to Doha to extract a clear declaration that public health and access to medicines are more important than protecting commercial interests of pharmaceutical companies. At the end of the day, opposition from rich countries crippled the legally binding language sought by the majority of WTO countries,' noted Asia Russel of Health GAP Coalition (Act Up Paris 2002).

There is no doubt that the real success of the negotiations will ultimately depend on the willingness of the developed countries to desist from exerting strong economic or legal pressures on poor countries to prevent them from exercising the rights given to them by TRIPS and to push them to accept policies that may adversely affect their national health systems. This will probably prove to be very difficult, as competitive pressures in the global economy remain intense. Indeed, the negotiations had scarcely ended when U.S. officials and pharmaceutical representatives made public statements denigrating the Doha Declaration as merely a political statement that did not have any relevance to disputes which might arise when a government decided to override an existing patent.

By 20 November 2001, only one week after the end of the Doha meeting, developing countries were further alarmed over a bill, the Trade Promotion Authority, which was introduced into the U.S. House of Representatives and which was explicitly designed to restrict their abilities to address public health needs (Kamath 2001). This bill suggested that, once again, the concessions made on paper would not be translated into actual rights that could be exercised by developing country governments. Indeed, if passed, this bill would run roughshod over Doha since it called for accelerated implementation of TRIPS and the elimination of all measures such as price controls and reference pricing that inhibit full market access for American firms (ibid.). Clearly, little of substance had changed.

By the time the final version for the Trade Promotion Authority was drafted, a bad situation had become worse. Unfortunately it seems, however, that this language is reflective of the U.S. position in discussions over international agreements. As it stands 'the text requires the USTR to push for patent monopoly protection far in excess of WTO rules, and negates much of the value of the Doha Declaration on TRIPS and Public Health that enabled the launch of the new round' (Davis 2001). According to a *New York Times* editorial, 'the rules governing poor countries' ability to get affordable medicines,' were described as a 'mess'; it went on to state that 'last November in Doha, Qatar, Washington agreed to more flexible language. But drug companies have reinstated old formulas into the bill' (2002). Thus, one year after Doha, an Oxfam (2002) review of Washington's bilateral policies on patents and medicines found that, 'overall the number of bilateral complaints against developing countries relating to patents and medicines made by the pharmaceutical companies to the U.S. government has not fallen; nor has the number of complaints which the U.S. government takes up.' In fact, the review found that the American government included 66 per cent of the countries identified by PhRMA's annual submission in its Section 301 report, compared with 61 per cent in 2001.

The unrelenting hard line taken by the United States and several other developed countries in and after the negotiations underscores the need for the developing countries to adopt and defend their own positions in these international decision-making processes. Although the developing countries always had the right under TRIPS to enact and to implement intellectual property policies in support of their national health policies, so long as these policies were consistent with that agreement, the Doha Declaration did heighten awareness of and support for these rights. It did not, however, offer anything more than what was already largely permissible under TRIPS. In addition, it did not introduce any means of enforcement that might make the powerful members of the WTO live up to the spirit, not just the letter, of that agreement.

Even the solution reached in August 2003 concerning paragraph 6 of the Doha Declaration presented only modest benefits for the developing countries. Under extreme pressure from big pharmaceutical firms and their protagonists in the global trade arena, the developing countries maintained strong opposition to attempts by the United States, Japan, the EU, and the WTO Secretariat to limit the scope of diseases for compulsory licencing, and the requirement that this instrument could only be used in very circumscribed situations of extreme urgency. Ideally, this achievement should permit developing countries to use the new system to deal with health problems that *they* deem important. Critics have argued, however, that the agreement comes with significant costs and uncertainties. According to James Love, director of the Consumer Project on Technology: 'The persons who have negotiated this agreement have given the world a new model for explicitly endorsing protectionism. The United States, Europe, Canada, Australia, Japan and other developed economies will be allowed to bar imports from developing country generic suppliers [when the former issue compulsory licenses] – under completely irrational protectionist measures that are defended by the WTO Secretariat and its most powerful members as a humanitarian gesture' (Love 2003a). The Doha Declaration and the negotiations that followed concerning paragraph 6, did not address the potentially adverse implications of TRIPS on the development of local industries and, by association, public health. Because the debate was so narrowly circumscribed, it tended to obscure wider concerns related to technology, innovation, and diffusion, the raison d'être of TRIPS. This, in turn, created the false impression that the so-called policy flexibilities within TRIPS could only be legitimately used to address public health emergencies. In the final hours prior to the General Council's decision regarding the implementation of paragraph 6 of the Doha Declaration, the chairman of the TRIPS Council conceded to U.S. demands that the system will not be used to promote industrial policy objectives (Love 2003b). In other words, concerns related to the development of local pharmaceutical industries were now effectively treated as inadmissible.

Recent Changes in Egyptian Patent Policy

On 29 May 2002, after two years of deliberations, the People's Assembly (lower house of the legislature) passed Egypt's new IPRs law, Law No. 82/2002. An analysis of two key provisions in the law's chapter concerning patents shows how those who drafted the law aimed to take full advantage of the flexibilities provided for in TRIPS in order to balance Egypt's obligations with the need to promote the development of the local pharmaceutical industry and to protect public health. These provisions concern (1) acts that shall not constitute infringements and (2) compulsory licences.

On the first point, Article 10, which outlines Egypt's exhaustion regime, defines the limits of the patent holder's rights. In other words, it determines what rights the patent holder may or may not retain over the use of a product once it has been sold in the patent-protected market. As noted above, controversy frequently arises when firms sell patented products at different prices in different markets, which creates an incentive for the 'higher price' country to import from the 'lower price' country. Egypt's law insists that the original patent holder's rights are fully extinguished by the first transaction, leaving purchasers free to use and resell the patented product at their discretion. Specifically, Article 10 states that 'the patentees rights to exclude others from importing, using, selling or distributing the product shall be exhausted if the patentee marketed and/or licensed the invention to third parties.' In short, the law defines an international exhaustion regime under which the right holder's first transaction or sale exhausts its rights to control the subsequent exploitation of the product: selling, using, distributing, or importing the product shall not constitute infringements thereafter. This provision is critically important because it allows the admission of parallel imports from third countries where a drug is marketed at a lower price.

With regard to compulsory licences, Article 23 of Law No. 82 of 2002 boldly establishes wide-ranging grounds for the issuance of compulsory licences as permissible under TRIPS Article 31 and confirmed in the Doha Declaration. It also draws on the allowance in Article 8 of TRIPS that members may in 'amending their laws and regulations, adopt measures necessary to protect public health and nutrition, and to promote the public interest in sectors of vital importance to their socio-economic and technological development.' Law No. 82 therefore stipulates that such licences may be granted by the Patent Office, after approval by a ministerial committee, when the product is (1) for non-commercial public use for the purpose of preserving national security, as well as for promoting health, nutrition, and environmental safety; (2) used to deal with emergency situations or situations of extreme urgency; and (3) used to promote the public interest by promoting sectors of vital importance to socioeconomic and technological development.

In seeking to clarify the government's intentions with regard to the ways in which the provisions for compulsory licensing of pharmaceutical inventions should be interpreted, Article 23 suggests that rather broad definitions are intended. It states that in the event of 'insufficient supply of a patented drug to satisfy the country's needs, or because of a decline in its quality, or irregular increases in its price, or in the event that a drug is related to critical cases, or chronic or endemic diseases,' a compulsory licence may be issued if deemed necessary. Article 23 also states explicitly that compulsory licences can be issued in cases where IP holders do not 'adequately work' their patents in the domestic market, a provision similar to the one that instigated the dispute settlement procedure between Brazil and the United States, as discussed earlier.

In addition to these key provisions that affect the content of the new patent policy, certain changes in the law also affect the regulatory structure. An important institutional change gives the Ministry of Health (MOH) firm control over all patents related to public health and makes it responsible for strategic IP decisions in this sphere. Thereby the MOH now has central responsibilities in the implementation of the patent regime as it affects pharmaceutical products and other medical inventions, with the power to approve or oppose patent grants. The concentration of this power in the hands of the health ministry is significant because it is the ministry responsible for ensuring drug accessibility, and it is in the best position to assess the impact of specific pharmaceutical patents on public health, in conformity with Article 2 of the new patent law. Here, the law prohibits from patentability any invention that 'harms the life or health of humans, animals or plants.' The MOH is most keenly aware of the needs of the public health system, particularly at a time when it is undertaking major reforms as part of is Health Sector Reform Program (HSRP), which calls for the creation of a comprehensive national policy to encompass all aspects of the pharmaceutical sector in Egypt, including the provision of IPRs for pharmaceutical products.

The new authority vested in the Ministry of Health has been a major point of contention with American trade officials, who insisted that the government address certain 'deficiencies' in the law. In the words of the U.S. Trade Representative, 'the United States continues to strongly urge Egypt to correct the reported deficiencies in the draft copyright and patent laws before these laws are enacted by the legislature. The United States remains concerned, in particular, about the possible insertion in the draft patent law of a previously rejected provision calling for health-related patents to be reviewed by the Ministry of Health which would appear to contradict the TRIPS requirement to provide patent protection without discrimination as to the field of technology' (2002). In fact, as the Egyptian authorities pointed out, this provision does not discriminate against pharmaceuticals as such or as a 'field of technology'; it merely establishes a procedure for patent approvals in this sector to take account of their impact on public health.[11] It remains to be seen what the USTR will do now that the new law has been enacted with this provision still intact.

The law has come under further attack from the head of the USAID SIPRE (Strengthening Intellectual Property Rights in Egypt) project, Ms Judy Winegar Goans, who alleges that it violates TRIPS in other regards. She contends that although the law 'accomplishes a number of important improvements ... the legislation contains a number of items that are not consistent with the TRIPS,' especially in its provisions for compulsory licensing and parallel imports (Fawzy 2002). While Egyptian officials have rejected these charges, they are clearly concerned that the application of the law may create many problems (ibid.). The extent of such problems and the willingness and ability of the government to deal with them, however, remains to be seen.

On balance, it seems that the pressures to persuade the developing countries to forgo many of the rights that they had negotiated in TRIPS continue to be exerted by those who would like to see an accelerated, full implementation of the agreement. Doha was meant to resolve those issues, but as we have seen, its potential to do so was greatly diluted. Now Egypt will be one of the first test cases to see whether any real progress was made. In this regard, the Commission on Intellectual Property Rights recently reminded the industrial countries that 'so far as possible developing countries should not be deprived of the flexibility to design their IP systems that developed countries enjoyed in earlier stages of their own development, and higher IP standards should not be pressed on them without a serious and objective assessment of their development impact' (2002, 10). This should serve as a timely reminder that industrial countries, and particularly the United States, need to accept that developing countries have the right to try, as best as they can within limits imposed by TRIPS, to ensure that their new IP regimes foster, rather than hinder, the development of their innovative capabilities, their local pharmaceutical industries, and their levels public health. It is important for the developed countries to honour the spirit of the Doha Declaration by complementing their great wealth with humanity by valuing the basic human rights of the people living in developing countries.

Conclusion

This chapter has argued that despite the notable improvement in the negotiating strength of the developing countries since the Uruguay Round, the industrial countries are still able to define the terms of reference for negotiations over possible links between TRIPS and public health which were upheld during the Fourth WTO Ministerial Conference in Doha. Thus, although the developing countries were successful in getting many of their most pressing concerns onto the agenda, they were not as successful in shaping the scope and substance of the negotiations or in determining the outcome. As a result these countries ultimately gained much less from the negotiations than was hoped for and needed given the tremendous public health burdens currently being faced by many of them.

The greatest benefit to the developing countries may have been the experience gained in establishing and maintaining a strong and united coalition throughout these negotiations. Their ability to develop a common policy position sent a clear message to the industrial countries indicating that they were serious about defending their interests in the WTO. Unfortunately, the potential harm of having agreed repeatedly within these negotiations that TRIPS formed an important part of the solution to their public health concerns may ultimately outweigh the benefits that accrued from the entire process. The problem is that the terms of these negotiations were so narrowly defined that the question of the impact of TRIPS on the scope for development of a strong local pharmaceutical industry, to underpin a government's public health policies, was simply ruled out of court. Yet this should have been a major focus of the discussion since that is where the impact of TRIPS is potentially greatest.

In reality it was the industrial countries that emerged victorious from these negotiations. By using their power, their extensive resources, and their access to sophisticated negotiating tactics, these countries were successfully able to create much ado about nothing. From the outset, they made it clear that their willingness to participate in these discussions depended on the acceptance of their terms of reference, which made it impossible to reopen the 'sacred text' of TRIPS, leaving the discussions to deal solely with the flexibilities in that agreement. Ultimately, the developed countries conceded nothing that TRIPS did not already permit, while they managed to persuade the developing countries to renew their public commitment to TRIPS in its present form. However, despite all this, the Doha Declaration also attests to and confirms the policy options available to national legislators under TRIPS. The debate surrounding TRIPS has heightened the awareness of developing country policymakers of the substance of TRIPS and of its potential implications for their economies and public health systems. Yet, in the absence of a fundamental renegotiation of the core provisions of TRIPS, it is up to national legislators to ensure that their national IPR laws takes full advantage of the policy flexibility reaffirmed in the Doha Declaration and in the later decision concerning paragraph 6. This appears to be the case with Egypt's new patent law where key provisions concerning parallel imports and compulsory licensing have aimed to take full advantage of the policy options permitted under TRIPS.

Although there is little doubt that the Egyptian government has only reluctantly adopted relatively high intellectual property standards, including the provision of a twenty-year patent term and onerous compulsory licensing procedures at an early stage in its development, the new patent law seeks to make full use of provisions in TRIPS to protect and promote national interests. Nevertheless, the inherent limits imposed by the agreement's minimum standards represent a serious obstacle to the future development of innovation in the country's pharmaceutical sector. The problem is almost certainly worse than a simple reading of the law would suggest. This is because the law merely seeks to define the legal ramifications of certain actions associated with intellectual property protection. Law No. 82 of 2002 cannot, however, guarantee effective implementation given the pressures that will inevitably be exercised by the other protagonists in this ongoing struggle.

8 Conclusion

This study examined the implications of the WTO's Agreement on Trade-Related Intellectual Property Rights for Egypt's pharmaceutical industry and public health sector using a national system of innovation approach. The study was centred on four main points: (1) there is no robust method of determining the appropriate balance between innovation and technological diffusion, known as the core intellectual property trade-off, without specifying numerous parameters, which tends to subject intellectual property policies to political influence rather than economic calculation; (2) attempts to establish positive and reliable links between strong IPRs and research and development, foreign direct investment, technology transfer, and trade have not yielded robust conclusions so that they are often qualified by references to other significant national factors; (3) thus, to adequately understand the implications of stronger patent protection for the pharmaceutical industries of developing countries, we must consider relevant aspects of each country's national system of innovation; and (4) the intimate relationship of the pharmaceutical industry to public health warrants a consideration of stronger IPRs from this perspective.

The study was born of an interest in examining the implications of an international agreement about which there continues to be considerable disagreement. Chapter 2 was concerned with exactly how this *agreement* came into existence and to this end, it examined the policy process through which it was created. The discussion revealed that the global pharmaceutical industry has been aggressively pursuing changes in the international IPRs regime since the 1980s. The intensification of these efforts can be attributed to changes in technology and to intensifying global competition from generic drug producers in the developed and the developing countries. Even though generic drug producers generally provide more affordable alternatives for consumers around the world, the strength of the global pharmaceutical industry, when combined with that of other so-called IPR-sensitive industries, has allowed it to gain the upper hand in the international policy process. Indeed, it has allowed the industry to play an unprecedented role in the history of the General Agreement on Tariffs and Trade. Ultimately, however, it was the willingness of the United States government to threaten, or impose, sanctions on countries that refused to accept the demands for stronger patent protection, and the broad support of the World Bank and the International Monetary Fund for such policy changes, that had a definitive impact on the creation of a strong global IPRs regime. Under such significant pressures, the developing countries only reluctantly accepted negotiation of a new global IPRs regime in the Uruguay Round. Many countries, including Egypt, believed that the inclusion of the more traditional areas like agriculture and textiles would somewhat balance industrial country demands for new rules regarding IPRs and services. This did not, however, alleviate major concerns over the potential adverse implications of stronger patent protection for local pharmaceutical industries and for public health. This is why the Egyptian government chose to take full advantage of the grace period allowed by TRIPS.

To assess the claims of the proponents of a stronger and globally harmonized IPRs regime and the concerns of its opponents, chapter 3 analyzed the theoretical foundation of IPRs with a focus on patents. It was argued that striking a balance between innovation and technological diffusion, the basic IPRs trade-off, depends on the specification of numerous parameters in any particular setting. Because of the complexity of this task different analysts have often reached conflicting conclusions regarding the optimal strength of patents, that is, their duration and scope. This ambiguity has meant that in the real world patent policies cannot simply be derived from economic analysis but are significantly subject to the influence of competing special interests, as demonstrated in chapter 2. From this perspective it becomes clear that the demand for pharmaceutical patents, as embedded in TRIPS, is not primarily based on insights from economic theory. Indeed, economic studies that have sought to establish the link between stronger patent regimes and R&D, FDI, technology licensing, and trade have failed to establish consistent or reliable conclusions and to provide a convincing economic justification for the new IPRs regime, particularly for the developing world. Instead, these studies have served to draw attention to the importance of the wide range of factors that collectively influence the nature of these four relationships. Both the theory and the evidence reviewed suggest that any serious evaluation of the likely impact of TRIPS must be based on a broad understanding of a particular technology and sector, key aspects of the national environment within which they are embedded, and the nature of the innovation process in the particular developing country's setting. In essence, it was established that innovation is far too complex a process to be attributed to any one particular incentive, including patents, as most mainstream intellectual property models would imply.

Chapter 4 developed a national system of innovation approach to assessing the implications of stronger patent protection for the pharmaceutical sectors of developing countries. The NSI approach views patents and IPRs more broadly and as only one element in the complex system of institutions and incentives that are embedded in the historical, linguistic, and cultural experience of a nation and which, consequently, shape its technological and economic performance. In particular, the NSI approach highlights the importance of three key factors that must all be assessed in order to determine whether a developing country will be capable of capturing some of the potential benefits (or of minimizing some of the potential costs) associated with stronger IPRs regimes: (1) the structure and capabilities of its pharmaceutical firms; (2) the scientific and technological infrastructure, including its universities and public research institutions; and (3) the existence of coherent and stable government policies relating to the pharmaceutical industry. The diversity of such an approach makes generalizations regarding the specific implications of TRIPS very difficult; however, it does permit a contextualization of patent policy reform and offers a more realistic view of the complexity of the innovation process.

Our discussion of the innovation process revealed that it is actually an evolutionary process, as opposed to the linear view of technical change that is implicit in most mainstream IP analyses, one that is based on a complex and interactive process of learning, searching, exploring, and utilizing existing knowledge. From such a perspective diffusion is not something separate that happens after innovation has occurred, but something that tends to play a significant role in innovation itself. In fact, the international diffusion of technology is almost certainly closely related to innovation, technological progress, and economic growth, especially in the developing countries where innovation is initially generally based on imitation, which is facilitated by lax patent regimes, among other things.

In chapters 5 and 6 this framework is applied to the case of Egypt in order to assess the implications of TRIPS on its pharmaceutical industry and on its health sector. Chapter 5 focused on examining key aspects of the evolution of Egypt's pharmaceutical industry, since that has shaped the context for contemporary responses and outcomes of TRIPS-related patent policy reforms. Basically, five phases characterize the evolution of the pharmaceutical industry. An examination of each phase showed that Egypt's domestic industry has undergone revolutionary changes as it has sought to cope with the radically different policies of three different military regimes, ranging from state-led import substitution policies to market-led export promotion policies. A relatively weak pharmaceutical patent policy has been instrumental in fostering the emergence of a vigorous domestic industry that has come to satisfy a great proportion of domestic demand; however, it was only during a brief episode in the 1960s, when this patent policy was complemented with a comprehensive pharmaceutical plan, that the innovative potential of the industry was revealed. The industry that emerged in this process achieved approximate national self-sufficiency in ways that were desirable from a public health point of view, in that it supplied needed drugs relatively reliably and at affordable prices. Finally, the industry that emerged in this way had limited innovative capacities, not surprisingly given the strategy that was adopted starting with the 'open door' policies of the Sadat regime. These historical realities have conditioned domestic response to a strengthened patent regime today.

Chapter 6 was concerned with an examination of how Egypt's pharmaceutical industry was affected by the country's traditional IP policy given some of the key pharmaceutical/health aspects of the national system of innovation. Egypt's traditionally lax pharmaceutical patent policy had been partially responsible for fostering a domestic pharmaceutical industry with the significant participation of locally owned private and public sector firms. The lax patent regime enhanced the ability of these firms to imitate foreign pharmaceutical products and processes and to benefit from important learning effects as a result. Over time this contributed to domestic competition and to public health. Initially, the industry was able to develop very successfully. Indeed, by the late 1990s it supplied 93 per cent of domestic needs at relatively low prices while remaining one of the more profitable industries in the country. But, although these firms had been among the greatest beneficiaries of Egypt's lax patent regime, together with the consumers of pharmaceuticals, their longer-term prospects were limited by major weaknesses in the country's scientific and technological support structure and the absence of key government policies. Today, those weaknesses are more visible and more critical because they will prevent the local industry from being able to benefit significantly from the new TRIPS-related IPRs regime.

These conclusions are particularly disturbing for Egypt's fragile public health system, which is currently undergoing significant reforms. Reliance on pharmaceutical products is expected to grow in the coming years, and much of this expenditure will continue to come directly out of household budgets. Because of the expected negative impact on the prices of pharmaceutical products, the implementation of TRIPS is likely to make the challenge of obtaining treatments even more desperate for the poor. It is unlikely that these costs will be offset by significant improvements in research on local diseases, or that technology transfer will accelerate, or that the country will be able to strengthen the pharmaceutical/health aspects of its NSI. For the moment, Egypt continues to maintain strict price controls; however, it is uncertain how long it will be able to resist growing pressures and threats to dismantle this system.

The potential adverse implications of stronger pharmaceutical patent protection for public health have struck a sensitive cord with developing country governments and with public health advocates worldwide. International concern over TRIPS has mainly focused on its likely impact on access to health-related treatments for the poor, rather than its likely impact on innovation and industry. Chapter 7 examined recent international events that transpired as a result of continuing disagreement between the developing and the developed countries over the impact of TRIPS on national pharmaceutical industries and on public health systems. Key changes in Egypt's new patent law were designed to address concerns over these issues. Despite the notable improvement in the negotiating strength of the developing countries since the Uruguay Round, the industrial countries are still able to define the terms of reference for the negotiations over possible links between TRIPS and public health, as shown by what happened before and during the Fourth WTO Ministerial Conference in Doha. Although the developing countries did get many of their most pressing concerns onto the agenda, they were not nearly as successful in shaping the scope and substance of the negotiations or determining their outcome. Ultimately, these countries gained much less from these negotiations than they had hoped for and need given their tremendous public health burdens.

The greatest benefit of Doha to the developing countries may have been the experience that they gained in establishing and maintaining a strong and united coalition. Their ability to develop a common policy position sent a clear message to the industrial countries indicating that they were serious about defending their interests in the WTO. Unfortunately, the potential harm of having agreed repeatedly within these negotiations that TRIPS formed an important part of the solution to their public health concerns may ultimately outweigh the limited benefits that accrued from the entire process. The terms of these negotiations were so narrowly defined that of the impact of TRIPS on the development of a strong local pharmaceutical industry which would underpin a government's public health policies could not even be tabled. This should, however, have been a major focus at Doha since that is where the impact of TRIPS is potentially greatest.

Nevertheless, the Doha Declaration attests to and confirms the policy options that are available to national legislators under TRIPS. The debate surrounding TRIPS has fostered greater awareness in developing countries of the substance of TRIPS and of its potential implications for their economies and public health systems. In the absence of a fundamental renegotiation of the core provisions of TRIPS, it is up to national legislators to ensure that their national IPR laws takes full advantage of the policy flexibility reaffirmed in the Doha Declaration and the later decision concerning its paragraph 6. This would appear to be the case with Egypt's new patent law where key provisions concerning parallel imports and compulsory licensing take full advantage of the TRIPS-permitted policy options.

There can be little doubt that the Egyptian government only reluctantly adopted relatively high intellectual property standards, including the provision of a twenty-year patent term and onerous compulsory licensing procedures. It is significant, therefore, that at an early stage in its development the new patent law seeks to make full use of provisions in TRIPS to protect and promote national interests. Nevertheless, the inherent limits imposed by the agreement's minimum standards represent a serious obstacle to the future development of innovation in Egypt's pharmaceutical sector. The problem is almost certainly worse than a simple reading of the law would suggest because the law merely seeks to define the legal ramifications of certain actions associated with intellectual property protection. The law cannot, however, guarantee effective implementation given the pressures that will inevitably be exercised by the other protagonists in this ongoing struggle.

More than four decades of relatively lax intellectual property policy in Egypt have nurtured a domestic pharmaceutical industry that has contributed invaluably to public health. This industry has been maturing, but successive governments have failed to address the developmental problems of its growth. Some changes in the policy on intellectual property were warranted to improve the industry's innovative performance and competitiveness; however, the imposition of industrial country standards is not appropriate given the current state of the key pharmaceutical/health aspects of Egypt's national system of innovation, and, more generally, its economic situation. In this environment it is likely that most local firms will adjust production and resort to even greater licensing activities, while foreign firms will continue with business as usual, only with guaranteed higher profits. No one is likely to embark on research projects of national relevance because of the changes in IP policy. In the end, consumers will have to suffer a greater burden as drug costs increase without significant social benefits in return. Unfortunately, the inadequacy of the TRIPS transition period is likely to magnify the social costs associated with this policy shift, particularly given the current state of the economy. In light of these circumstances, there is little doubt that TRIPS represents an illusive trade-off both in the short term and in the foreseeable future.

Appendix

Brief Description of Methodology

This study relied on both primary and secondary data, including a wealth of largely qualitative information gathered during several months of field research in Cairo. The first round of interviews occurred during the periods December 1998 to January 1999, July 1999 to October 1999, and January 2000 to February 2000. A brief follow-up was conducted in 2001. The second round of interviews, which was performed primarily for other research but upon which this study drew, took place during August 2003 to October 2003. Data were gathered from interviews and from various official and unofficial sources. In all seventy-one interviews were held. These systematically covered all of the stakeholders directly involved in the pharmaceutical patent debate in Egypt and especially those knowledgeable about the pharmaceutical sector. Interviews employed both structured and unstructured methods depending on the request of the interviewees, interview time constraints, and the nature of the data being collected.

The people interviewed can be categorized as members of the following groups: academia and research institutes; media; banking; private consulting; the American Chamber of Commerce; the U.S. Embassy; Nathan Associates Inc. (a consulting firm sponsored by USAID); government ministries; local industry; and foreign industry. Where it was deemed impossible because of the researcher's limited time to interview all of the individuals identified in a particular category, the most important personalities were selected, based on the press and the opinion of other interviewees. While the majority of interviewees wished to remain anonymous, many of them agreed to be listed in the study's list of interviewees, which follows. Direct quotations have been used in the study only with the interviewee's express permission. Some quotations have been used without identification of the interviewees but still with their permission.

Apart from the interviews, information was gathered from a wide range of sources, including a variety of official documents, including confidential ones. These were used in addition to the secondary literature drawn from the extensive literature on IPRs, Egypt, and developing countries. Although the study draws heavily on these secondary sources, much of the material concerning Egypt is original, and the argument relies extensively on corroboration through interviews and original documents. This is particularly the case in chapters 5 and 6, where published material is very sparse. Chapter 5 in particular benefited from information provided by four interviewees who had played key roles in the pharmaceutical industry during both the Nasser and Sadat regimes. The author was also the leading intellectual property policy specialist for the Canadian International Development Agency in the run-up to the fourth WTO ministerial conference in Doha, Qatar (November 2001) and so relies extensively on this experience, particularly in Chapter 7. During the course of the study the researcher has had to translate numerous government documents, newspaper articles, conference submissions, meeting minutes, and academic papers from Arabic to English.

Persons Interviewed Who Agreed To Be Named and Date of Interview

First Round of Interviews

Dr Moustafa El Hadary
Chairman, Drug Policy and Planning Centre and Member of the
    National Committee on the Follow-up to the Results of the Uruguay
    Round
Ministry of Health and Population (9 Aug. 1999)

Dr Samia Salah
Vice Chairwoman, Drug Policy and Planning Centre and Member of
    the National Committee on the Follow-up to the Results of the Uruguay Round
Ministry of Health and Population (9 Aug. 1999 and 2 Feb. 2000)

Dr Gamal El Bayoumi
Assistant Minister for Foreign Affairs
Chief Negotiator, European-Egyptian Free Trade Agreement
Ministry of Foreign Affairs (26 Jul. 1999)

Dr Mohamed Taysir El Sawi
Director General, National Information Centre for Health and
Population
Ministry of Health and Population (12–14 Sept. 1999)

Dr Wageeda Anwar
Advisor to the Minister of Health on Matters of Scientific Research and
   Foreign Relations
Ministry of Health and Population (14 Aug. 1999)

Mr Alaa Z. Youssef
Second Secretary of Cabinet of the Minister of Foreign Affairs
Responsible for TRIPS Council work Jan. 1995 to Jan. 1999
Ministry of Foreign Affairs (13, 16 Sept. 1999)

Dr Hossam Loutfy
Chairman, Parke-Davis Egypt (19 Sept. 1999)

Dr Mohamed Baha-El-Din Fayez
Former Director of the National Centre for Scientific Research,
   National Research Centre
Professor Emeritus of Pharmaceutical Chemistry
Head of the National Subcommittee on IPRs (4 Sept. 1999)

Dr Hassan El Badrawy
Justice in the Court of Appeals
Member of the National Subcommittee for the Follow-up to the Results
   of the Uruguay Round
Chief Architect of National Patent and Competition Policies
Ministry of Justice (8 Sept. 1999)

Dr Ahmed Aboul Enein
Chairman, SEDICO
Former Advisor to UNIDO (29 Sept. 1999)

Dr Gamal Ghali
Chairman, Arab Medical Packing Company (29 Sept. 1999)

Dr Abdel Azziz El Sayed
Director, R&D Quality Control, EIPICO (26 Sept. 1999)

Dr Sarwat Bassily
Chairman and CEO, Amoun Pharmaceuticals Company (22 Sept. 1999)

Dr Galal Ghorab
Chairman, Pharmaceutical Holding Company (21 Jul. 1999, 1 Sept.
    1999, and 25 Jan. 2000)

Mrs Judy Winegar Goans
Chief of Party, SIPRE Project, Nathan Associates Inc. (9 Sept. 1999)

Mrs Jaleen Moroney
Deputy Chief of Party, SIPRE Project, Nathan Associates Inc. (9 Sept.
    1999)

Dr Zakaria Gadd
Chairman, Medical Unions Pharmaceuticals
President of the Syndicate of Egyptian Pharmacists (22 Jul. 1999)

Dr Hany Hamroush
Scientific Affairs Specialist, Embassy of the United States of America
    (1 Sept. 1999)

Mr Roger Freeman
First Secretary, Embassy of the United States of America (1 Sept. 1999)

Mr Jeffrey Kemprecos
Director, External Affairs Healthcare Middle East
Merck, Sharp and Dhome (22 Sept. 1999)

Ms Sherine El Saba
Communications Manager, Glaxo Wellcome Egypt (4 Aug. 1999)

Dr Osama El Saady
Chairman, Hoechst Marion Roussel Egypt (6 Sept. 1999)

Dr Negad El Shaarawi
Chairman, Glaxo Wellcome Egypt
Former President of Squibb Egypt (5 Sept. 1999)

Dr Hossam Kamel
Chairman, Merck, Sharp and Dhome Egypt (19 Sept. 1999)

Dr Ahmed El Hakim
Director, External Affairs and Health Policy, Pfizer Egypt (21 Jul. 1999)

Dr Mahmoud Mohieldin
Senior Advisor to the Minister of Economy (2 Aug. 1999)

Dr Gamilla Mousa
Undersecretary of Pharmaceutical Affairs
Ministry of Health (29 Jul. 1999)

Mr Sayed El Bous
Minister Plenipotentiary, Commercial Affairs
Advisor to the Minister of Economy (18 Sept. 1999)

Dr Fawzie El Refaie
Acting Vice President for Technology Development and Scientific
    Services
Head of the Patent Office (11 Sept. 1999)

Dr Mounir Zahran
Ambassador, Head of Egyptian Delegation to the Uruguay Round
Ministry of Foreign Affairs (13 Sept. 1999)

Ms Mahitab Orabi
Research Analyst, EFG-Hermes (19 Jul. 1999)

Mr Amr El Kady
Head of Research EFG-Hermes (19 Jul. 1999)

Mr Hisham Shuair
Egyptian-European Partnership Unit
Ministry of Foreign Affairs (9 Aug. 1999)

Dr Magda Shahin
Deputy Assistant, Minister for International Economic Relations
Ministry of Foreign Affairs (27 Jul. 1999)

Dr Essam Galal
Professor of Pharmacology, Development, and Strategic Studies
Former Head of the General Organization for Pharmaceuticals under
    the Nasser regime
Former Third World Negotiator in UNCTAD and WHO (18 Aug.
    1999)

Second Round of Interviews

Dr Venice Kamal Gouda
Former Minister of State for Scientific Research Affairs (15 Sept. 2003)

Dr Fawzie El Refaie
President, Academy of Scientific Research and Technology
Ministry of Scientific Research and Technology (4 Sept. 2003)

Professor Dr Hassan Moawad
Former Director, Mubarak City for Scientific Research and Technology
  Applications
Dean, Agricultural Division, Microbiology Department, National
  Research Centre (7 Sept. 2003)

Dr Medhat Seif El-Nasr
President, Mubarak City for Scientific Research and Technological
  Applications (15 Sept. 2003)

Dr Maha A. El-Demellawy
Associate Professor and Director, Medical Biotechnology Department
Genetic Engineering and Biotechnology Research Institute (GEBRI)
Mubarak City for Scientific Research and Technology Applications
  (15 Sept. 2003)

Dr Moustafa El Awady
Professor of Molecular Biology and Biochemistry
Chairman, Department of Biomedical Technology, National Research
  Center (26 Aug. 2003)

Dr Wageeda Anwar
Director, Genetic Engineering and Biotechnology Center
Ain Shams University (9 Sept. 2003)

Miss Zeinab El Sadr
Manager, User Services Department
Egyptian National STI Network
Academy of Scientific Research and Technology (22 Sept. 2003)

Mrs Ola Wagih Lawrence
Director, Egyptian National STI Network
Egyptian National STI Network
Academy of Scientific Research and Technology (22 Sept. 2003)

Dr Samia Salah
Chairperson, Drug Policy and Planning Centre
Ministry of Health (18 Sept. 2003)

Dr Abdallah Molokhia
Chairman, National Organization for Drug Control and Research
Ministry of Health (23 Sept. 2003)

Dr Madiha Omar
Chief Quality Assurance Specialist, National Organization for
    Drug Control and Research
Ministry of Health (23 Sept. 2003)

Mr Motaz A. Moneim
Director, Biotechnology Information Centre Egypt (25 Aug. 2003)

Mrs Fagr El Sissy,
Assitant Director Biotechnology Information Centre Egypt (25 Aug.
    2003)

Dr Ahmed Darwish
Senior Advisor, Social Fund for Development
Egyptian Incubator Association
Government of Egypt (17 Sept. 2003)

Mr Magdy Wahba
Project Manager, Egyptian Incubator Association (17 Sept. 2003)

Dr Yehia El Agami
President, Small Enterprise Development Organization
Social Fund for Development (17 Sept. 2003)

Dr Hani Hamroush
Science Advisor, U.S. Embassy (11 Sept. 2003)

Mrs Joan Mahoney
Science and Technology Program Coordinator, U.S. Embassy (11 Sept.
    2003)

Mr Sabry El Nabawy
Chief Public Relations Officer, National Bank of Egypt (18 Sept. 2003)

Mrs Bothina Abdelhamid
Scientific Editor, *Al Gomhoreya* Daily Newspaper (24 Sept. 2003)

Dr Hatem Sidqui
Member Bioethics Committee UNESCO, Cairo
Member Bioethics Committee, National Research Center
Member Bioethics Committee, Cairo Univeristy
Chief Editor Assistant and Head of Science and Environment Section
   Al Ahram National Newspaper (25 Sept. 2003)

Dr Galal Ghorab
President, Holding Company for Pharmaceuticals (2 Sept. 2003)

Dr Kadria Ali Abdel-Motaal
Director, Technology Management and Marketing, VACSERA (14 Sept.
   2004)

Dr Zein El-Abeden M. El-Kilany
Microbiology Ph.D.
General Manager of Biotechnology Department, Nile Co. for
   Pharmaceuticals (11 Sept. 2003)

Dr Mohammed Khater
Biotechnology and Oncology Business Unit Manager
The Nile Co. for Pharmaceuticals (11 Sept. 2003)

Dr Mohamed Shawky El Sayed
Head, Biotechnology Department
Egyptian International Pharmaceutical Industries Company (10 Sept.
   2003)

Dr Abdel Aziz Saleh
Special Adviser (Medicines)
World Health Organization
Regional Office for the Eastern Mediterranean (17 Sept. 2003)

Dr Mohammad Abdur Rab
Regional Adviser
Research Policy and Cooperation
World Health Organization EMRO (17 Sept. 2003)

Interview Structure

1 Professional background of the person being interviewed. How
   long have they been involved with Egyptian pharmaceuticals
   and/or intellectual property policy? Within which organizations
   and which institutional positions?

2 Who is pioneering patent policy reform in Egypt? What influence has this had on the policy process?

3 Who are the main actors in the pharmaceutical sector in Egypt? What are their roles?

4 Do the actors in the pharmaceutical sector form a cluster? What is the extent and nature of linkages between key actors (both national and international)? How is your institution linked with other actors in the system?

5 What is the government's assessment of the potential implications of patent policy reform on the pharmaceutical sector and public health? Do officials in the Ministry of Health have a different position than those in the Ministry of Trade, the Ministry of Foreign Affairs, or the Ministry of Scientific Research?

6 What do you see as the role of the national pharmaceutical industry? Are there any indications that the local industry is ready for changes in Egypt's patent regime?

7 What are the main sources of innovation in the pharmaceutical sector? What role do patents play in your organization? What is the significance of patent reform for your organization?

8 How can we explain the institutional changes proposed in the draft patent law currently under consideration – broadening of industrial applicability to include inventions in the fields of foodstuffs, agriculture, medical drugs, and pharmaceutical compounds, stipulating strict conditions for the use of compulsory licensing, providing a twenty-year term of protection, requiring certain extensive examination procedures, making patents available irrespective of where the invention was made?

9 What are the circumstances that led to the perception that Law No. 132 of 1949 was no longer adequate for national development priorities and policies? What are the justifications for these proposed changes?

10 Can it be deduced from the proposed changes in Egypt's patent law that the government is shifting orientation from a policy based predominantly on the local production and supply of drugs to one based on the acceptance of foreign domination of the drug market and possibly greatly increased drug imports?

11 What have been the most critical periods of patent reform historically and in particular since the signing of the Marrakech Agreement in January 1995? Has the government had to make concessions to patent reform opponents? What has been the nature of these concessions?

12 How is foreign direct investment in the pharmaceutical sector viewed within the government?
13 In what ways does the government plan to promote local development and production of pharmaceuticals in Egypt under the new regime? Is it plausible to believe that joint ventures and licensing agreements can and will be designed in ways that will permit the domestic industry to continue to make a significant contribution to the country's health care needs?
14 When did the idea of patent reform begin to grow within the government? How strong is the government's commitment to the proposed changes? What is the greatest concern with this policy shift?
15 What are the greatest challenges to be faced by the local pharmaceutical sector on account of the pending changes in patent policy in the near future? In relation to the scope and pace of the changes in Egypt's patent law, is the policy likely to be beneficial for economic growth and social development in the short run and/or long run?
16 Which social groups support an unchanged policy? Which groups support the changes? Are the supporters and opponents homogeneous groups?
17 How do you assess the behaviour of the Egyptian government during the Uruguay Round of Multilateral Trade Negotiations with regard to the inclusion of the intellectual property rights? What in your opinion was the final balance of gains and losses? Who gained, who lost, and what were the gains and losses?
18 How did the Egyptian strategy develop throughout the negotiations? How did the government relate to the issues at stake during the negotiations? Did the Egyptian delegation act with a clear strategy? Was there any disagreement among the delegates?
19 To what extent was becoming a WTO member and hence automatically becoming party to TRIPS the result of the fact that there were good grounds for believing that the agreement would have beneficial impacts on the economy and society?
20 How did the representatives of the Egyptian pharmaceutical industry participate in the negotiations? What was the role of external (foreign) pressure, both from bilateral partners and multilateral agencies and financial institutions? What is the role of these parties in extending technical cooperation and cost sharing of implementation of the reform program?
21 Do you think that the reform program will be implemented in a

timely and effective manner? If not, how might this be justified? What measures is the government taking to ensure that changes to the patent regime will have the least possible disruptive effect on the nation's public health system?

22 Given the imminent changes to Egypt's patent regime, what do you think about the prospects of the local industry?

Notes

1 Introduction

1 FDI is defined as the 'act of establishing or acquiring a foreign subsidiary over which the investing firm has substantial management control' (Maskus 1998; 8).

2 Prior to the creation of the WTO-TRIPS the GATT, which did not include significant disciplines on IPRs, did not permit signatory states to use trade retaliation to protest against inadequate IPR systems of other signatory states. Moreover, even after the promulgation of the TRIPS in 1995 the developing countries still had until 2005 to implement the agreement in areas that had not been previously protected within their jurisdictions, without external pressures or risking conflict with other trading partners who desired stronger IPR protection.

3 National treatment means that each member will accord the nationals of other members treatment no less favourable than that it accords to its own nationals with regard to intellectual property protection. MFN means that if a member extends any special or preferential treatment regarding IPRs to another member then that same treatment will have to be accorded to all other members without discrimination.

4 A compulsory license entails the use of the subject matter of a patent without the authorization of the right holder. A national administrative or judicial authority usually grants this allowance. The right holder normally receives an agreeable percentage of sales in royalties when a compulsory license is granted to a third party. More will be said about compulsory licensing later in the study.

2 Establishing the New Global IPRs Regime

1 Unless otherwise indicated, all dollar figures in this study refer to U.S. dollars.
2 This included the software, electronics, chemicals, publishing, and film industries.
3 The IPC was a coalition of eleven to fourteen major U.S. companies whose mission was to ensure that the TRIPS would respond to their needs. In 1986 the original members of the IPC included Bristol Myers, CBS, General Electric, General Motors, Hewlett Packard, IBM, Du Pont, Johnson and Johnson, Merck, Monsanto, and Pfizer. Rockwell International, Time Warner, Digital Equipment Corporation, FMC, and Procter and Gamble joined in 1994, by which time CBS, Du Pont, and General Motors ceased their participation.
4 See Hudec (1987) for a comprehensive review of the history of developing countries in the GATT system.
5 In Egypt the Ministry of Foreign Affairs monopolizes all international negotiations. The rules that govern who can participate in international negotiations on behalf of Egypt and how incumbents can do so are very strict. This systemic rigidity or inflexibility made it impossible for experts from civil society or industry to participate in the process directly.
6 It is important to note that the TRIPS only provides guidelines for the formulation of domestic law, it does not replace it. Thus, ratification of the TRIPS is only the first step in the domestic reform process, after which there is the formulation of the new draft IPRs law, approval by Cabinet, debate and ratification by the People's Assembly, publication in the Official Gazette, and finally executive or presidential assent. This process was completed in May 2002.
7 This is approximately $800 million using the prevailing exchange rate of LE 6.25 per U.S. dollar.
8 PhRMA is an American organization whose membership comprises approximately a hundred U.S. pharmaceutical companies that primarily engage in research activities. The organization's main role is to act as the industry's watchdog.
9 'Pipeline' protection is a type of retroactive protection preferred by the proponents of stronger IPRs. It basically means that 'pipeline' countries (those in the process of reforming their IPR regimes) grant patent protection to pharmaceutical products that had been patented in other WTO member states but had not yet been marketed domestically as soon as the TRIPS is given legal effect. The TRIPS, however, does not require this extension.

The agreement applies only to products created after its date of entry into force.

3 Intellectual Property Theory and TRIPS

1 The idea behind the exhaustion of an IP right is that once a product has been legitimately commercialized in any given market, the rights of the patent holder are exhausted since their rights have been exercised. The principle of exhaustion thus allows a member state to then import the patented product from other countries where it has also been legitimately marketed. This is widely referred to as parallel importing. This is usually practiced to restore price competition. Article 6 has left the determination of IPRs exhaustion to national legislation; i.e., national decisions cannot be subject to dispute settlement under the agreement.

2 Establishment trade includes sales by U.S. foreign affiliates in host markets.

4 A National System of Innovation Approach

1 This means that foreign-owned firms are a part of both home and host country systems (Lundvall 1992, 18).

2 Adapted from Stiglitz in Mytelka (1998, 4).

3 England extended patent protection in 1949, France in 1960, Germany in 1968, Japan in 1976, Switzerland in 1977, and Sweden and Italy in 1978 (Nogues 1990, 82). The countries that refused to grant any patent protection until the Uruguay Round included Australia, Brazil, Colombia, Malawi, Mexico, New Zealand, Zambia, and Zimbabwe (Nogues 1990, 82). Those countries that refused to grant product but granted process patents for pharmaceuticals included Argentina, Bolivia, Bulgaria, Canada, Chad, China, Cuba, Czechoslovakia, Ecuador, Egypt, Finland, Ghana, Greece, Hungary, Iceland, India, Iran, Korea, Lebanon, Libya, Monaco, Mongolia, Morocco, Norway, Pakistan, Peru, Poland, Romania, Russia, Syria, Thailand, Tunisia, Turkey, Uruguay, Venezuela, Vietnam, and Yugoslavia (Nogues 1990, 82).

5 Patent Policy and the Evolution of Egyptian Pharmaceuticals

1 Please refer to the appendix for details regarding the research methodology of chapters 5, 6, and 7, as well as the list of interviewees, and the interview structure.

2 These firms included Hoechst Orient (German/Egyptian), Pfizer (U.S./

Egyptian), and Ciba and Sandoz (Swiss/Egyptian) who were attracted by the size of the market and the desire to counter each other's presence.

3 Among the private firms established during this period were Pharco, Squibb, and the ACDIMA group of companies. ACDIMA or the Arab Company for Drug Industries and Medical Appliances was established as a pharmaceutical holding company with the goal of creating a vertically integrated company with affiliates throughout the Arab world. Support for the projects by other Arab countries, however, was withdrawn when Egypt forged peace with Israel. The result was that most of the affiliated companies ended up being established in Egypt rather than throughout the Arab world.

4 It must be kept in mind that the size and structure of these companies are continually changing through mergers and acquisitions. By the end of this study several of these companies had merged, which has in some cases been accompanied by name changes. For instance, Hoechst Marrion Roussel merged with Rhone Poulenc to form Aventis in 1999 and more recently Glaxo Wellcome merged with Smith Kline Beecham to form Glaxo Smith Kline.

5 EMRs obligate a country to accept the filing of all new patent applications during the transition period, and to grant each applicant an EMR for up to five years, or until the patent application has been granted or rejected. In order for the applicant to qualify for such an EMR the invention must merely have been granted a patent, and have received market authorization, in any other WTO member country. In effect, this nullifies the significance of the transition period and this has been a source of much confusion for developing country policy makers seeking to take advantage of the transition period.

6 Stronger IPRs and Egypt's (Bio)Pharmaceutical Innovation System

1 Based on statistics compiled from the Academy of Scientific Research and the Ministry of Health and Population.

2 Ibid.

3 Ibid.

4 Ibid.

5 Ibid.

6 These include insulin, anti-cancer drugs or cytotoxics, cardiovascular medications, and eye disease treatments.

7 Confidential source.

8 This section on linkages draws extensively on a study completed in 2004 by the author for the University of Toronto's Joint Centre for Bioethics on the

emergence of biotechnology in Egypt. A short article based on this work was subsequently co-authored and published in *Nature Biotechnology* on 6 December 2004. Please see the bibliography for complete reference.

9 By this we mean that one party of a partnership has highly qualified personnel while the other does not, which not only discourages the former from 'doing their part' but indeed makes project completion very challenging if at all possible.

10 CIPR (the Commission on Intellectual Property Rights) is a group of international experts appointed by the British Government in May 2001 to examine how IPRs and development policy can be integrated with the aim of reducing poverty.

11 Dr Ismail Sallam was replaced by Dr Mohamed Awad in 2002.

12 Confidential source.

13 Confidential source.

14 According to the Ministry of Economy (2000, 12), GDP per capita in 1999 totaled LE 3,830 or U.S.$1128.

7 Policy Options under TRIPS: Realty or Illusion?

1 From here on the Declaration on the TRIPS and Public Health will simply be referred to as the Doha Declaration.

2 These countries included Korea, New Zealand, Hungary, Israel, Pakistan, the United Arab Emirates, Brazil, Canada, the Dominican Republic, Australia, China, Hong Kong, Indonesia, the Philippines, Thailand, Vietnam, the Czech Republic, Estonia, Lithuania, Poland, Russia, the Slovak Republic, Slovenia, Kuwait, Lebanon, Saudi Arabia, South Africa, Turkey, the Andean Community (Bolivia, Colombia, Ecuador, Peru, and Venezuela), and Uruguay.

3 Available on the CPT Page on Brazil: http://www.cptech.org/ip/health/c/brazil/statement06252001.html (accessed 3 Nov. 2002).

4 Please note that when I refer to the developing country coalition it includes least developed country members of the WTO as well.

5 A non-paper is a document that is proposed informally with the understanding that its specific language is open to negotiation.

6 The developing country draft proposal can be view at http://www.wto.org/english/tratop_e/trips_e/mindecdraft_w312_e.htm (accessed 20 Oct. 2001).

7 A preamble in international agreements is 'used to ascertain the intention of the parties in the process of interpretation, and is part of the context of the agreement' (Abbott 2002).

8 Please see chapter four for a complete discussion of these concepts and relevant provisions under the TRIPS.

9 This proposal can be viewed on the WTO website at http://www.wto.org/english/tratop_e/trips_e/mindecdraft_w313_e.htm (accessed 15 Oct. 2001).

10 For a list of these conditions see http://www.wto.org/english/tratop_e/trips_e/implem_para6_e.htm (accessed 10 Oct. 2003).

11 Indeed, pharmaceuticals are not the only 'field of technology' singled out under the new patent law as the USTR statement implies. Under the law, if patents are related to 'military affairs, or military production, or national security' they are to be reviewed and approved or rejected by the ministries of Defence, Military Production, and the Interior, respectively. In each case the specialized ministry is given final adjudication authority over such patents given their sensitive subject matter and hence the need for specific expertise.

References

Abdelgafar, Basma, Halla Thorsteinsdóttir, Uyen Quach, Peter Singer, and Abdallah S. Daar (2004). 'The Emergence of Egyptian Biotechnology from Generics.' *Nature Biotechnology* 22 (12 Supp 1.).

Abdelghaffar, Mohamed (2001). 'Danger Threatens Pharmaceutical Production.' *Akhbar Al Yom*, 29 Sept., 10.

Abbott, Frederick (2002). 'The Doha Declaration on the TRIPS and Public Health: Lighting a Dark Corner at the WTO.' *Journal of International Economic Law* 5(2): 469–505.

Act Up Paris (2002). 'Accelerating Access: Serving Pharmaceutical Companies and Corrupting Health Systems.' Press Release, 15 May. www.actupp.org/article498.html (accessed 20 May 2002).

Aghion, Philippe, Nicholas Bloom, Richard Bludell, Rachel Griffith, and Peter Howitt (2002). 'Competition and Innovation: An Inverted U Relationship.' http://post.economics.harvard.edu/faculty/aghion/papers/comp_and_innov.pdf (accessed 5 Oct. 2002).

Aith, Marcio (2000). 'Patent Laws Can Generate Conflict with U.S.' *Folha de Sao Paulo*, 12 Feb. http://www.cptech.org/ip/health/c/brazil (accessed 15 Oct. 2002).

Al Ahram (2001). 'Flying Machines and Electric Toothbrushes.' *Al Ahram Weekly Online*, no. 539, 21–7 June.

Al Alam Al Yom (1999). 'After the Minister of Economy Insists on the Grace Period the Debate over Drug Production Intensifies: Intensification of the Debate over the Future of Drug Production.' *Al Alam Al Yom*, 27 July, 3.

Al Ansari, Mahfouz (1999). 'Mubarak and Drugs, Egyptian Health, the NATO Alliance and the Copenhagen Alliance.' *Al Ahram*, 27 Feb., 13.

Al Bassil, Abd Al Azim et al. (2002). 'Problems Re: Drug Access and Public Health in Egypt – Beyond IP.' *Al Ahram Special Report*, 15 June, 20–1.

Alden, Edward, Geoff Dyer, Ken Warn, and Bettina Wassener (2001). 'Manufacture of Antibiotics: Bayer Urged to Cut Price of Drugs to Help America in Its Fight Against Anthrax.' *Financial Times*, 24 Oct., 4.

Ali El Din, Baha, and Mahmoud Mohieldin (2001). 'On the Formulation and Enforcement of Competition Law in Emerging Economies: The Case of Egypt.' Egyptian Center for Economic Studies, Working Paper No. 60.

Alt, James E., Randall L. Calvert, and Brian D. Humes (1986). 'Game Theory and Hegemonic Stability: The Role of Reputation and Uncertainty.' Political Economy Working Paper 106. St Louis: Washington University, Center for Political Economy.

Andersen, Esben Sloth, and Bengt-Ake Lundvall (1988). 'Small National Systems of Innovation Facing Technological Revolutions: An Analytic Framework.' In Christopher Freeman and Bengt-Ake Lundvall (eds.), *Small Countries Facing the Technological Revolution*, 9–36. London: Pinter.

Arrow, Kenneth (1962). 'Economic Welfare and the Allocation of Resources for Invention.' In Universities–National Bureau Committee for Economic Research (ed.), *The Rate and Direction of Inventive Activity: Economic and Social Factors. A Conference of the Universities–National Bureau Committee for Economic Research and the Committee on Economic Growth of the Social Science Research Council*, 609–25. Princeton, NJ: Princeton University Press.

Baba, Yasunori, and Ken-ichi Imai (1992). 'Systemic Innovation and Cross Border Networks: The Case of the Evolution of the VCR Systems.' In Frederick M. Scherer and Mark Perlman (eds.), *Entrepreneurship, Technological Innovation, and Economic Growth: Studies in the Schumpeterian Tradition*, 141–52. Ann Arbor: University of Michigan Press.

Banta, David (2000). 'Increase in Global Access to Essential Drugs Sought.' *Journal of the American Medical Association* 283(3), 19 Jan.

Bale, Harvey (1988). 'A Computer and Electronics Industry Perspective.' In Charles E. Walker and Mark A. Bloomfield (eds.), *Intellectual Property Rights and Capital Formation in the Next Decade*, 119–26. London: University of America Press.

Barr, Stephen (1999). 'Pfizer Defiant – How David Shedlarz Challenges the Analysts.' *CFO: The Magazine for Senior Financial Executives*, July, 36–42.

Barzel, Yoram (1968). 'Optimal Timing of Innovations.' *Review of Economics and Statistics*, Aug., 348–55.

Bayer (2001). 'Bayer to Supply Government by Year End with 100 Million Tablets for $95 Million.' Bayer Press Release, *Bay News International*. www.news.bayer.com/News/News.nsf/id/01–0350. Accessed 24 Oct. 2001.

Benko, Robert P. (1987). *Protecting Intellectual Property Rights*. Washington, DC: American Enterprise Institute for Public Policy Research.

Bessen, James, and Eric Maskin (2000). 'Sequential Innovation, Patents and Imitation.' Working Paper No. 100–01, Department of Economics, MIT.

Bonin, Bernard (1991). 'Oligopoly, Innovation, and Firm Competitiveness.' In Jorge Niosi (ed.), *Technology and National Competitiveness: Oligopoly, Technological Innovation, and International Competition*, 267–81. Montreal: McGill-Queen's University Press.

Brown, Lawrence A. (1981). *Innovation Diffusion: A New Perspective.* London: Methuen.

Chambers, R. (1983). *Rural Development: Putting the Last First.* London: Longman.

Chesnais, François (1991). 'Technological Competitiveness Considered as a Form of Structural Competitiveness.' In Jorge Niosi (ed.), *Technology and National Competitiveness: Oligopoly, Technological Innovation, and International Competition*, 142–76. Montreal: McGill-Queen's University Press.

– (1992). 'National Systems of Innovation, Foreign Direct Investments and Other Operations of Multinational Enterprises.' In Bengt-Ake Lundvall (ed.), *National Systems of Innovation: Toward a Theory of Innovation and Interactive Learning*, 265–95. London: Pinter.

CIPR (2002). *Integrating Intellectual Property Rights and Development Policy: Report of the Commission on Intellectual Property Rights.* London: Commission on Intellectual Property Rights. http://www.iprcommission.org (accessed 20 Sept. 2002).

Clemente, C.L. (1988). 'A Pharmaceutical Industry Perspective.' In Charles E. Walker and Mark A. Bloomfield (eds.), *Intellectual Property Rights and Capital Formation in the Next Decade*, 127–34. London: University of America Press.

Correa, Carlos A. (1995). 'Intellectual Property Rights and Foreign Direct Investment.' *International Journal of Technology Management.* Special Issue on the Management of International Intellectual Property, 10(2/3): 173–99.

– (1998). 'Implementing TRIPS in Developing Countries.' http:"www.twnside.org.sg/souths/twn/title/ment–cn.htm (accessed 25 April 1998).

– (2000). 'The Strengthening of IPRs in Developing Countries and Complementary Legislation.' Report prepared upon request of DFID (UK), Oct.

– (2001). 'Some Assumptions on Patent Law and Pharmaceutical R&D.' Occasional Paper No. 6. Geneva: Quaker UN Office.

Costa, Mauricio E.C. (1988). 'A View from Brazil.' In Charles E. Walker and Mark A. Bloomfield (eds.), *Intellectual Property Rights and Capital Formation in the Next Decade*, 57–64. London: University of America Press.

Dasgupta, Partha (1986). 'The Theory of Technological Competition.' In Joseph Stiglitz and G. Frank Mathewson (eds.), *New Developments in the Analysis of Market Structure*, 519–47. Cambridge, MA: MIT Press.

- (1988). 'The Welfare Economics of Knowledge Production.' *Oxford Review of Economic Policy*, 4(4): 1–12.

Davis, Paul (2002). 'Re: Urgent: Fast Track Vote against Affordable Meds and PWAs Probable Today.' Ip-health listserv. http:"lists.essential.org/pipermail/ip-health/2002-July/003330.html (accessed 26 July 2002).

de Almeida, Paulo R. (1995). 'The Political Economy of Intellectual Property Protection: Technological Protectionism and Transfer of Revenue among Nations.' *International Journal of Technology Management*, Special Issue on the Management of International Intellectual Property, 10(2/3): 214–29.

Deardorff, Allan V. (1992). 'Welfare Effects of Global Patent Protection.' *Economica*, 59: 35–51.

de Jonquières, Guy (2001). 'All Night Haggling in Doha Ends in Agreement.' *Financial Times*, 15 Nov., 6.

Doern, Bruce G., and Markus Sharaput (2000). *Canadian Intellectual Property: The Politics of Innovating Institutions and Interests*. Toronto: University of Toronto Press.

Dosi, Giovanni (1988). 'Sources, Procedures, and Microeconomic Effects of Innovation.' *Journal of Economic Literature*, 26 (Sept.): 1120–71.

Dyer, Geoff, and Adrian Michaels (2001). 'A Bitter Pill for the Drug Makers.' *FT.com Financial Times*, 24 Oct. www.ft.com (accessed 26 Oct. 2001).

Eggertson, Thrainn (1990). *Economic Behaviour and Institutions*. Cambridge: Cambridge University Press.

El Essawi, Ibrahim (2000). 'From Reform to Recession.' *Al Ahram Weekly Online*, 27 Apr.–3 May, Issue No. 479. http://www.ahram.org.eg/weekly/2000/479/op2.htm (accessed 22 Oct. 2002).

El Sawy, Tayseer M. (1997). *TRIPS and the Egyptian Drug Market: Final Report*, 1 May. Cairo: National Information Centre for Health and Population.

Ernst, Dieter, Lynn K. Mytelka, and Tom Ganiatsos (1998). 'Technological Capabilities in the Context of Export-led Growth: A Conceptual Framework'. In Dieter Ernst, Tom Ganiatsos, and Lynn Mytelks (eds.), *Technological Capabilities and Export Success in Asia*, 5–45. London: Routledge.

Essam El-Din, Galal (2000). 'The Wrong Prescription.' *Al Ahram Weekly Online*, 20–6 Apr., Issue No. 478. www.ahram.org.eg/weekly/2000/478/ec2.htm (accessed 1 Nov. 2002).

Evans, Robert (2001). 'Drug Companies Warn AIDS Research Could Dry Up.' *Reuters Limited*, 19 Sept. http:"www.spectrum.ieee.org/news/cache/ReutersOnlineScience/09_19_2001.romta1116-story-bcsciencescienceaids-drugsdc.html (accessed 21 Sept. 2001).

Evenson, Richard E. (1990). 'Survey of Empirical Studies.' In Wolfgang E. Siebeck with Robert E. Evenson, William Lesser, and Carlos A. Primo Braga (eds.). *Strengthening Protection of Intellectual Property in Developing Countries: A Survey of the Literature,'* 33–46. Washington, DC: World Bank.

Fawzy, Nahla (2002). 'New Law Strengthens Investment Climate.' Egyptian State Information Service, 29 July. www.sis.gov.eg (accessed 21 Sept. 2002).

Fayez, Baha El Din (1997). *Implications of WTO Rules for Technology Transfer to the Pharmaceutical Industry in ESCWA Member Countries, with Emphasis on the the Case of the Arab Republic of Egypt.* Cairo: National Research Centre.

Ferrantino, Michael J. (1993). 'The Effect of Intellectual Property Rights on International Trade and Investment.' *Weltwirtschaftliches Archiv* 129: 300–31.

Freeman, Christopher (1987). *Technology Policy and Economic Performance: Lessons from Japan.* London: Pinter.

Freeman, Christopher, and John Hagedoorn (1992). Globalization of Technology. MERIT Research Memorandum 92-013. Maastricht.

Freeman, Christopher, and Carlotta Perez (1988). 'Structural Crises of Adjustment: Business Cycles and Invesment Behaviour.' In G. Dosi, C. Freeman, R. Nelson, G. Silverberg, and L. Soete (eds.). *Technical Change and Economic Theory,* 38–66. London: Printer.

Freeman, Christopher, and Luc Soete (1997). *The Economics of Industrial Innovation.* Cambridge, MA: MIT Press.

Frischtak, Claudio R. (1989). 'The Protection of Intellectual Property Rights and Industrial Technology Development in Brazil.' Industry and Energy Department Working Paper, Industry Series Paper No. 13. Washington, DC: World Bank. 29 Sept.

Fuhrmans, Vanessa, and Gautam Naik (2002). 'In Europe Drug Makers Fight against Mandatory Price Cuts.' *Wall Street Journal Online.* http://online.wsj.com/article/011SB102341006255711560100.html?mod=Pagepercent200n (accessed 5 Oct. 2002).

Gadbaw, Michael R., and Timothy Richards (1988). *Intellectual Property Rights: Global Consensus, Global Conflict?* London: Westview.

Galal, Essam E. (1983). 'National Production of Drugs: Egypt.' *World Development,* 11(3) pp. 237–41.

Galal, Nourhan (1999). *The Egyptian Pharmaceutical Sector.* Cairo: Commercial International Brokerage Co.

Gallini, Nancy (1992). 'Patent Policy and Costly Imitation.' *Rand Journal of Economics* 23: 52–63.

Gilbert, Richard, and Carl Shapiro (1990). 'Optimal Patent Length and Breadth.' *Rand Journal of Economics* 21: 106–12.

Grabowski, Henry, and John Vernon (1986). 'Longer Patents for Lower Imitation Barriers: The 1984 Drug Act.' *R&D, Innovation, and Public Policy* 76(2): 195–8.

Grossman, Gene, and Elhanan Helpman (1991). *Innovation and Growth in the Global Economy.* Cambridge, MA: MIT Press.

Haagsma, Auke (1988). 'A View from the European Community.' In Charles E. Walker and Mark A. Bloomfield (eds.), *Intellectual Property Rights and Capital Formation in the Next Decade*, 65–76. London: University of America Press.

Hagedoorn, John, and Jos Schakenraad (1991). 'The Internationalization of the Economy, Global Strategies and Strategic Technology Alliances.' *Nouvelles de la ssience et des technologies* 9(2): 29–41.

Harmsen, Richard, and Arvind Subramanian (1994). 'Economic Implications of the Uruguay Round.' In Naheed Kirmani (staff team leader), *International Trade Policies: The Uruguay Round and Beyond*, vol. 2, *Background Papers*, 1–31. Washington: International Monetary Fund, 1–31.

Hassan, Tarek Mohamed Ali (1997). 'Strategic Planning for the Improvement of Quality in Egyptian Drug Production in the Shadow of the WTO.' Unpublished MA dissertation, Ain Shams University, Cairo.

Hemsley, Devlin J. (1997). 'Management Views on Industry Issues, Pressures and Consultants.' *Script Magazine*, 17 June.

Henderson, Rebecca, Luigi Orsenigo, and Gary Pisano (1999). 'The Pharmaceutical Industry and the Revolutions in Molecular Biology: Interactions among Scientific, Institutional and Organizational Change.' In David Mowery and Richard Nelson (eds.), *Sources of Industrial Leadership: Studies of Seven Industries*, 267–311. Cambridge: Cambridge University Press.

Hoekman, Bernard (1994). 'Services and Intellectual Property Rights.' In Susan M. Collins and Barry Bosworth (eds.), *The New GATT: Implications for the United States*, 84–122. Washington, DC: Brookings Institution.

Hudec, Robert E. (1987). *Developing Countries in the GATT Legal System.* Sydney: Gower.

– (1991). *Enforcing International Trade Law: The Evolution of the Modern GATT Legal System.* Austin: Butterworth.

Ibrahim, Mohsen M. (1996). 'Future of Research in Hypertension in Developing Countries.' *Eastern Mediterranean Health Journal* 2(2): 202–5. http://www.emro.who.int/Publications/EMHJ/0202/02.htm (accessed 16 Nov. 2002).

ICTSD (2002a). 'Divisive Debate over TRIPS and Public Health Continues in TRIPS Council.' *Bridges Weekly Trade News Digest* 6(9). http://www.ictsd.org/weekly/02-03-12/story2.htm (accessed 20 Mar. 2002).

ICTSD (2002b). 'Access to Medicines in Spotlight at TRIPS Council.' *Bridges*

Weekly News Digest 6(24). http://www.ictsd.org/weekly/02-06-26/ story3.htm (accessed 20 Mar. 2002).

Industry Canada (1997). *Sector Competitiveness Frameworks: Pharmaceutical Industry, Part 1, Overview Prospects*. Ottawa: Industry Sector Health Industries.

Jacobzone, S. (2000). 'Pharmaceutical Policies in OECD Countries: Reconciling Social and Industrial Goals.' Labour Market and Social Policy – Occasional Papers No. 40. Paris: OECD.

Jaffe, Adam (2000). 'The U.S. Patent System in Transition: Policy Innovation and the Innovation Process.' *Research Policy* 29: 531–57.

Kamath, Gauri (2001). 'U.S. Bill May Deprive Developing Nations of Cheap Drugs.' *Economic Times*, 20 Nov. http://economictimes.indiatimes.com/ cms.dll/xml/comp/default? (accessed 20, 2001).

Keefauver, William L. (1988). 'Communications: An Industry Perspective.' In Charles E. Walker and Mark A. Bloomfield (eds.), *Intellectual Property Rights and Capital Formation in the Next Decade*, 143–50. London: University of America Press.

Keohane, Robert (1984). *After Hegemony: Cooperation and Discord in the World Political Economy*. Princeton: Princeton University Press.

Kirim, Arman (1985). 'Reconsidering Patents and Economic Development: A Case Study of the Turkish Pharmaceutical Industry.' *World Development* 13(2): 219–36.

Klemperer, Paul (1990). 'How Broad Should the Scope of Patent Protection Be?' *Rand Journal of Economics* 21: 113–30.

Lall, Sanjaya (1974). 'The International Pharmaceutical Industry and Less Developed Countries with Special Reference to India.' *Oxford Bulletin of Economics and Statistics* 36(3): 143–72.

Leahy, Patrick J. (1988). 'U.S. Congressional Approaches to Reconciling Intellectual Property Rights.' In Charles E. Walker and Mark A. Bloomfield (eds.), *Intellectual Property Rights and Capital Formation in the Next Decade*, 77–82. London: University of America Press.

Lesser, William (1990). 'An Overview of Intellectual Property Systems.' In Wolfgang E. Siebeck et al. (eds.), *Strengthening Protection of Intellectual Property in Developing Countries*, 5–15. Washington, DC: World Bank.

Lipsey, Richard (1991). *Economic Growth: Science and Technology and Institutional Change in a Global Economy*. Toronto: Canadian Institute for Advanced Research.

Loury, Glenn C. (1979). 'Market Structure and Innovation.' *Quarterly Journal of Economics* 93(3): 395–410.

Love, James (2001). 'Access to Medicine and Compliance with the WTO TRIPS

Accord: Models for State Practice in Developing Countries.' Paper prepared for the U.N. Development Program, 21 Jan. www.cptech.org/ip/health/cl/recommendedstatepractice.html (accessed 31 Mar. 2001).

– (2002). 'Access to Medicines: Solving the Export Problem under TRIPS.' *Bridges* 6(4): 3. http://www.cptech.org/ip/wto/bridges-exports.html (accessed 5 June 2002).

– (2003a). 'CPTech Statement on WTO Deal on Exports of Medicines – August 30, 2003.' *Patent Exception for Exports to Address Health Needs – Letters, Statements and Press Releases.* http://www.cptech.org/ip/wto/p6/ (accessed 5 Jan. 2005).

– (2003b). 'TRIPS Council to Meet on August 28, at 4:30.' IP-Health List Serve. http://lists.essential.org/pipermail/ip-health/2003-August/005171.html (accessed 5 Jan. 2005).

Lundvall, Bengt-Ake (1992). 'Introduction.' In Bengt-Ake Lundvall (ed.), *National Systems of Innovation: Towards a Theory of Innovation and Interactive Learning*, 1–22. London: Pinter.

Mabry, Marcus (1999). 'Give Us This Day Our Daily Meds.' *Newsweek International* 134(1): 22–5.

Macan-Markar, Marwan (2001). 'Trade: Asian Governments Want Clear WTO Agenda.' *IPS*, 28 Sept.

Malecki, Edward J. (1997). *Technology and Economic Development: The Dynamics of Local, Regional and National Competitiveness.* Edinburgh: Longman.

Mansfield, Edwin (1988). 'Intellectual Property Rights, Technological Change, and Economic Growth.' In Charles E. Walker and Mark A. Bloomfield (eds.), *Intellectual Property Rights and Capital Formation in the Next Decade*, 3–26. London: University of America Press.

Mansfield, Edwin, John Rapoport, Jerome Schnee, Sam Wagner, and Michael Hamburger (1971). *Research and Innovation in the Modern Corporation.* New York: Norton.

Maskus, Keith (1998). 'The Role of Intellectual Property Rights in Encouraging Foreign Direct Investment and Technology Transfer.' *Duke Journal of Comparative International Law.* 9(1): 109.

Maskus, Keith, and Mohan Penubarti (1995). 'How Trade-Related Are Intellectual Property Rights?' *Journal of International Economics* 39: 227–48.

Mc Donagh, Patrick (2001). 'Taking McGill to Market.' *McGill News Alumni Quarterly* 80(4). http://www.mcgill.ca/news/archives/winter2000/market/ (accessed 10 May 2001).

McKelvey, Maureen (1991). 'How Do National Systems of Innovation Differ? A Critical Analysis of Porter, Freemen, Lundvall and Nelson.' In Geoffrey

Hodgson and Ernesto Screpanti (eds.), *Rethinking Economics: Markets, Technology and Economic Evolution*, 117–37. Aldershot: Edward Elgar.

Michaels, Adrian (2001). 'The Race for a Drug Is a Close One.' *Financial Times*, 2 Sept., 12.

Ministry of Economy. (1998). *A New Business Environment for a Great Country.* Qalyoub: Al Ahram Commercial Press.

– (2000). *Egypt 2000*. Cairo: Ministry of Economy.

Ministry of Scientific Research (MOSR) (1997). 'Final Overview Report for Project on Improving the Science and Technology Policy and Management in Egypt: A World Bank–IDF Funded Project, WB28836.' Cairo.

Mohieldin, Mahmoud. (2002). 'A Stitch in Time.' *Al Ahram Weekly Online*, 21–7 Mar., issue no. 578.

Moreau, Ron (1999). 'Thailand Plays by the Rules.' *Newsweek International*, 5 Jul., 24.

Mostafa, Hadia (2004). 'Overdose?' *Business Today Egypt*, www. businesstodayegypt.com/arttemplate.asp?ArtID=2&IssueNo=05& IssueNo=05&IssueYear=04&MagID=BT (accessed 12 May 2004).

Mowery, David and Nathan Rosenberg (1989). *Technology and the Pursuit of Economic Growth*. Cambridge: Cambridge University Press.

MSF, Oxfam, TWN (2001). 'Re: TRIPS Council Special Discussion on Access to Medicines, September 19, 2001.' Ip-health listserv. http://lists.essential.org/ pipermail/ip-health/2001-September/001874.html (accessed 20 Sept. 2001).

Mytelka, Lynn K. (1998). 'Competition, Innovation, and Competitiveness: Learning to Innovate under Conditions of Dynamic Industrial Change.' Paper prepared for the International Conference: The Economics of Industrial Structure and Innovation Dynamics, Centro Cultural de Belem, Lisbon, 16–17 Oct.

– (1999). *Competition, Innovation and Competitiveness in Developing Countries*. Paris: OECD.

Namfua, Macel W., and Abdulqawi A. Yusuf (1991). *Africa and the TRIPS Negotiations in the Uruguay Round*. UNCTAD/UNDP Project RAF/87/157.

Nelson, Richard (1993). *National Innovation Systems: A Comparative Analysis*. New York: Oxford University Press.

– (1996). *The Sources of Economic Growth*. Cambridge: Harvard University Press.

Nelson, Richard, and Nathan Rosenberg (1993). 'Technical Innovation and National Systems.' In Richard Nelson (ed.), *National Innovation Systems: A Comparative Analysis*, 3–28. New York: Oxford University Press.

New York Times. (2002). 'A Fairer Trade Bill.' *New York Times on the Web*, 25 Jul., www.nytimes.com/2002/07/25/opinion/25THU3.html?pagewanted= print&position=bottom (accessed 28 July 2002).

Nogues, Julio (1990). 'Patents and Pharmaceutical Drugs: Understanding the Pressures on Developing Countries.' *Journal of World Trade* 24(6): 81–104.

– (1993). 'Social Costs and Benefits of Introducing Patent Protection for Pharmaceutical Drugs in Developing Countries.' *The Developing Economies* 31(1): 24–53.

Nordhaus, William S. (1969). *Invention, Growth and Welfare: A Theoretical Treatment of Technological Change.* Cambridge, MA: MIT Press.

OECD (1971). *The Conditions for Success in Technological Innovation.* Paris: OECD.

– (1992), *Technology and the Economy: The Key Relationships.* Paris: OECD.

Orabi, Mahitab, and Mohamed Nour El Din (1999). *Egypt: Pharmaceutical Sector Review.* Cairo: EFG-Hermes.

Ostry, Sylvia (1990), *Governments and Corporations in a Shrinking World: Trade and Innovation Policies in the United States, Europe and Japan.* New York: Council on Foreign Relations Press.

Ostry, Sylvia, and Richard Nelson (1995). *Techno-Nationalism and Techno-Globalism: Conflict and Cooperation.* Washington, DC: Brookings Institution.

Oxfam (2001). 'Fatal Side Effects: Medicine Patents under the Microscope.' Oxfam GB Policy Paper, Feb. www.oxfam.org.uk/cutthecost/downloads/ policy3.rtf (accessed 10 July 2001).

– (2002). 'U.S. Bullying on Drug Patents: One Year After Doha.' Oxfam Briefing Paper, No. 33, Nov. http://www.oxfam.org.uk/policy/papers/ 33bullying/33bullying.pdf (accessed 16 Nov. 2002).

Pack, Howard, and Larry Westphal (1986). 'Industrial Strategy and Technological Change: Theory Versus Reality.' *Journal of Development Economics* 22: 87–128.

Pavitt, K., and P. Patel (1988). 'The International Distribution and Determinants of Technological Activities.' *Oxford Review of Economic Policy* 4(4): 35–55.

Pearl, Daniel (1996). 'No Quick Cure, Big Drug Makers Push Egypt, Other Nations to End Their 'Piracy.'' *Wall Street Journal*, 17 Dec., 1 and 12.

Perez, Carlota (1988). 'New Technologies and Development.' In Christopher Freeman and Bengt-Ake Lundvall (eds.), *Small Countries Facing the Technological Revolution*, 85–97. London: Pinter.

Pharmaceutical Research and Manufacturers of America (PhRMA) (2000). 'Submission of PhRMA for the 'Special 301'' Report on Intellectual Property Barriers,' 18 Feb. http://www.phrma.org/policy /aroundworld/special301 (accessed 25 Feb. 2000).

Pollard, Stephen (2001). 'Business Europe: Big Pharmaceuticals take the Gloves Off.' *Wall Street Journal Europe*, 17 Dec.

Porter, Michael (1990). *The Competitive Advantage of Nations*. New York: Free Press.

Primo Braga, Carlos A. (1990). 'Guidance from Economic Theory.' In Wolfgang E. Siebeck et al. (eds.), *Strengthening Protection of Intellectual Property in Developing Countries*, 17–32. Washington: World Bank.

– (1991). 'The North-South Debate on Intellectual Property Rights.' In Murray G. Smith (ed.), *Global Rivalry and Intellectual Property: Developing Canadian Strategies*, 173–82. Halifax: Institute for Research on Public Policy.

Primo Braga, Carlos A., and Carsten Fink (1997). 'The Economic Justification of the Grant of Intellectual Property Rights: Patterns of Convergence and Conflict.' In Frederick Abbott and David J. Gerber (eds.), *Public Policy and Global Technological Integration*, 99–122. London: Kluwer Law International.

– (2000). 'International Transactions in Intellectual Property and Developing Countries.' *International Journal of Technology Management* 19(1/2): 35–56.

Primo Braga, Carlos A., Carsten Fink, and Claudia Paz Sepulveda. (1998). 'Intellectual Property Rights and Economic Development: Background Paper to the World Development Report 1998.' http://www.vita.org/technet/iprs/ipr-dcom.htm (accessed 1 May 1998).

Pruzin, Daniel (2001). 'WTO Talks on TRIPS, Public Health Declaration Stalls over Compromise Text.' *International Trade Daily*, 24 Oct. http://www.bna.com/products/corplaw/tdln.htm (accessed 25 Oct. 2001).

Rath, Amitar (1990). 'Science, Technology, and Policy in the Periphery: A Perspective from the Centre.' *World Development* 18(11): 1429–43.

Richards, Timothy (1988). 'Intellectual Property Rights: Reconciling Divergent Views.' In Charles E. Walker and Mark A. Bloomfield (eds.), *Intellectual Property Rights and Capital Formation in the Next Decade*, 93–8. London: University of America Press.

Rifkin, Jeremy (1998). *The Biotech Century*. New York: Penguin Putnam.

Rodrik, Dani (1999). 'The New Global Economy and Developing Countries: Making Openness Work.' Policy Essay No. 24. Washington, DC: Overseas Development Council.

Romer, Paul (1994). 'Two Strategies of Economic Development: Using Ideas and Producing Ideas.' *Proceedings of the World Bank Annual Conference on Development Economics*. New York: Word Bank, 63–91.

Rosegger, Gerhard (1986). *The Economics of Production and Innovation: An Industrial Perspective*. New York: Pergamon Press.

Rosenberg, Nathan (1976). *Perspectives on Technology*. Cambridge: Cambridge University Press.

Rozek, Richard, and Ruth Berkowitz (1998). *The Effects of Patent Protection on the Prices of Pharmaceutical Products: Is Intellectual Property Protection Raising the Drug Bill in Developing Countries?* Washington, DC: National Economic Research Associates.

Sabater, Luisa (1995). 'Multilateral Debt of Least Developed Countries.' UNCTAD Discussion Paper No. 107. Geneva: UNCTAD.

Salama, Adel Mohsen (1997). 'The Game of the Giants in Drug Manufacture.' *Al Ahram*, March.

Saxenian, Helen (1994). 'Getting the Most out of Pharmaceutical Expenditures.' Human Resources Development and Operations Policy Working Paper No. 37, Sept. www.worldbank.org/html/extdr/hnp/hddflash/hewp/hrwp033.html (accessed 10 Mar. 1999).

Scherer, F.M. (1977). *The Economic Effects of Compulsory Patent Licensing*. New York: New York University Press.

Schumpeter, Joseph (1934). *The Theory of Economic Development*. Cambridge: Harvard University Press.

– (1942). *Capitalism, Socialism and Democracy*. New York: Harper.

Scotchmer, Suzanne, and Jerry Green (1990). 'Novelty and Disclosure in Patent Law.' *Rand Journal of Economics* 21 (1, Spring): 131–46.

Segal, Aaron (1987). *Learning by Doing: Science and Technology in the Developing World*. Boulder, CO: Westview.

Sell, Susan (1998). *Power and Ideas: North-South Politics of Intellectual Property and Anti-trust*. New York: State University of New York Press.

Shahidullah, Shahid M. (1991). *Capacity Building in Science and Technology in the Third World*. Boulder: Westview.

Sherwood, Robert M. (1996). 'The TRIPS: Implications for Developing Countries.' Study on the Financial and Other Implications of the Implementation of the TRIPS for Developing Countries, commissioned by the World Intellectual Property Organization, Sept.

Singh, Ajit (1995). 'How Did East-Asia Grow So Fast? Slow Progress toward an Analytical Consensus.' UNCTAD Discussion Paper No. 97. Geneva: UNCTAD.

Singh, Ajit, and Rahul Dhumale (1999). 'Competition Policy, Development and Developing Countries.' Trade-Related Agenda, Development and Equity Working Paper No. 7, Nov. Geneva: South Centre.

Stalson, Helena (1987). *Intellectual Property Rights and U.S. Competitiveness in Trade*. Washington, DC: National Planning Association.

Stiglitz, Joseph (1986). 'Theory of Competition, Incentives and Risk.' In Joseph Stiglitz and G. Frank Mathewson (eds.), *New Developments in the Analysis of Market Structure*, 399–446. Cambridge, MA: MIT Press.

– (2002). 'Globalism's Discontents.' *American Prospect*, 14 Jan. www. globalpolicy.org/globaliz/econ/2002/0114stiglitz.htm (accessed 10 Feb. 2002).

Stoneman, Paul (1987). *The Economic Analysis of Technology Policy.* Oxford: Clarendon.

Stoneman, Paul, and J. Vickers (1988). 'The Assessment: The Economics of Technology Policy.' *Oxford Review of Economic Policy* 4(4): i–xvi.

Story, Alan (2000). 'The Oxfam 'Access to Essential Medicines" Project: Some Patent and Research and Development Issues.' Report prepared for Oxfam International. London: Oxfam International.

Subramanian, Arvind (1995). 'Putting Some Numbers on the TRIPS Pharmaceutical Debate.' *International Journal of Technology Management, Special Issue on the Management of International Intellectual Property* 10(2/3): 252–68.

Subramanian, Arvind, and Mostafa Abdel-Latif (1997), 'The Egypt-EU Partnership Agreement and the Egyptian Pharmaceutical Sector.' Working Paper No. 11, Mar. Cairo: Egyptian Center for Economic Studies.

Sykes, Allan O. (1992). 'Constructive Unilateral Threats in International Relations: The Limited Case for Section 301.' *Law and Policy in International Business* 23(2): 263–330.

Taylor, Christopher T., and Aubrey Silberston (1973). *The Economic Impact of the Patent System: A Study of the British Experience*. Cambridge: Cambridge University Press.

Toft, A. (1990). 'The New Roles and Facilities of the World Bank.' *IDS Bulletin* 21(2): 38–41.

United Nations Conference on Trade and Development (UNCTAD) (1997). *The TRIPS and Developing Countries*. New York: United Nations.

– (1999), *Investment Policy Review: Egypt*. Geneva: United Nations.

– (2001). Competition Policy and the Exercise of Intellectual Property Rights: Revised Report by the UNCTAD Secretariat. Geneva: UN.

United Nations Development Programme (UNDP) (1999). *Human Development Report*. New York: Oxford University Press.

– (2001). *Human Development Report 2001: Making New Technologies Work for Human Development*. Oxford: Oxford University Press.

– (2003). *The Arab Human Development Report*. New York: United Nations Development Programme, Regional Bureau for Arab States.

United States Trade Representative (USTR) (2000). U.S. Trade Representative Special 301 Report for 2000. U.S. Department of State's Bureau of International Information Programs. Washington, DC. http://usinfo.state.gov/ei/Archive/2003/Dec/31-708465.html (accessed 1 Mar. 2006).

– (2002). 'Special 301 Country Reports – Priority Watch List.' USTR/Sectors Intellectual Property. www.ustr.gov/reports/2002/special301-pwl .htm#egypt (accessed 13 Oct. 2002).

von Wartensleben, Aurelie (1983). 'Major Issues Concerning Pharmaceutical Policies in the Third World.' *World Development* 11(3): 169–75.

Waldmeir, Patti (2001). 'Patents and Panics.' *Financial Times*, 1 Nov., 14.

Williamson, John (1994). *The Political Economy of Policy Reform*. Washington, DC: Institute for International Economics.

World Bank (1992). 'World Bank Support for Industrialization in Korea, India, and Indonesia.' A World Bank Operations Evaluation Study. Washington, DC: OED World Bank.

– (2001). *Global Economic Prospects and the Developing Countries 2002: Making Trade Work for the World's Poor*. New York: World Bank.

Yerkey, Gary G., and Daniel Pruzin (2001a). 'United States Drops WTO Case against Brazil over HIV/AIDS Patent Law.' Washington, DC: Bureau of National Affairs Inc., 26 June. http://www.cptech.org/ip/health/c/brazil/ bna06262001.html (accessed 2 Nov. 2002).

– (2001b). 'WTO Provisional Agreement on TRIPS Reached at WTO Ministerial in Doha.' *International Trade Reporter*. http://www.bna.com/itrnews/ story7.htm (accessed 5 Nov. 2002).

Zein El Abedien, Ghada (2001). 'TRIPS for Drugs – Between Patents and Monopoly.' *Akhbar Al Yom*, 11 June, 3.

Index

countries, 22–4, 147–64, 170–2,
175–7, 183–4; and Doha Declaration, 150–1, 153, 154; double standards of, 163–4; and drugs, 17, 128;
and intellectual property rights, 3–
4, 9–10, 61–2, 71, 73, 139; patent
protection in, 48–9, 139; R&D in,
48–9, 75, 113; and technology
transfer, 94; and TRIPS, 142
industrialization, 48, 60, 64–5, 91
industry: academia vs, 90, 118–19,
123–5; and innovation, 63, 64–5,
68–70; linkages in, 123–5; subsidies
for, 75–6, 90. *See also* multinational
enterprises; pharmaceutical industry
innovation: definition, 40; in developing countries, 55–61, 64–5; and
diffusion, 56–61; disincentives to,
38–9, 56; funding for, 75–6; imitation and, 51, 59–60; industry and,
63, 64–5, 68–70; intellectual property rights and, 56, 59–60, 64, 168;
markets and, 38–9, 64; patents and,
40–1, 47–50, 57–8, 60, 64, 67; in
pharmaceutical industry, 62, 68–9;
policies on, 82; as process, 41, 57,
59, 82; production engineering
and, 66–7; R&D and, 66, 68–9. *See
also* knowledge; R&D
insulin, 110
Intellectual Property Committee, 19
intellectual property rights (IPRs),
35–6, 56; balancing, 39–41; and
competition, 72, 73; developing
countries and, 10, 20–1, 23–4, 59–
60, 71–2, 139; exhaustion of, 37,
156, 158–61, 167, 173–4; GATT and,
19, 20–4; industrial countries and,
3–4, 9–10, 61–2, 71, 73, 139; Inter-

national Monetary Fund and, 3–4,
32, 180; pharmaceutical industry
and, 3–4, 36–7, 71; strength of, 32–
3; and trade, 20, 29, 46–7, 161;
trade-off in, 4, 37–9, 41–4, 56–61,
147–8; United States and, 9–10, 19–
20; World Bank and, 138, 180. *See
also* intellectual property rights
policies
intellectual property rights policies,
20, 36, 103–40, 181; demand for
stronger, 3, 9–10, 19–20, 99; in
Egypt, 64, 92–3, 95, 99–101, 174–5,
177–8; framework for, 61–2, 70–81;
implementation of, 70–2; industrial countries and, 3–4, 61–2; and
innovation, 56, 59–60, 64, 168; lax,
21, 71–2, 101, 108–10, 138, 182–3;
multinational enterprises and, 18,
43, 99; and national context, 61,
138–9; national system of innovation and, 61–2; pharmaceutical
industry and, 18–19, 43–50, 134;
public health and, 61–2; reform of,
16–19, 20–1, 23–4; requirements of,
35–6, 61–2. *See also* TRIPS
International Code of Conduct for
the Transfer of Technology, 76–7
International Dispensary Association, 80
International Federation of Pharmaceutical Manufacturers Associations, 44, 157
International Monetary Fund (IMF),
9, 94–5, 97; and IPRs, 3–4, 32, 180
International Organization for
Genetic Engineering, 126
investment, 38–9, 48, 75, 105–6, 130;
in pharmaceutical industry
(Egypt), 92, 98, 105–6, 109–10; in

Studies in Comparative Political Economy and Public Policy